DOS Answers: Certified Tech Support

Mary Campbell

Osborne **McGraw-Hill**
Berkeley · New York · St. Louis
San Francisco · Auckland · Bogotá
Hamburg · London · Madrid · Mexico
City · Milan · Montreal · New Delhi
Panama City · Paris · São Paulo
Singapore · Sydney · Tokyo · Toronto

Osborne **McGraw-Hill**
2600 Tenth Street, Berkeley, California 94710, USA

For information on software, translations, or book distributors outside of the U.S.A., please write to Osborne McGraw-Hill at the above address.

DOS Answers: Certified Tech Support

1234567890 DOC 9987654

ISBN 0-07-882030-8

Contents at a Glance

1	Top Ten Tech Terrors	1
2	Setup	11
3	Fast Fixes	39
4	File and Disk Management	53
5	Other DOS Commands	77
6	Utilities	97
7	DOS Shell	115
8	DoubleSpace	131
9	Memory	161
10	Configuration Issues	187
11	Interoperability	229
12	Networking	249
13	Error Messages	261
A	Glossary	281
	Index	311

Contents

Foreword		**v**
Acknowledgments		**ix**
Introduction		**xix**

1	**Top Ten Tech Terrors**	**1**
	How do I remove DoubleSpace?	2
	MemMaker starts every time I boot my machine. How can I stop this?	3
	I installed MS-DOS 6.2 and now I get "EMM386: Unable to start enhanced Windows mode due to invalid path specification for EMM386" when I try to start Windows. What's wrong?	4
	I have installed DOS 6.x and when I enter BACKUP I get a message stating "Incorrect DOS version." What should I do?	5
	I backed up my hard drive with MS Backup, reformatted it, and then reinstalled DOS. Now I can't restore my files. What's wrong?	6
	After I installed DOS 6.x and ran DoubleSpace, my computer starting saying that I had "insufficient memory" when I tried running memory-intensive programs. What's wrong?	6
	When I boot my machine, it says "CVF is damaged." What should I do now?	7
	As I'm booting up, I see the message "Cannot run SMARTDrive 4.0 with DoubleSpace." Isn't SMARTDrive compatible with DoubleSpace?	8
	I just installed MS-DOS 6.x on my IBM PS/1. When I boot my computer, I receive an "Incorrect DOS version" error message and/or "Invalid COMMAND.COM." Did I do something wrong?	8

When I run Stepup for MS-DOS 6.2, it says that it can't update
    some of my DOS files. Why not?   9

2 Setup   11

My Setup disk doesn't seem to be working. Should I return it?   12

Why should I keep my Uninstall disk?   13

Do I need to back up my data before I upgrade to DOS 6.*x*?   13

My computer got turned off while it was still running Setup.
    What do I do?   14

Is there any way to interrupt Setup once I have started it?   15

I started Setup, but can't read the screens that are appearing.
    Did I buy the wrong version of DOS?   15

I was running Setup to install DOS and I got the message
    "Cannot find a hard disk on your computer." What
    happened?   16

I was in the process of setting up DOS 6.*x*, and I received an
    error message about a virus. I chose not to continue. Are
    my DOS disks infected with a virus?   17

I was running Setup and got the message "There is not
    enough free space on drive C to install MS-DOS." Can I
    still install DOS on my hard disk?   17

I was told I need to install DOS manually. How do I do this?   18

When I originally installed my MS-DOS 6.*x* upgrade, I only
    installed the Backup, Undelete, and Anti-Virus utilities for
    one platform (DOS or Windows). Do I have to reinstall
    DOS to get the utilities for the other platform?   19

I have an older computer that I would like to upgrade to DOS
    6. Should I be considering anything else before I upgrade?   20

When trying to run Setup for the MS-DOS 6.*x* upgrade, the
    error message "Root directory of your hard disk contains
    some of your original DOS files" is displayed and the
    upgrade won't install. What original DOS files is the
    message referring to?   21

I have a critical program that just won't run on MS-DOS 6.*x*.
    I want to return to my old version of DOS, but I ran
    DoubleSpace. Is there any way for me to do this?   21

I have DR-DOS and want to upgrade to DOS 6.2. Is there
    anything I should consider before I begin?   22

When I run Stepup for MS-DOS 6.2, it says that it can't update
    some of my DOS files. Why not?   22

Can I use the MS-DOS 6.*x* upgrade to upgrade my current
    IBM PC-DOS?   23

I accidentally deleted all my files in the DOS directory. I know
    how to use the Undelete command but I cannot
    remember all the DOS file names. Do I have to reinstall
    DOS again?   23

I typed A:\SETUP to start the upgrade, and DOS displayed the
    message "Not ready reading drive A." Are my disks
    corrupted?   24

I have the MS-DOS 6.2 Stepup program and one of my DOS
    files has been corrupted. When I try to run Stepup, it tells
    me that it cannot update that file. How can I correct this
    problem?   24

The only floppy drive I have is drive D. Can I run Setup from
    that drive and if so, how?   25

When I run Setup, I get the message "Your computer uses a
    disk-compression program." Is this going to be a problem?   26

What do I need to do after replacing my SCSI hard drive to
    have it set up for DOS?   27

Can I use DOS 6.x on my Quantum Hardcard?   27

I just ran the Stepup upgrade for DOS 6.2. When I boot the
    computer, I get a DoubleGuard Alarm error and the
    computer hangs up. I am using QEMM386 for my
    memory management functions. What's wrong?   27

I just installed MS-DOS 6.x on my IBM PS/1. When I boot my
    computer, I receive an incorrect DOS version error
    message and/or an invalid COMMAND.COM. Did I do
    something wrong?   28

I have a Compaq computer with DOS 2.11. I'm trying to
    upgrade to MS-DOS 6.2 and I'm getting the message
    "Your version of DOS cannot be upgraded with Setup."
    The Upgrade package says I should be able to upgrade,
    so what's wrong?   28

I am having difficulty running DOS 6.x on my Hyundai
    computer. Did I install it incorrectly?   29

How can I find out what's new in MS-DOS 6.2?   29

The MS-DOS 6.x Setup program insists on creating an
    Uninstall disk in the A drive. How can I get around it?   30

How much disk space is required to install DOS 6.0 or 6.2?   30

Even with my Uninstall disk I am not able to go back to my
    old release of DOS. What is wrong?   31

I was installing DOS 6.x, and got the message "Incompatible
    hard disk or device driver." Can I install DOS, and if so,
    how?   31

Do I need to keep the OLD_DOS.1 subdirectory?   32

I heard that I can get a free copy of Stepup for DOS 6.2. What do I need to do? 33

Why did MS-DOS 6.2 change the Buffers statement in my CONFIG.SYS file to 10,0 during the upgrade? 33

I'm running Setup and get the "Too Many Primary Partitions" screen. What do I need to do to set up DOS? 33

I made backups of my MS-DOS Setup disks as soon as I got the program. When I tried reinstalling DOS with those disks, Setup kept asking for the disk I put in the drive, just as if it were the wrong disk. I can read the disks, so they aren't corrupted, but I can't install them. What's wrong? 34

How can I upgrade to DOS 6.0 if the Setup disks won't work in my A drive and I do not have a previous version of DOS installed on my hard disk? 35

After I start the Setup program, I get a message that says in order to run the single disk upgrade, you must already have MS DOS 6.0 installed. 35

I have a Toshiba machine. When I run MS-DOS 6.2 Stepup, I get an error message saying that Stepup cannot identify the IO.SYS file. What's wrong? 36

I just ran the MS-DOS 6.2 Stepup program and I now have trouble using any application that needs the EMM386.EXE memory manager. What do I do? 36

I just bought a new hard drive for my computer. My version of DOS 6.x is labeled as an upgrade. Does this mean I have to install my old version of DOS on this new hard drive before I can install DOS 6.x? 36

My hard drive is divided into several 32MB partitions, since I have an old version of DOS. Now that I'm upgrading, is there an easy way to convert the hard drive to a single partition? 37

3 Fast Fixes   **39**

My system locked up while running a program. After I rebooted my system, there were no files on drive C except COMMAND.COM. Where are my files? 40

I accidentally deleted all my files in a directory. Can I get them back? 41

I know I saved a file, but I can't remember what directory it's in or what I named it. How do I find it without doing a DIR command in every directory on the system? 42

I can't print. Is it the fault of DOS, my printer, or my program? 43

I was unable to boot from my hard drive, so I booted from my MS-DOS 5.0 boot disk. Now I don't see any files on my disk. Did I lose all my information? 44

I can't read data from my floppy disks. Where is my data?   45

I ran out of disk space while running a program. What do I do?   46

I am working with data and my system stopped responding.
Do I have to reboot?   46

I can't boot from my hard disk because one of the lines in
CONFIG.SYS or AUTOEXEC.BAT causes the system to
freeze. How do I start my computer?   47

I can't turn my computer on. How do I get it to work?   48

My computer is broken. Did I lose my data?   49

I just formatted the wrong floppy disk. Is there any way I can
get my data back?   49

Why do I get the "Non-system disk or disk error" message
when I start my computer?   50

I was looking at the files on my hard drive and came across a
bunch of files with weird looking characters. It says they
occupy a few hundred megabytes of disk space. I don't
have that much room on my hard drive. I am trying to
delete these files but I don't seem to have any luck with
the DELETE command. I have also tried Norton's
Disk-Doctor. How do I get rid of them?   51

4   File and Disk Management   **53**

How can I see if I have any hidden files?   55

What's the difference between the ERASE and DEL commands?   55

I tried to use MOVE to move a subdirectory on my hard drive
to a different parent directory. Why did I get the message
"Unable to open source?"   55

I just copied a file into a new directory and accidentally gave it
the same name as a file already in that directory. How can
I get the original file back?   56

How can I delete read-only or hidden files?   57

I have several files on my hard drive with a .TMP extension.
What are they and can I delete them?   57

When I ran CHKDSK /F, it found errors and corrected them.
Now some of my programs are acting as if files are
damaged. Why?   58

What is the difference between RAM and my hard disk space?   58

My system has high-density disk drives. Can I format a
low-density disk for use on another computer?   59

I'm trying to rename my \TEXTDATA directory, but I keep
getting the messages "Invalid parameter" or "Invalid path
or file name." Can't I rename a directory?   59

When I enter CHKDSK /F I am asked "Convert to file?" Do I
answer Yes or No?   60

When I try to delete a file on my hard disk, I get the message "File name is invalid." Why? 60

Somone said that I shouldn't put all of my files and programs in the root directory. Why? 61

Whenever I format a disk, DOS asks me if I want to give the disk a volume label. What is a volume and why might it be useful? 61

I accidentally deleted a group of files using the DOS Shell. When I used UNDELETE, I couldn't get them back. Why? 62

I was taught to park my hard drive heads before turning my computer off. My new computer has MS-DOS 6.x and the PARK command doesn't seem to work. How do I park the hard drive heads? 63

What is a file allocation table? 63

The online MS-DOS Help says that DOS 6.2's DISKCOPY performs a one-pass DISKCOPY. I get an error message saying "Error creating image file. DISKCOPY will revert to a multiple-pass copy." What's wrong? 63

How do I get a large file that will not copy to one floppy disk onto disks? 65

I am trying to clean up my hard disk and I can't delete a directory. What am I doing wrong? 65

How do lost allocation units and cross-linked clusters develop? 66

What are the limitations of DOS's FDISK command when used to partition a hard drive? 66

When I run CHKDSK, it reports that my files are using more disk space than when I use DIR and add all of the file sizes together. Why? 66

When I use XCOPY to copy a group of files, only a few or no files get copied and the message "Access Denied" appears on the screen. At this point XCOPY terminates and doesn't copy any more files. What is causing this? 67

Can I copy multiple files from nested subdirectories without using Backup? 67

When I use DIR I like it to show the files in a specific way. How can I set the DIR command to always show its results this way? 68

Can I erase the .CHK files in the root directory of my hard disk? 69

I know I have corrupted files on my disk, but I don't know which ones. How can I find out without reloading all my programs? 70

Do I use FDISK to format my hard disk? 70

How do I stop the COPY command from prompting before overwriting a file? 70

How can I remove a directory and all of its files quickly? 71

I installed a second hard drive and set my old one as my D
     drive. With FDISK, I see that I have two active partitions,
     one on each hard drive. Is this dangerous, and, if so, how
     can I fix it?   71

How do I combine multiple partitions?   72

I have about 20 small text files that I want to combine into
     one big file. Is there a quicker way to combine all the files
     versus "insert file" with my text editor?   75

An employee says the files on her floppy disk keep
     "disappearing" while she's at lunch. She thinks someone
     may be using her system and deleting the files. What can
     I do to find out what happened and/or recover the work?
     HELP!!!   76

5   Other DOS Commands   77

The time on my computer did not change for daylight saving
     time. Can I change the time?   78

Is there any way to stop a DOS command while it's running?   78

My coworker's DOS prompt shows the directory she is in, but
     my prompt just shows the active drive. How can I change
     my prompt?   78

How can I tell which version of DOS I currently have installed
     on my computer?   80

I just installed DOS 6.*x* and when I use the DIR command, I
     see "Volume in drive C is MS-DOS 5."   80

I just tried to copy files with XCOPY and saw the message "Bad
     command or file name." I've verified that the file exists
     with the DIR command. What's wrong?   81

How do I find out about the DOS commands? There isn't very
     much information in the manual.   81

What's the difference between the CD and CHDIR commands?   81

How can I add a new directory to my Path statement?   82

Is there any way to print out what DOS displays on my screen,
     such as the results of my DIR command?   84

I see CLS in my AUTOEXEC.BAT file. What does that do?   85

What is a batch file, exactly?   85

My coworker can make her last command appear by pressing
     the UP ARROW key. I can't. Why?   86

Can I use the DOS MODE command to redirect my printer
     ports from LPT1 to LPT2?   88

Is there any way to quickly find out what the contents of a file
     are from DOS without starting the program I used to
     create the file?   88

Is there any way to print files without starting a program?   89

When I turn my computer on, all the lines in the
AUTOEXEC.BAT file appear. Is there anyway to keep them
from appearing? 89

Is there any way to slow down the output of a DOS command
like DIR or TYPE? 90

Is there a faster way to make a bootable DOS disk than the
DOS FORMAT /S command? 90

I get "Cannot find file QBASIC.EXE" when I attempt to access
the online help or edit a file with the EDIT command.
What is wrong? 91

Can I include lines that do not execute in my batch file so that
I can explain to other users what the executing lines do? 91

Is there a screen saver utility that comes with DOS? 91

I have problems reading the screen in DOS because of bad
eyesight. Is there anything I can do? 92

Is there any way to make DOS execute a batch file one line at
a time? 93

How can I tell a batch file to execute different commands
depending on the outcome of a CHKDSK? 93

I need to write some batch files that get user input to choose
from a menu. Is there a way to do this? 93

How can I create the escape character when trying to use
ANSI escape sequences? 94

How can I use a function key to start a program? 95

6 Utilities **97**

Do I have to format disks before using them as backup disks? 99

Are the old BACKUP and RESTORE commands compatible
with the new MS Backup utility? 99

Why do I need to run the compatibility test before using MS
Backup for the first time? 99

How do DOS 6's deletion protection levels work? 99

What does Defrag actually do to my disk and why do I want
to use it? 101

I installed DOS 6.x. Now when I type BACKUP and press ENTER
I get the message "Incorrect DOS version." How do I back
up my files? 102

What exactly are viruses and why are they a problem? 103

Can the new Anti-Virus program protect me from all viruses? 103

I copy all the files in my \WORKING directory to a backup disk
each day. Is there a way to copy only the files that have
changed since yesterday? 104

The scroll bars in the DOS Editor disappeared. What can I do
to get them back?   105

I got an "out of memory" message when I tried to open a
document in the DOS Editor. Why?   106

Can you set margins in the DOS Editor?   107

I used the Comp utility to verify the integrity of files after
saving them to floppy disks. Why do I get the message
"Bad command or file name" with DOS 6.x?   107

What is the difference between MSAV and Vsafe, the two virus
utilities that came with MS-DOS 6.x?   108

Why does RESTORE tell me I have no files to restore, when I
can see the backup files on the disks when I use the DIR
command?   108

I used the RESTORE command, but none of the files from my
second or later disks were restored. What can I do?   109

When I run the Backup utility in Windows, it works up to a
point and then my computer just stops responding. What
is going on?   109

My computer cannot pass MS Backup's compatibility test
when I'm in Windows' Enhanced Mode, but passes with
no problem in DOS or in Windows' Standard Mode. Why?   110

I backed up my entire hard drive, then installed a new hard
drive with MS-DOS 6.x already on it. How do I restore the
data I backed up with MS-DOS 5.0's BACKUP command?   110

ScanDisk reported that it fixed my file errors, but I still can't
run some of my programs. Why?   110

I need to make backup copies of some important files, but I
only want to copy files made since Monday. Can I do it?   111

I backed up my hard drive with MS Backup, reformatted it,
and reinstalled DOS 6.x. Now I can't restore my files. How
do I get my files back?   111

I program in Assembly language and use EXE2BIN.EXE to
convert my Assembly programs to .COM files. I can't find
this utility with MS-DOS 6.x. How do I create my .COM files?   112

Can I use the MS-DOS 6.x utilities with other versions of DOS?   112

How do I get MS Backup to put the catalogs into a different
directory?   112

How often should I run Defrag?   113

I keep getting "Insufficient memory" messages when trying to
run Defrag on my 2GB external hard drive. What's wrong?   113

7 DOS Shell   **115**

How can I set up DOS Shell to open Windows?   116

I don't have a mouse cursor in DOS Shell, but I do have one in
my DOS applications. Why?   116

How can I get DOS Shell to work with my mouse? 117

I use DOS Shell and I have noticed that when I restart my computer, I have new batch files in my DOS directory. What is creating these files and can I safely delete them? 117

Why is my AUTOEXEC.BAT file deleted when I delete files from a subdirectory with DOS Shell? I'm not deleting from the root directory and the file I intended to delete is not named AUTOEXEC.BAT. 118

When I start DOS Shell, I don't see the display I'm used to seeing. What could be causing this and how do I fix it? 119

Is there any way to prevent DOS Shell from reading all the files and directories on my disk while starting? 121

Every time I leave DOS Shell I get the error message "Unable to update DOSSHELL.INI." Why? 121

Every time I try to use the Command Prompt item from my Main group I get the message "Bad command or file name" and never get to the DOS prompt. What's wrong? 122

I load DOS Shell in my AUTOEXEC.BAT file. Every time, it immediately switches to the DOS prompt. Why? 122

When I try to switch between programs, DOS Shell just stops functioning, and I need to reboot my computer. Why? 122

I added all my frequently used DOS programs to the Main group in DOS Shell. Everything is OK for a while, then some or all of my program items disappear. What's wrong? 123

I tried to get into DOS Shell after installing MS-DOS 6.2 and it wasn't there. What happened? 123

I heard I can start a program from DOS Shell by selecting the data I want to use. How do I do it? 124

How do I add my own programs to the Program List? 126

I noticed that I have both a DOSSHELL.COM and a DOSSHELL.EXE file in my DOS directory. Why? 127

When I try to start a program from DOS Shell, I get the error message "Unable to load COMMAND.COM or DOSSWAP.EXE." Why? 128

Task swapping isn't working with some of the programs I use with DOS Shell. Am I setting something wrong? 128

How can I speed up task swapping with DOS Shell? 129

Is there a way to switch the mouse buttons in DOS Shell? 129

8   DoubleSpace   131

I have Stacker but I want to use DoubleSpace. How can I convert? 134

How do I change from XtraDrive disk compression to
DoubleSpace disk compression? 135

I have DoubleSpace on my machine. I am installing a new
program. Do I run DoubleSpace again to compress this
program? 135

Do I need to back up the host drive for my DoubleSpace
compressed drive to completely back up the hard drive? 135

Can I use DoubleSpace on my floppy disks? 136

How can I compress a floppy drive and not compress my hard
drive? 136

Are there any special steps I need to take when I copy a file
from my hard drive to a floppy disk after running
DoubleSpace? 138

DoubleSpace broke my hard drive. What happened? 138

When I start DoubleSpace, I see the message "Your computer
might be running software that is incompatible with
DoubleSpace." How do I run DoubleSpace? 138

Why, since I ran DoubleSpace, do I receive the error message
"You must specify the host drive for a DoubleSpace drive"
every time the computer boots up? 139

How do I get my disk that I compressed with DoubleSpace
back the way it was? 140

Are the files put into a DoubleSpaced drive compressed as you
load them? 141

Can I store more information on backup disks if I first
DoubleSpace the disks and then back up to those disks
using MS Backup? 141

My buddy and I each have the same computer with the same
size hard drive. We both have roughly the same amount
of data, yet he got more free space when he ran
DBLSPACE than I did. Why? 141

I tried to uncompress using the command "DBLSPACE
/UNCOMPRESS C:" and received a message that there
were files in the root directory of both the compressed
drive and the host drive with identical names. The
uncompress process said that it couldn't continue until
there were no common names. Now what? 142

Can I use DoubleSpace if I am part of a network? 142

I just put some files in my compressed drive. The files must
take up more room than their size since I have a lot less
free space. What happened? 142

Can I make my compressed drive larger so I can put more
data there? 143

I tried to change the size of my compressed drive but was told
that it is too fragmented. I ran Defrag but I still get the
same message. Why?   143

Does the Defrag utility work on compressed drives?   145

How do I know which disk is my compressed disk?   145

I just ran DoubleSpace, but now I need to free up more room
on my uncompressed drive. What can I do?   146

DBLSPACE /CHKDSK reports that it found no errors, but some
of the programs are acting as if files are damaged
(program hangs, data error, etc.). Why am I having this
problem?   146

I want to format my hard drive and have it compressed with
DoubleSpace. When I type FORMAT C:, DOS displays the
message "You must use DBLSPACE /FORMAT C: to format
that drive." When I type DBLSPACE /FORMAT C:, it
doesn't work either. How can I format my hard drive
without removing DoubleSpace?   146

Every time I boot my machine, it goes into DoubleSpace. Why?   147

I have a large 1Gb hard drive. I just ran DoubleSpace but it
only gave me a 512MB DoubleSpaced drive. I expected
to get 2Gb. What went wrong?   147

I have DOS 6.0 and I used DoubleSpace on some floppy disks.
I can't access the data on the disks while in Windows. For
each floppy disk, I must exit Windows, manually mount
the disk, and then restart Windows. What am I doing
wrong?   147

I added a second hard drive and my DoubleSpaced drive C is
now drive D. However, I cannot see any of my files on
drive D. How can I regain access to my files?   148

Why is my system running slower after installing DoubleSpace?   149

I just got a DoubleGuard Alarm message. Is something wrong
with my disk?   149

I just got the message "Compressed drive C is currently too
fragmented to mount." How do I use this drive's data?   150

I just saw the message "DoubleSpace could not mount drive C
due to problems with the drive." What is wrong?   151

Can I change the level of compression used by DoubleSpace
to make more space available?   152

I installed DOS 6.2 on an older machine (8088/286) with
512K of total RAM. Why can't I run DoubleSpace?   152

Why does DoubleSpace use more memory under MS-DOS 6.2
than it did under MS-DOS 6.0?   152

When I try to shrink the size of my compressed drive, DoubleSpace gives me a maximum free space on the uncompressed drive that I can change, but it is not enough. I deleted some files from the compressed drive but the maximum size for the uncompressed drive still did not change. Why? 153

I think my application doesn't like DoubleSpace. How can I check? 153

Can I use DoubleSpace to compress my Hardcard? 157

How do I change the letter of my compressed disk? 158

9 Memory **161**

What is the difference between RAM and ROM? 164

The games I used in DOS 5 worked fine in DOS 6 until I installed DoubleSpace. Why am I getting an "Insufficient memory" error message? 164

How do I know what kind of memory I have on my computer? 165

The message "Expanded memory services unavailable" displays when I start my computer. How can I use some of my upper memory? 166

When I ran MemMaker, I chose to not set aside any EMS memory for my applications. How can I reconfigure my memory to include EMS memory for an application that requires it? 167

How can I increase the 640K memory limit I have on my computer? Can running a DOS utility, adding more memory, or buying a newer computer help? 168

Every time I boot my machine it goes into MemMaker. What's wrong? 169

My CONFIG.SYS file has DOS=HIGH, yet when I turn my computer on, I see the message "HMA not available; Loading DOS low." How do I get DOS to load high? 169

I get the message "EMM386 Exception Error #6" when I try to run an application. The application ran fine the last time I used it. What does this message mean? 170

I ran DoubleSpace on my 286 computer with 2MB of RAM, now I get "Insufficient memory" messages from other applications. Why don't I have enough memory? 170

What is the difference between the EMM386.EXE options, RAM, and NOEMS? 171

I have 8MB of RAM on my computer. How do I tell MemMaker to use all of my RAM? 171

How can I tell if DOS loaded into the high memory area? 172

After upgrading to DOS 6.*x*, CTRL+ALT+DEL does not reboot my machine. How do I get this key combination to work?   172

I have DOS=HIGH in my CONFIG.SYS file, but none of my terminate-and-stay-resident (TSR) programs seem to be loading into high memory. What am I doing wrong?   172

My computer has a 512K cache and a 1MB video RAM. Why doesn't this memory get included by the MEM command?   173

What does the HIGHSCAN parameter on the EMM386.EXE line in my CONFIG.SYS file do?   174

When I boot, I get the error message "Size of expanded memory pool adjusted. Press any key when ready...", but then it says "EMM386 successfully installed." I am specifying 8MB of expanded memory and I know that I have 8MB in my machine. Am I getting expanded memory or not?   174

Since running MemMaker I have been receiving a parity error on my computer. How can I get rid of this error?   175

How do I find out what is using my computer's conventional memory?   176

After upgrading my Packard Bell computer to DOS 6.*x*, Microsoft Windows will not run in 386 Enhanced mode. I am using the new version of EMM386.EXE. Windows ran fine with my previous version of DOS. What happened?   177

Why did MemMaker put DOS=UMB and DOS=HIGH on separate lines?   177

I just added more memory to my 486 EISA computer so now I have more than 16MB total RAM. I am using DOS's HIMEM.SYS for my extended memory manager. However, DOS's MEM command only reports 16MB. Why doesn't MEM show all of the memory?   178

I get the error message "Bad or missing *file name*" listed for EMM386.EXE and HIMEM.SYS every time I boot up. I am running Stacker on my computer. Doesn't Stacker work with high memory?   178

When running a program, my computer displays the message "EMM386 DMA buffer is too small." What is causing this and how can I prevent it?   179

Can I manually optimize and improve on MemMaker's UMB configuration?   180

Why does EMM386.EXE tell me "Cannot establish page frame"?   180

I have already optimized my memory but I need "just a little more." How can I get it?   182

I am unable to load SHARE at all. Is something wrong with the SHARE command?   183

I was running a terminal emulator for an IBM 3270 to connect my computer to a mainframe, and I was downloading a big file when my computer hung. Is this a memory problem?   184

Since I upgraded to DOS 6.2, my computer hangs with a DoubleGuard message. What is going wrong?   184

I received a "WARNING: EMM386 installed without a LIM 3.2 compatible page frame" message when I booted my computer, and my programs don't recognize the expanded memory that EMM386 created. What is wrong?   185

10   Configuration Issues   187

I have an application whose Setup program requires installation from floppy drive A, but my disks fit in my floppy drive B. Is there any way to install the program?   189

Every time I boot my computer since installing MS-DOS 6.2, HIMEM.SYS says there are problems with my RAM. If I boot without HIMEM.SYS, it runs fine. How do I turn off this warning?   190

What is a "clean boot" and why would I need it?   191

I created a "clean boot" system disk and rebooted my machine with it in drive A, but my system ignored it and just booted from drive C. Did I do something wrong?   193

I just installed MS-DOS 6.2 on my computer, and now it hangs every time I try to access my A or B drive. Why?   193

I have heard coworkers use the term "cash" when referring to their computer. What is it?   194

What does it mean when DOS displays "Bad command or file name"?   194

What is the BUFFERS command used for in the CONFIG.SYS file?   195

What is SMARTDrive and how will it benefit my system?   195

What does the FCBS command in the CONFIG.SYS mean?   196

I always see the line "@ECHO OFF" in AUTOEXEC.BAT files. If I don't add that line, what will happen?   196

When I booted my computer, I got the message "Unrecognized command in CONFIG.SYS line" and a line number. How do I fix this problem?   197

I'm getting the "Bad or Missing Command Interpreter" message, but then I get a DOS prompt. Still, nothing seems to work. I've seen the error message in MS-DOS 5 before, but I was never able to get a DOS prompt. What's going on?   197

Sometimes, when exiting programs like Windows, I get the
    message "Invalid COMMAND.COM." What's causing this?   198

I get the error message "Out of environment space." What's
    environment space and how can I get more?   198

Can I change the drive letter of my RAM drive?   199

After performing an MS-DOS upgrade, I receive the "Incorrect
    DOS version" error message whenever I try to execute
    some DOS commands. Why?   199

I heard someone mention something called CMOS. What is it
    and do I have one?   199

I hate the comma separators when I do a DIR in DOS 6.2.
    How can I get the output to look like 5.0?   200

After I make a change to my AUTOEXEC.BAT file, do I have to
    reboot my machine to get those changes to show up?   200

I just changed my AUTOEXEC.BAT or CONFIG.SYS file. When I
    boot my computer, either file displays strange characters
    and no longer works. What happened?   200

I upgraded from MS-DOS 3.1 to 6.2 and now my floppy
    drives don't format properly. Why?   201

I just installed 6.2 on my machine and when I reboot, I see
    "HIMEM is testing extended memory ..." and my machine
    stops. It does not go any further. What has happened?   202

I'm running MS-DOS 6.2 and I'm having problems accessing
    my floppy drives. I don't understand it. Everything was
    fine under 6.0. Now what?   203

What is a RAM drive and how do I get one?   203

I heard that I can speed up my applications by placing my
    temp files on a RAM drive. How do I do this?   204

DOS is black and white. How can I make it color?   205

When I boot my machine up I get the error message "Cannot
    run SMARTDrive 4.0 with DoubleSpace." I have a
    SMARTDRV.EXE file in my Windows and DOS directories.
    Which one should I use?   206

The computer executes the CONFIG.SYS, but then freezes
    without giving me a DOS prompt. Why?   206

I have just upgraded to DOS 6 and the Num Lock light is on!
    It never used to be on. How can I make it go away?   207

At bootup, I get the error message "Missing operating
    system." Why?   207

How do I use SMARTDrive from DOS 6.2 to cache my
    CD-ROM drive?   208

After I turn it on, my computer freezes during the list of
    programs loading into memory. Why?   208

How can I use my computer's upper memory area (UMA)? 209

I am running out of memory. Can DOS use less so my other programs have more? 210

Why does booting take longer with DOS 6? 211

I heard that I can set DOS to extend my laptop's battery usage. How? 211

In my multiple configuration, how can I have a choice in my submenu to return me to the previous menu? 212

Why does my multiple configuration menu flash on and off when I use the MENUCOLOR command to set the color of the multiple configuration menu? 214

I just got the message "Inconsistency between startup and MemMaker STS file." What is this problem and how do I solve it? 215

How do I set up a path with more than 127 characters? 215

I want to run Interlnk but when I try to use it, it tells me I must install it. I thought Interlnk was installed when I installed DOS. What's wrong? 216

What is the top transfer rate if I am using Interlnk with a serial cable? 216

I am trying to install Interlnk and I continue to get the "Connection not established" message. Why? 217

Is Interlnk faster with a serial or parallel cable? 217

I recently upgraded to a 400MB hard drive. After I restored all of my data, something's changed! Why does CHKDSK report that the data that used to fit on my 200MB drive now uses 230MB? 218

My computer says that "SMARTDrive cannot cache a compressed drive." I want to cache my C drive, so what can I do? 219

What is a Master Boot Record? 219

I set up CONFIG.SYS and AUTOEXEC.BAT perfectly. How do I prevent someone else from skipping over their contents by pressing F5 or F8? 219

I just got an "EMM386 exception error #12" message. What does that mean and what can I do? 220

I just got an "EMM386 exception error #13," what can I do? 220

I have installed MS-DOS 6.x and compressed both drives C and D using DoubleSpace. Now my computer tells me there are "Too many block devices." What is a block device? Why do I now have too many? 220

Since installing DOS 6.*x*, my CD-ROM drive is not working properly. I also see the message "Incorrect DOS version" during bootup. Is there something that I need to do in DOS to make it function again?   221

I think I have a problem with DBLSPACE.BIN. Can I boot without loading it?   222

I want to use different CONFIG.SYS and AUTOEXEC.BAT files. Do I need to create separate boot disks for each set of CONFIG.SYS and AUTOEXEC.BAT files?   222

I have multiple startup configurations, and I have problems running MemMaker. Can this be done?   224

How do I set up my computer to use an alternate keyboard layout and character set for international use?   226

One of my programs has problems recognizing which key I am pressing. Is something wrong with my keyboard?   227

I loaded something with DEVICEHIGH or LOADHIGH but it didn't work because the programs I loaded high are in conventional memory. What happened?   228

11   Interoperability   229

I just installed DOS 6.*x* on my IBM PS/1 computer. A four-quadrant IBM screen used to appear when I started the computer, but now I only see the DOS prompt. Why?   231

I have 4MB of RAM. Since upgrading to MS-DOS 6.*x*, Windows tells me that there is not enough memory to start in Enhanced mode. Why?   232

After installing MS-DOS 6.*x* and DoubleSpace, Windows is much slower. What happened?   232

My mouse stopped working in my DOS applications and the MS-DOS Editor. However, it still works in Windows. How can I fix this?   233

I get a message saying "Permanent swap file is corrupt" when I start Windows. I create a new one in Windows, but when I restart Windows I get the same message again. Am I doing something wrong?   234

I can't use the DOS-based MS Backup when I'm in Windows. Why not?   234

What is a BIOS and how do I know what type and date I have?   235

When I run Setup for any program, the Setup program won't accept the second Setup disk, but continually asks for it to be inserted. How can I install my program?   236

I have a program with a built-in backup feature designed to back up its data files. Since upgrading to DOS 6.*x*, the backup feature doesn't work. Why?   238

I installed MS-DOS 6.2 and now I get "EMM386: Unable to start enhanced Windows mode due to invalid path specification for EMM386" when I try to start Windows. What's wrong? 239

Why do I get the error message "Incorrect DOS version" when I attempt to go to the DOS Prompt program item in Windows? This started after upgrading to DOS 6.*x*. 240

Windows and some other programs will not start since I upgraded to MS-DOS 6.*x*. Why? 240

My printer isn't working. Is there a reliable way to test the printer to see if the problem is either hardware- or software-related? 241

Why did I lose my compressed Stacker drives after upgrading to MS-DOS 6.2? 242

I have an older version of Norton Utilities/PC Tools. It worked fine with MS-DOS 5.0. Why do I need to upgrade, now that I have upgraded to MS-DOS 6.*x*? 242

When I try to start a DOS program from Windows, I get the message "Insufficient File Handles." What can I do? I'm on a network. 243

Why can't Interlnk share my CD-ROM drive? 243

How do I configure Lotus 1-2-3 3.*x* to work in DOS Shell? 244

When I start Windows 3.0, I see the message "You must have the file WINA20.386 in the root of your boot drive to run Windows in Enhanced Mode." How do I run Windows? 244

I keep getting the error message "Memory parity error" when I open an application in Windows. How do I get rid of this message? 245

I want to delete a non-DOS partition on my hard drive. Can I do it with DOS? 246

I'm having trouble with my Clipper database after installing MS-DOS 6.*x*. Any ideas about what to do? 246

I'm using a virus detection program other than MSAV. It detects a virus infecting one of the MSAV files. Is my system in trouble? 246

I installed MS-DOS 6.*x* and no longer have the OS/2 Boot Manager. How do I get it back? 247

Why can't I load DOS into high memory on my Zenith SuperSport? 247

Each time I start my system it stops responding after loading Above DISC. What can I do to fix this? 248

12 Networking **249**

Will DOS 6 work with my network? 251

Can I add a program item to DOS Shell for my network? 252

Does MemMaker work if I am on a network? 252

My programs do not run correctly when they use expanded
memory and I am connected to a network. How do I get
my programs to work? 253

I'm on a LANtastic or 10Net network and can't run
DoubleSpace on my local hard drive. How can I compress
my local drive? 253

I'm on a LANtastic network and I can't run ScanDisk to check
my local hard drive. How do I run ScanDisk? 254

Why, after installing MS-DOS 6.0 and DoubleSpace, do I get
the error message "Invalid drive specification" when I try
to go to my login drive on my Novell network? 254

How can I run MSD on my computer that is on an ArcNet
network? 256

I cannot run my AT&T StarGroup network after running DOS
6 Setup. How do I get my network running? 256

After upgrading to DOS 6.x, I frequently see the message
"Incorrect DOS version" when I use DOS commands on a
network. What causes this error message? 257

When attempting to load my NETX.COM for my Novell
network, why do I get an "Incorrect DOS version" or "Not
running on DOS V3.0 through V5.0" message? 258

Can I back up my Novell network drive using DOS 6's Backup? 259

I'm running into several problems since I upgraded my Novell
network. Did I do something wrong? 259

I'm trying to load the hard disk driver for my Novell NetWare
server but no matter what I do, it says that the file does
not exist. I checked my DOS partition and it's there. What
is happening? 260

I am running Novell's NetWare Lite and now every time I try
to use certain drives, I get the "Not ready" error message.
What is wrong? 260

13 **Error Messages**   **261**

Abort, Retry, Fail, Ignore? 262

Access denied 262

Allocation error. Size adjusted. 262

Bad command or file name 263

Bad or missing C:\directory\filename.ext
Error in CONFIG.SYS line x 263

Bad or missing command interpreter 263

Cannot find file QBASIC.EXE 264

Cannot load COMMAND.COM, system halted   264

Cannot make directory entry   264

Cannot move multiple files to a single file   265

Cannot run SMARTDrive 4.0 with DoubleSpace   265

A CVF is damaged   265

Data error   266

Directory already exists   266

Disk unsuitable for system disk   266

Divide overflow   266

DoubleGuard Alarm #nn   266

Drive not ready   267

Drive or diskette types not compatible   267

Duplicate file name or file not found   267

EMM386 DMA buffer is too small   267

EMM386 Exception Error #6   267

EMM386 Exception Error #12   268

EMM386 Exception Error #13   268

EMM386 Not Installed - Protected Mode Software Already
    Running   268

EMM386: Unable to start enhanced mode Windows due to
    invalid path specification for EMM386   268

Error creating image file. Diskcopy will revert to a
    multiple-pass copy   269

Error in EXE file   269

ERROR: missing parameter.   269

Expanded memory services unavailable   270

An extended memory manager is already installed   270

File allocation table bad   270

File cannot be copied onto itself   270

File creation error   270

File not found   271

Format terminated. Format another (Y/N)?   271

From DoubleSpace: There is not enough free conventional
    memory   271

General failure reading/writing to drive X: 271

Incorrect DOS version   272

Insufficient disk space   272

Insufficient memory   273

Internal stack overflow. System halted   273

Invalid COMMAND.COM   273
Invalid date   273
Invalid directory   274
Invalid drive specification   274
Invalid media type or track 0 bad - Disk unusable   274
Invalid number of parameters   274
Invalid parameter   274
Invalid path, not directory, or directory not empty   275
Missing operating system   275
No room for system on destination disk   275
Non-system disk or disk error   275
Not ready reading/writing drive *X:*   276
Out of environment space   276
Parameters not supported by drive   276
Path not found   276
Probable Non-DOS disk. Continue (Y/N)?   276
Required parameter missing   277
Syntax error   277
Target disk bad or incompatible   277
Too many parameters   277
Unable to create directory   277
Unable to load COMMAND.COM or DOSSWAP.EXE   278
Unable to write BOOT   278
Unrecognized command in CONFIG.SYS
    Error in CONFIG.SYS line *X*   278
Unrecoverable read/write error on drive A, side 1, track 29   278
WARNING: EMM386 installed without a LIM 3.2 compatible
    page frame. Press any key to continue   279
Write failure, diskette unusable   279
Write Fault error reading/writing to device XXX: 279
Write Protect Error   279
You must specify the host drive for a DoubleSpace drive   279

A   Glossary   **281**

Index   **311**

Foreword

Few things are as frustrating as having a computer problem that you can't solve. Computer users often spend hours trying to find the answer to a *single* software question! That's why the tech support experts at Corporate Software Incorporated (CSI) have teamed up with Osborne/McGraw-Hill to bring you the **Certified Tech Support Series**—books designed to give you all the solutions you need to fix even the most difficult software glitches.

At Corporate Software, we have a dedicated support staff that handles over 200,000 software questions every month. These experts use the latest hardware and software technology to provide answers to every sort of software problem. CSI takes full advantage of the partnerships that we have forged with all major software publishers. Our staff frequently receives the same training that publishers offer their own support representatives and has access to vendor technical resources that are not generally available to the public.

Thus, this series is based on actual *empirical* data. We've drawn on our support expertise and sorted through our vast database of software solutions to find the most important and frequently asked questions for MS-DOS. These questions have also been checked and rechecked for technical accuracy and are organized in a way that will let you find the answer you need quickly— providing you with a one-stop tech support solution to your software problems.

No longer do you have to spend hours on the phone waiting for someone to answer your tech support question! You are holding the single, most authoritative collection of answers to your software questions available—the next best thing to having a tech support expert by your side.

We've helped millions of people solve their software problems. Let us help you.

Randy Burkhart
Senior Vice President, Technology
Corporate Software Inc.

Acknowledgments

I would like to thank all the staff at Corporate Software who enthusiastically committed so much time and knowledge to this effort. So many of them spent time on weekends and after hours to search their data banks for the best questions and answers. They also spent untold hours reviewing manuscript and pages and responding to all of our requests for help. Without all of their hard work, this book would not exist. I would like to personally thank each of the following people for their assistance.

Alan S.	Jordan B.	**Special thanks to:**
Anthony L.	Laura C.	Jan R.
Brian K.	Michael L.	Jay C.
Caren C.	Paul P.	Kim A.
Daniel G.	Robert B.	Tom B.
Dan D.	Robert E.	Doug F.
David D.	Ronald P.	Chiu fai S.
David K.	Steve W.	Kathy M.
David M.	Tim L.	
Dennis D.	Ty G.	
Haik S.	Virginia M.	

The staff at Osborne was also an important part of this book. Because it was the first book in the series, with design and other issues to work out, there was limited time to get it all done. Without exception, they all did more than their share to insure that we met all the important deadlines. I would like to extend special thanks to: Larry Levitsky, Publisher, for the idea to do the series and all of his work with Corporate Software to make the idea a reality; Scott Rogers, Acquisitions Editor, who took the time to read each chapter and made excellent suggestions for improvements; Sherith Pankrantz, Editorial Assistant, who helped to organize all the components of the project; Claire Splan, Project Editor, who managed the editorial process and did an excellent job of editing the manuscript; and Marla Shelasky and all of the Production staff, who created not one, but several book designs to find the one that made the information as accessible as possible.

Lastly, I would like to thank my assistants, Gabrielle Lawrence and Elizabeth Reinhardt. They contributed extensively to the book's contents and art work, and proofed the final pages to help catch technical and grammatical errors.

Introduction

There is no good time to have a problem with your computer or the software you are using. You are anxious to complete the task you started and do not have time to fumble through a manual looking for an answer that is probably not there anyway. You can forget about the option of a free support call solving your problems since most software vendors now charge as much as $25 to answer a single question. *DOS Answers: Certified Tech Support* can provide the solution to all of your MS-DOS problems. It contains the most frequently asked DOS questions along with the solutions to get you back on track quickly. The questions and answers have been extracted from the data banks of Corporate Software, the world's largest supplier of third-party support. Since they answer over 200,000 calls a month from users just like you, odds are high that your problem has plagued others in the past and is already part of their data bank. *DOS Answers: Certified Tech Support* is the next best thing to having a Corporate Software expert at the desk right next to you. The help you need is available seven days a week, any time you have a problem.

   DOS Answers is organized into 13 chapters. Each chapter contains questions and answers on a specific area of MS-DOS. Within each chapter you will find the simplest questions at the beginning, progressing to intermediate and advanced questions as you move through the chapter. With this organization, you will be able to read through questions and answers on particular topics to familiarize yourself with them before the troubles actually occur. An excellent index makes it easy for you to find what you need even if you are uncertain which chapter would cover the solution.

Throughout the book you will also find the following elements to help you sail smoothly through your DOS tasks whether you are a novice or a veteran user:

- **Frustration Busters:** Special coverage of DOS topics that have proven confusing to many users. A few minutes spent reading each of these boxes can help you avoid problems in the first place.

- **Tech Tips and Notes:** Short technical helps that provide additional insight to a topic addressed in one of the questions.

- **Tech Terrors:** Pitfalls you will want to steer clear of.

- **Frequently Used DOS Terms:** DOS has a lingo all its own. If you are new to DOS, you will want to browse through the terms in Appendix A. Learning to speak a little of DOS's language will put you a step ahead when DOS error messages do appear on your screen.

Top Ten Tech Terrors

Every computer user experiences technical problems at some time. We've tapped the data banks and consultant expertise at Corporate Software and identified the ten most common problems people encounter when using DOS. These are problems that *thousands* of users have run into. You may find it worthwhile to read through this list as a preventive measure, so that you can avoid these problems altogether.

The problems presented in this chapter are varied. DoubleSpace and MemMaker are represented because they are new features of DOS 6 which many users are unfamiliar with. Other problems relate to incompatibilities of the new release of DOS with an older version of other products or your particular hardware configuration. You can think of these answers to the ten most common problems plaguing DOS users as insurance. If these things do go wrong in the future, you will know exactly how to fix the problem.

How do I remove DoubleSpace?

DoubleSpace increases the disk's storage capacity by compressing the information stored on a disk. However, you may want to remove DoubleSpace if you find that it does not work with your hardware configuration or your software. You may also want to replace DoubleSpace with a third-party disk compression program.

To remove DoubleSpace with MS-DOS 6.2 you must first start DoubleSpace;

1. Type **DBLSPACE** at the DOS prompt and press ENTER.

2. Select Uncompress from the Tools menu and select Yes to uncompress the highlighted compressed drive.

3. Select Exit from the Drive menu to leave DoubleSpace.

In MS-DOS 6, you cannot automatically remove DoubleSpace, but will have to do so manually, using these steps:

1. Use MS Backup to back up the files on the compressed drive. You will want to make sure that MS Backup is copied to a floppy disk or another drive, such as your host drive.

   The program files for MS Backup include:

DEFAULT.SET	MSBACKFG.OVL	MSBACKUP.LOG
MSBACKDB.OVL	MSBACKFR.OVL	MSBACKUP.OVL
MSBACKDR.OVL	MSBACKUP.EXE	MSBACKUP.RST
MSBACKFB.OVL	MSBACKUP.INI	

   To save time when you perform the backup, you may only want to back up your data files, not your program files, assuming that you still have the disks for all of your programs.

2. Type **DBLSPACE** at the DOS prompt and press ENTER.

3. Select the Info command from the Drive menu and make a note of which drive contains the file for the compressed drive.

4. Copy the file COMMAND.COM (usually found in the \DOS directory) from your compressed drive to the root directory of your uncompressed drive.

5. From your uncompressed drive, type **DELTREE DBLSPACE.*** and press ENTER.

6. Restart your computer by pressing CTRL+ALT+DEL.

7. Use MS Backup to restore your backed-up files.

If your program files are on floppy disks, you need to copy them to the hard disk or reinstall them.

Tech Tip: MS Backup knows where to place the restored files on your hard drive because it saves a catalog file which records the files that were backed up. If you don't copy this file to your uncompressed drive or a floppy disk, you will need to restore it from your backup disks before you restore the other files. To do so, select Restore, then Catalog in the MS Backup utility.

2 MemMaker starts every time I boot my machine. How can I stop this?

This problem indicates that your sytem's memory was not successfully optimized by MemMaker. During the MemMaker process, MemMaker information lines are temporarily added to the CONFIG.SYS and AUTOEXEC.BAT files. If there was some type of conflict, MemMaker might not have been able to complete the process. This will leave the MemMaker lines in the CONFIG.SYS and AUTOEXEC.BAT files, because MemMaker was unable remove the lines. Any program that starts from the AUTOEXEC.BAT file and does not immediately return control of the system, such as a menu program, can cause this problem. You will see a message like the one in Figure 1-1. To correct it, you need to edit the AUTOEXEC.BAT file. To do this:

1. Exit MemMaker.

2. Type **CD ** and press ENTER to move to the root directory.

3. Type **EDIT AUTOEXEC.BAT** and press ENTER.

4. Add **REM** to the beginning of any line that executes a menu or other program, except terminate-and-stay-resident programs (TSRs).

5. Select Save from the File menu to save the file.

6. Select Exit from the File menu to return to the DOS prompt.

7. Press CTRL+ALT+DEL to reboot your system.

```
Microsoft® MemMaker
-----------------------------------------------------------------------


Your computer system was restarted before MemMaker finished determining
the memory requirements of your device drivers and memory-resident
programs.

   If MemMaker was interrupted accidentally, or if you are not
   sure what happened, choose "Try again with the same settings."


   If you restarted your computer because it was not working
   properly, choose "Cancel and undo all changes." MemMaker
   will stop optimizing your computer's memory and will restore
   your original system files. To fix the problem, see the
   Troubleshooting section of the "Making More Memory Available"
   chapter in the MS-DOS User's Guide.

   Try again or cancel? Cancel and undo all changes



ENTER=Accept Selection       SPACE=Change Selection        F1=Help
```

FIGURE 1-1   If MemMaker starts each time you reboot, this message displays.

If your system reboots directly to a DOS prompt after executing the AUTOEXEC.BAT file, then you are ready to run MemMaker. After MemMaker is complete, you can remove the REM statements from the AUTOEXEC.BAT file.

I installed MS-DOS 6.2 and now I get "EMM386: Unable to start enhanced Windows mode due to invalid path specification for EMM386" when I try to start Windows. What's wrong?

This error message is rather deceiving because very often it has nothing to do with whether your Path statement is correct. In fact, it often appears because of your Anti-Virus software. The Microsoft Anti-Virus utility keeps track of every file on your hard drive using what are called Checksums. After the Stepup installation, many DOS files have been changed, including EMM386.EXE. Your Anti-Virus software now sees these changed files as possibly being infected by a virus.

To fix this problem, you must either re-scan your hard drive with the Anti-Virus software and choose Update when it stops on your DOS files, or disable VSafe, the memory resident portion of the Anti-Virus software. Since VSafe is typically started in your AUTOEXEC.BAT file, you can disable it by simply adding **REM** at the beginning of the line in your AUTOEXEC.BAT file that starts VSafe. Then, reboot your system for your change to take effect.

If you are using the Windows version of the Anti-Virus utility, you use different steps to fix this problem.

1. Start Windows in Standard mode by typing **WIN /S** and pressing ENTER.

2. Start your Microsoft Anti-Virus utility.

3. Select Set Options from the Options menu and make sure the Create New Checksums check box is selected. (It should be filled with an X.)

4. Select OK, then choose Detect.

5. Anti-Virus detecting will pause on the modified DOS files with a warning.

6. Choose Update to update the Anti-Virus software with the new file conditions. You should then be able to run Windows in 386 Enhanced mode again.

I have installed DOS 6.x and when I enter BACKUP I get a message stating "Incorrect DOS version." What should I do?

BACKUP.EXE is not included on the version 6.x disks. DOS 6.x ships with two new backup programs, one for DOS and one for Windows. If there is a BACKUP.EXE in your DOS directory it is from a previous version of DOS. You need to use the Setver command to include Backup, as in:

```
SETVER BACKUP.EXE 5.00
```

This will add Backup to the Setver table and allow it to work with DOS 6.*x*.

I backed up my hard drive with MS Backup, reformatted it, and then reinstalled DOS. Now I can't restore my files. What's wrong?

MS Backup stores information about each backup you make in the BACKUP set catalog. Ordinarily, the catalog files are in the DOS directory. However, since you reformatted the hard drive, the file is gone. You'll need to:

1. Start MS Backup. You will probably need to rerun the compatibility test.

2. Choose Restore, then Catalog, then Retrieve.

3. Select the correct disk drive and insert the last disk of the backup set, which contains the catalog.

MS Backup then retrieves the catalog and places it in your \DOS directory. After this step is completed you can load the catalog. You can now choose Select Files and choose the files you want to restore. You do not have to restore your DOS directory since you have already reinstalled DOS.

After I installed DOS 6.*x* and ran DoubleSpace, my computer starting saying that I had "insufficient memory" when I tried running memory-intensive programs. What's wrong?

DoubleSpace consumes between 38K and 52K of memory, depending on your configuration. For memory-hungry applications such as games or graphics programs, this loss of conventional memory can cause real problems. One way to free memory is to disable drivers for anything not needed to run your current program, such as fax boards or CD-ROM drivers.

■ You can disable individual drivers by adding REM to the beginning of the lines that start those drivers in your

Tech Tip: If you are unsure of what a particular driver is for, do not remove it. Call the software company for assistance.

AUTOEXEC.BAT or CONFIG.SYS file, then restarting your system.

■ You can create a boot disk with no CONFIG.SYS or AUTOEXEC.BAT file, and use that disk to boot your system before using memory-intensive programs. To do so, put a formatted disk in drive A, type **SYS A:**, and press ENTER. If the memory-intensive program you wish to run is saved on your host drive, rather than your compressed drive, delete the hidden file, DBLSPACE.BIN, from the boot disk to free the memory that DoubleSpace would usually use.

■ You can bypass your AUTOEXEC.BAT or CONFIG.SYS file by pressing F5 when you start your computer and your screen displays "Starting MS-DOS".

Tech Tip: Your memory-intensive program may use devices, such as a mouse, that require that the device drivers be installed. If it does, and you choose to completely bypass your AUTOEXEC.BAT and CONFIG.SYS files, then you will need to manually install those drivers at the DOS prompt before using the program. You may want instead to boot your computer and press F8 to select which device drivers are loaded.

When I boot my machine, it says "CVF is damaged." What should I do now?

The "CVF is damaged" message appears to warn you that data corruption is starting to appear on your compressed hard drive. If the situation is allowed to continue, the damage may worsen, possibly to the point where data is lost. To avoid this:

1. Make a backup of any important information of the drive.

2. Next, you need to check or repair the corruption.

   a. If you have MS-DOS 6.2, run ScanDisk. ScanDisk is able to repair most forms of file corruption.

   b. If you have MS-DOS 6.0, run Chkdsk by entering **CHKDSK /F** and pressing ENTER. Chkdsk may detect crosslinked files, and detect and repair lost allocation units or other errors. However, Chkdsk repairs these errors by deleting the file after the occurrence of the error, making its corrections often as damaging as the error.

If ScanDisk cannot repair the corruption, or if the damage detected with Chkdsk is severe, you may need to back up the drive with the corrupted files, reformat it, and restore your data. You can use the MS Backup utility with DOS 6.x to back up and restore your files.

As I'm booting up, I see the message "Cannot run SMARTDrive 4.0 with DoubleSpace." Isn't SMARTDrive compatible with DoubleSpace?

SMARTDrive is a disk-caching application which speeds up disk operations and lets you work with hard drive controllers that do not recognize extended memory. DoubleSpace compresses a hard drive so that it can hold more information. While the two programs can work together, the older versions of SMARTDrive do not know how to work with DoubleSpace. Therefore, you need to load the version of SMARTDrive that ships with MS-DOS 6.x for it to work with DoubleSpace. To do this, edit your AUTOEXEC.BAT file so that the line for SMARTDrive reads C:\DOS\SMARTDRV.EXE *parameters* in which *parameters* represents the settings for SMARTDrive. If SMARTDrive is loading from the \WINDOWS directory, you're probably loading the old version.

I just installed MS-DOS 6.x on my IBM PS/1. When I boot my computer, I receive an "Incorrect DOS version" error message and/or "Invalid COMMAND.COM." Did I do something wrong?

The IBM PS/1 has the original DOS on a ROM chip inside the computer. In order to solve this problem, you must disable the ROM DOS by using the Customize utility in the DOS directory. Turn off the computer, and hold ALT+PRINT SCREEN while turning the computer back on. This will bypass the ROM chip and allow the computer to boot off the hard drive. Then run CUSTOMIZ from the DOS prompt.

10 When I run Stepup for MS-DOS 6.2, it says that it can't update some of my DOS files. Why not?

The files are either missing or are not an exact match of the MS-DOS 6.0 file. Stepup checks each file to make sure that it is an original 6.0 file. If it is not, then Stepup will not update it. If you have the MS-DOS 6.0 upgrade, exit Stepup, reinstall MS-DOS 6.0 by entering **SETUP /Q** and pressing ENTER, then rerun Stepup.

If your copy of MS-DOS 6.0 came pre-installed on your machine—an OEM (Original Equipment Manufacturer) version—try the above process. If Stepup still fails, call the manufacturer to see if they have a special version of Stepup. The Microsoft version will update some, but not all, OEM versions of DOS 6.0.

Setup

Before you can use a new version of MS-DOS on your computer you must install the new DOS files on your hard disk. Microsoft refers to this installation process as setup. The setup process:

- analyzes the hardware and software you have and notifies you of problem conditions

- creates an Uninstall disk that allows you to boot your system or revert to the old DOS version

- creates a subdirectory for the old DOS files (OLD_DOS.x) and copies them to that directory

- expands the files on the Setup disk

- copies the files to your hard disk

- installs the Anti-Virus, Backup, and Undelete utilities

The setup procedure requires only a few minutes of your time and ties up your computer system for no more than 20 minutes. If you don't have a current backup of your data, you may want to invest additional time to complete the needed backup procedures first. To minimize your frustration and the total time committed to the task, look at the suggestions in the Frustration Busters box.

FRUSTRATION BUSTERS!

There are many problems that you can circumvent with the proper preparation before you begin Setup. Perhaps the most important part of a successful setup procedure is making sure you have equipment and software that is compatible with MS-DOS 6.*x*. The following suggestions will help insure your success:

- Check to see that you have MS-DOS 2.11 or higher installed on your computer if you are using the upgrade kit, or DOS 6.0 if you are using the Stepup kit.

- Remove any virus protection, delete protection, and disk caching software that you may be running.

- Disable any other message services or terminate-and-stay-resident software that may be running. You may need to add **REM** at the beginning of lines in your AUTOEXEC.BAT and CONFIG.SYS files (using the DOS Editor), then reboot your system to temporarily disable these features.

- Have a blank disk that will work with drive A in case of an emergency. The disk may be formatted or unformatted.

My Setup disk doesn't seem to be working. Should I return it?

If your Setup disk isn't working, it's probably because you have a low-density drive that cannot read the high-density Setup disk. You can obtain a low-density disk replacement at no cost by completing and mailing in the Low-Density Disk Offer form at the back of the MS-DOS Upgrade book that came with your software. Be sure to specify whether you need 3.5" or 5.25" disks.

If you are uncertain if density differences are causing your problem, check the density of the drive you are using by trying to format a blank disk. Follow these steps:

1. Place a blank disk in the drive.

2. Type **FORMAT A:** and press ENTER.

If you are using a drive other than A, substitute that drive letter for A in step 2 above. DOS will attempt to format the disk with the highest density the drive supports. If you use a 3.5" disk and see that DOS is attempting to format 1.44MB, you will know you have a high-density disk. If you format a 5.25" disk and see that DOS is attempting to format 1.2MB, the drive is high density. Formatting either size disk in a low-density drive would display smaller megabyte sizes accordingly.

Ignore any error messages that you receive while formatting since your only interest is verifying the density supported by the drive.

Why should I keep my Uninstall disk?

It is helpful to keep the Uninstall disk because if for some reason you cannot boot from your hard disk, you can use it to boot your system. The Uninstall disk includes a record of how your hard disk and operating system were configured before the system was upgraded and is the recommended way to revert back to your previous version of MS-DOS.

Do I need to back up my data before I upgrade to DOS 6.*x*?

It is definitely a good idea to back up your files before you upgrade. Although Setup does not *require* you to back up your data and, theoretically, will do nothing to damage your data files, you will feel more comfortable knowing that your data is safe should any problems occur while setting up. If you are upgrading to DOS 6.*x*, and want to run DoubleSpace, the new disk-compression program, you should definitely make complete backups of your data. DoubleSpace reads all of your files, compresses them, and writes them back to the disk. If something should cause DoubleSpace to fail—incompatible hardware or an untimely power surge, for example—you will likely lose all of the data on your hard disk.

In fact, you should back up your data files if your hard drive uses any sort of disk-compression program. You cannot create an Uninstall disk if you use a disk-compression program. Therefore, if MS-DOS 6.x's Setup and your disk-compression program do not work well together, you will have no way to restore your data if your hard drive crashes.

Tech Tip: Creating a complete backup of your hard drive can take a while. If you make sure that you have reliable backups of all your programs, you can simplify the process by only backing up your data files, such as word-processing documents. However, you will lose any customization settings you have created for your programs if you have to reinstall from the original program disks.

My computer got turned off while it was still running Setup. What do I do?

There are two different procedures you can use when Setup is stopped before DOS is completely installed. The first thing you need to do is decide which procedure you need to use. To find out, follow these steps:

1. Take the floppy disks out of all of the drives.

2. Press CTRL+ALT+DEL.

If DOS prompts you for an Uninstall disk, place it in the appropriate drive and respond to the prompts on the screen. If DOS starts without prompting for an Uninstall disk:

1. Make sure you can still read your hard drive. To do this,

   a. Type **DIR C:\ /P** and press ENTER. You should see a listing of files and directories in the root directory of your hard drive. Since you used the /P switch, only one screen of file names will appear at a time. Press any key to continue the listing until it is finished.

   b. Type **DIR C:*DIRECTORY*** , in which *DIRECTORY* is the name of one of the directories on your hard disk, and

Tech Tip: If Setup just stopped without any warning, try restarting Setup by typing **A:\SETUP /I**. This disables the Setup feature that looks at your hardware and automatically determines what type you have. This may work if Setup is incorrectly analyzing your hardware configuration. Note that you will have to respond manually as Setup asks you about your hardware.

press ENTER. Again, you should see a listing of files and any subdirectories.

2. Now that you are sure you can access your hard drive, you will want to create a startup disk. To do this:

   a. Put a disk in your A drive.

   b. Type **FORMAT A: /S,** and press ENTER.

3. With the newly created startup disk in drive A, press CTRL+ALT+DEL.

You are restarting your computer with the new startup disk in order to avoid any settings that might have been changed in your AUTOEXEC.BAT or CONFIG.SYS file by Setup.

4. Once again, make sure that you can access your hard drive by checking the contents of the root directory and another directory, as described in step 1.

5. Put Setup Disk 1 in a floppy disk drive, then type **A:\SETUP** in which A is the name of the disk drive you are using.

Setup should start running again normally. If you receive a message about an incompatible partition, stop the program immediately. This message indicates that there may be some damage done to your hard drive. You will need to contact the manufacturer of your equipment or a computer repair service.

Is there any way to interrupt Setup once I have started it?

You can interrupt Setup at any time by pressing F3. You may need to press F3 twice, depending on what Setup is doing at that point. Do not interrupt Setup by turning your computer off.

I started Setup, but can't read the screens that are appearing. Did I buy the wrong version of DOS?

You probably have the right version of DOS unless the only operating system on your computer is OS/2. In this case, you will need to contact the vendor who sold you your computer for information about how to setup MS-DOS 6.*x*. However, if you already have DOS on your computer, your problem is most likely your hardware. Setup for 6.*x* automatically detects the type of hardware you have. This includes the type of monitor or keyboard you are using. If Setup misidentifies your hardware, it will send messages to the hardware that the hardware can't understand. If this is the problem, you can follow these steps:

1. Quit Setup by pressing F3 twice.
2. With the Setup Disk 1 in the drive, type **A:\SETUP /I**, in which A is the name of the drive you are using, and press ENTER. The /I switch disables the automatic hardware detection for Setup.
3. During Setup, you will be prompted to tell what type of hardware you are using. If you aren't sure what all the hardware parts are, you will want to find the manuals that came with your computer system and its components and look through them for the correct identification.

I was running Setup to install DOS and I got the message "Cannot find a hard disk on your computer." What happened?

You may have a real problem. There are only three reasons to see this message.

1. Your hard drive or its driver is incompatible with Setup. If this is true, you need to consult your computer's documentation or call the manufacturer of your computer to find out what to do.
2. Your hard drive isn't working correctly. In this case, you will need to contact a computer repair service to find out what's wrong and have your hard drive fixed or replaced.
3. Your computer is not correctly recognizing your hard drive. Again, the best solution to deal with this is to call your computer's manufacturer to find out what you need to change to let your computer recognize your hard drive.

Tech Tip: Your computer keeps track of the different hardware settings in a special location in memory called CMOS. If your CMOS settings are incorrect, then your computer won't know how to work with your hard drive correctly. Your hardware manufacturer can help you resolve this confusion.

I was in the process of setting up DOS 6.x, and I received an error message about a virus. I chose not to continue. Are my DOS disks infected with a virus?

No, your DOS disks are not infected. The exact message that is displayed probably looks like this:

```
Boot sector write error!
Possible virus!
Do you want to continue Y/N?
```

This message is from an anti-virus program detecting virus-like activity. The virus-like activity detected is the Setup program re-writing DOS system files as part of the installation process. Because viruses often try to update system files, the anti-virus program is flagging these attempted changes. However, these changes are necessary to let your computer start from DOS 6.x properly. To prevent these error messages during Setup, you should disable all anti-virus software before you install a new version of DOS.

If you are sure that you have no anti-virus software currently running on the computer, the most likely cause of the message is an anti-virus feature coming from the BIOS. American Megatrend's (AMI) BIOS dated 1992 or 1993 is likely to have a built-in virus scan. This anti-virus feature can be disabled in the computer's CMOS settings. See your computer's documentation for more information on how to make this change.

I was running Setup and got the message "There is not enough free space on drive C to install MS-DOS." Can I still install DOS on my hard disk?

What you need to do is delete any unnecessary files on your hard disk to make room for the new DOS files. This would be a good time to create archival or backup copies of any old files and remove them from your hard disk, since it is clear that you are low on hard disk space. To remove the unnecessary files, first exit Setup by pressing F3.

I was told I need to install DOS manually. How do I do this?

You may need to install DOS manually if you have incompatible partitions or some other difficulty with your system. Installing DOS manually means that you are just going to copy the MS-DOS 6.*x* files to your hard drive, without using some of Setup's other features. To do this:

1. Put your Setup Disk 1 or a startup disk in drive A and restart your computer with CTRL+ALT+DEL. If you are in Setup procedure, press F3 twice to exit Setup.

2. Copy the system files from your startup disk to your hard drive by entering **SYS A: C:** and pressing ENTER.

3. With the Setup disk in the drive, type **A:\SETUP /U /Q** and press ENTER. This command ignores any incompatible partitions that may exist on your disk and causes Setup to simply copy and expand the DOS files without running the full Setup program. This command does not install the MS Backup, Undelete, and Anti-Virus utilities.

4. Follow any instructions or prompts you see.

5. Put the Setup Disk 1 or the startup disk back in drive A and press ENTER.

6. Use Editor to check that your CONFIG.SYS and AUTOEXEC.BAT files correctly describe the location of device drivers and programs, and that AUTOEXEC.BAT's Path statement includes the directory the DOS files are in.

7. Restart your computer. DOS should be installed.

If you also want to install the MS Backup, Undelete, and Anti-Virus utilities:

1. Put your Setup Disk 1 in a drive.

2. Type **A:\SETUP /E**, in which A is the name of the drive you are using, and press ENTER.

3. Follow the instructions or prompts you see on the screen.

If you are installing MS-DOS 6.2 using Stepup instead of Setup, you have some further steps. Stepup is a special program which upgrades MS-DOS 6.0 to MS-DOS 6.2 by changing only those files that need to be upgraded. After installing the MS Backup, Anti-Virus, and Undelete utilities from the DOS 6.0 disks, you need to rerun Stepup to update these files for MS-DOS 6.2.

When I originally installed my MS-DOS 6.*x* upgrade, I only installed the Backup, Undelete, and Anti-Virus utilities for one platform (DOS or Windows). Do I have to reinstall DOS to get the utilities for the other platform?

No, you don't have to completely reinstall DOS. Adding the utilities you need is easy. Just follow these steps:

1. Put the Setup disk in drive A.

2. Make that drive current by typing **A:** and pressing ENTER.

You can substitute drive B for drive A in both steps 1 and 2 if you prefer.

3. Type **SETUP /E** and press ENTER.

This runs the Setup program to install the three utilities only. You have the option of choosing platforms of MS-DOS only, Windows only, or Windows and MS-DOS for utilities for both platforms.

You have a little more work if you installed DOS 6.2 using Stepup.

1. Before following the steps above, reboot your computer using a MS-DOS 6.0 system disk.

2. Then follow the steps above using your MS-DOS 6.0 Setup disks, not the Stepup disks.

3. After reconfiguring the utilities for the new platform, you will need to reboot your computer and rerun MS-DOS 6.2 Stepup to update the utilities for MS-DOS 6.2.

I have an older computer that I would like to upgrade to DOS 6. Should I be considering anything else before I upgrade?

Yes, you should check the date of the machine's BIOS. The BIOS is the program that communicates between your hardware (printer, keyboard, monitor) and DOS. If you have an older machine and an old version of DOS, you probably have an old BIOS. If the BIOS date is prior to 1990, you may have problems after upgrading to DOS 6.*x*, depending on the manufacturer of your computer's BIOS.

Unfortunately, there is not a single, fail-safe method for determining your BIOS date. You can try the following options:

1. Look at the contents of memory address FFFF. Although not all manufacturers store the date at this location, many do. You can check the address from the DOS prompt by following these steps:

    a. Type **DEBUG** and press ENTER.

    b. In response to the - prompt, type **D FFFF:5 C** and press ENTER.

    Your screen may display a date at the right side something like this:

```
C:\>DEBUG
-D FFFF:5 C
FFFF:0000   30 31 2F-31 38 2F 38 3901/18/89
```

2. Use a utility such as MSD, Norton Utilities, a utility or reference disk that came with your machine, or a utility packaged with another program.

3. Check the literature and materials that came with your computer.

Tech Tip: You can use the MSD utility included in DOS 6 to find out different information about your computer, including the BIOS date. Start this utility by typing **MSD** and pressing ENTER. Then select an option from the opening screen to choose the information you want to see.

4. Make a rough estimate by subtracting one year from the purchase date.

You may be able to contact your computer manufacturer for a BIOS upgrade. You will need to carefully consider whether you want to spend money upgrading the BIOS when you have other components such as a hard disk that may be outdated by today's standards.

When trying to run Setup for the MS-DOS 6.x upgrade, the error message "Root directory of your hard disk contains some of your original DOS files" is displayed and the upgrade won't install. What original DOS files is the message referring to?

This message tells you that the boot drive's root directory contains one or more of the following files:

FORMAT.COM	BASIC*.COM	SYS.COM
FORMAT.EXE	BASIC*.EXE	SYS.EXE
DISKCOPY.EXE	GWBASIC*.COM	
DISKCOPY.COM	GWBASIC*.EXE	

To proceed with the upgrade, you must rename, delete, or move these files from the root directory.

I have a critical program that just won't run on MS-DOS 6.x. I want to return to my old version of DOS, but I ran DoubleSpace. Is there any way for me to do this?

First, you'll need to remove DoubleSpace. If you're using MS-DOS 6.2, entering the command **DBLSPACE /UNCOMPRESS** and pressing ENTER will make removing it simple.

If you're using MS-DOS 6, you'll have to manually remove DoubleSpace. You can do this in two ways:

1. The best solution is to back up your data and reformat the host drive, the uncompressed drive that contains the compressed drive file.

2. You can also move files from your compressed drive to its host drive, using the MOVE or COPY command, and then make your compressed drive smaller. After copying all of the files out of the compressed drive, you can then delete the compressed drive. This method is usable, but not recommended, since it will take longer than simply backing up the data and reformatting. Also, if your compressed and host drives are close to full, there may not be enough space on the host drive to hold all of the files.

Once DoubleSpace is removed, you should be able to use the Uninstall disk to switch back to your previous version of DOS, provided you still have the OLD_DOS.x directory on the hard drive. To use the Uninstall disk, simply place it in drive A and reboot—the Uninstall program will prompt you to confirm that you want to uninstall, then do the job.

I have DR-DOS and want to upgrade to DOS 6.2. Is there anything I should consider before I begin?

Yes, Some of the DR-DOS utilities cause a conflict with the Setup program. Take these steps before beginning:

1. Purge and unload DELWATCH.

2. Disable the security program.

3. If you are using SUPER-STOR Compression, you need to back up your data and remove the compression.

When I run Stepup for MS-DOS 6.2, it says that it can't update some of my DOS files. Why not?

The files are either missing or are not an exact match of the MS-DOS 6.0 files. Stepup checks each file to make sure that it is an original 6.0 file. If it is not, then Stepup will not update it. If you have the MS-DOS 6.0 upgrade, exit Stepup, reinstall MS-DOS 6.0 by entering **SETUP** and pressing ENTER, then rerun Stepup.

   If your copy of MS-DOS 6.0 came pre-installed on your machine—an original equipment manufacturer (OEM) version—try the above process. If Stepup still fails, call the manufacturer to see if they have a special version of Stepup. The Microsoft version will update some, but not all, OEM versions of DOS 6.

Can I use the MS-DOS 6.*x* upgrade to upgrade my current IBM PC-DOS?

You can upgrade PC-DOS with MS-DOS but you need the full upgrade package, not just Stepup. The Stepup upgrade for MS-DOS 6.2 will only upgrade MS-DOS 6.0 and cannot upgrade any versions of IBM PC-DOS 6.

I accidentally deleted all my files in the DOS directory. I know how to use the Undelete command but I cannot remember all the DOS file names. Do I have to reinstall DOS again?

If you have deleted all of your DOS files in the DOS directory and do not want to reinstall DOS 6.*x* because the machine has been running fine, you can use the SETUP /Q option. This command will copy fresh DOS files to the hard drive without changing the CONFIG.SYS or AUTOEXEC.BAT file. It will not install the MS Backup, Undelete, or Anti-Virus utilities. You will need to run Setup a second time using the SETUP /E option to install those utilities.

I typed A:\SETUP to start the upgrade, and DOS displayed the message "Not ready reading drive A." Are my disks corrupted?

First, check that the disk drive light that goes on when you start the upgrade matches the disk drive you put the Setup disk into. If your disk is in drive B, run the setup program by typing **B:\SETUP**. If that isn't the problem, you probably are using the wrong density disk. If your computer cannot read high-density 1.44 or 1.2 MB disks, you may see this message. The upgrade is only available in the stores in a high-density format. There is a coupon in the back of the MS-DOS upgrade manual that you can send to Microsoft to receive the low-density versions of the upgrade.

If you know that you are using the right capacity disks, then try reading one of the other disks from the package. If you can read the information from the other disks in the package, but not the first one, then that one is probably damaged. Also try other disks, to see if you have problems reading all disks.

I have the MS-DOS 6.2 Stepup program and one of my DOS files has been corrupted. When I try to run Stepup, it tells me that it cannot update that file. How can I correct this problem?

The file that Stepup is trying to update may be damaged. Since Stepup only works when you have a usable copy of MS-DOS 6.0 already installed, you have to correct the corrupted file condition. You will need to rename the damaged file and then expand the file from the MS-DOS 6.0 Setup disks. The way to accomplish this would be to make your DOS directory active and rename the file. Follow these steps:

   1. Type **CD \DOS** and press ENTER.

   If your DOS files are in a directory other than \DOS you will need to substitute the name of your directory.

   2. Type **RENAME *FILENAME.???* *FILENAME.OLD*** and press ENTER.

In the step above, *FILENAME.???* is the name of the damaged file.

An example will help to clarify these steps. If REPLACE.EXE is the damaged file and your DOS files were in a directory called \SYSTEM, you would type **CD\SYSTEM** and press ENTER, then type **RENAME REPLACE.EXE REPLACE.OLD** and press ENTER.

Once this has been done you will need to expand a new copy of the damaged file from the MS-DOS 6.0 Setup disks. This is accomplished by placing the disk that contains the file into the appropriate drive and, while still in the DOS directory, using the EXPAND command. You might use the syntax **EXPAND *DRIVE:FILENAME.??? C:\DOS***. In this entry, *DRIVE:* represents the drive that the disk is in (usually either A or B), *FILENAME.???* represents the name of the damaged file, and DOS is the name of the directory where your DOS files are stored.

Tech Tip: Files on your Setup disks with an _ as the last character in the file extension are files that need to be expanded. Files with complete file names can just be copied.

For example, suppose the file is REPLACE.EXE and is on Disk 2 of the MS-DOS 6.0 Setup disks. Also, these disks fit in drive B and your DOS directory is named \DOS. You would insert Disk 2 into drive B and type **EXPAND B:REPLACE.EX_ C:\DOS**, then press ENTER.

The next step is to run Stepup again. This time Stepup is able to update the problem file.

The only floppy drive I have is drive D. Can I run Setup from that drive and if so, how?

To run Setup normally, your floppy drive must be A or B. Using the ASSIGN or SUBST command will not help, since Setup tries to read the drive identifier directly from the BIOS, rather than from DOS. One possible alternative would be to make a temporary directory on your hard drive, and copy the contents of each Setup disk to that directory with the command: **COPY D:*.* C:\SETUP**. Next, activate the temporary directory and run Setup from there.

When I run Setup, I get the message "Your computer uses a disk-compression program." Is this going to be a problem?

It might be. The problem is that since you are using a disk-compression program, Setup cannot create an Uninstall disk which would allow you to revert to your previous copy of DOS if something stops working after you install DOS 6.*x*. Therefore, if something does go wrong, you may lose all the data in the compressed drive.

To prevent this from happening, you should exit Setup and make a backup all of the data in your compressed drive. You won't need to back up your programs if you still have the program disks or archival copies of them. After doing this, you should create a startup disk with specific commands on it by following these steps:

1. Put a disk in drive A.

2. Create a startup disk by typing **FORMAT A: /S** and pressing ENTER.

3. Copy the FDISK.EXE, FORMAT.COM, and SYS.COM files to the new startup disk.

After creating the backup disks and the startup disk, you can simply run Setup as usual. You will only need the disks you created if a problem occurs with your hard drive after DOS 6.*x* is installed.

If the screen specifically says "Your computer uses SuperStor disk compression" then your problem is a little different. Set up cannot access your uncompressed drive if you use this disk-compression program, making it impossible to set up DOS. To make the uncompressed drive accessible and run Setup:

1. Insert the SuperStor disk that has the ADD2SWP.EXE on it in a disk drive.

2. Type **A:ADD2SWP *DRIVE:*,** in which *DRIVE:* is the name of your hard disk's startup drive.

3. Follow the instructions and prompts you see on your screen.

4. Restart your computer.

5. Run Setup again.

What do I need to do after replacing my SCSI hard drive to have it set up for DOS?

The steps for setting up a SCSI hard drive are similar to those for any other type of hard drive. Make sure the drive is recognized by the SCSI controller, partition the drive with FDISK, and, if it is to be a bootable drive, format the hard drive for DOS using the /S switch.

Can I use DOS 6.*x* on my Quantum Hardcard?

You will need the patch file ATPLUS.COM version 3.0 or later to patch the MS DOS system files. Contact Quantum for the ATPLUS.COM file to patch the operating system to recognize the Hardcard.

I just ran the Stepup upgrade for DOS 6.2. When I boot the computer, I get a DoubleGuard Alarm error and the computer hangs up. I am using QEMM386 for my memory management functions. What's wrong?

Under DOS 6.0, you were using DoubleSpace and QEMM386 with the STEALTH feature active. Older versions of QEMM386.EXE and STEALTH are incompatible with DOS 6.2's DoubleSpace. You will want to follow these steps:

Tech Tip: A better solution is to contact Quarterdeck Office Systems, the manufacturer of QEMM386, for an updated version which is compatible with DOS 6.2.

1. Restart the computer and press F5 when you see the message "Starting MS-DOS." This will bypass your CONFIG.SYS and AUTOEXEC.BAT files and take you directly to a DOS prompt.

2. Type **EDIT C:\CONFIG.SYS** and press ENTER to edit CONFIG.SYS using the DOS Editor.

3. Disable the STEALTH feature of QEMM386 (see your QEMM documentation for exact steps).

4. Save the modified version of CONFIG.SYS and reboot.

The DoubleGuard system is a new feature in MS-DOS 6.2. It constantly performs a checksum operation on the DoubleSpace program while it's in memory. If the program changes by being overwritten by another program, for example, DoubleGuard locks the system to prevent corrupt data from being written to the hard drive.

I just installed MS-DOS 6.*x* on my IBM PS/1. When I boot my computer, I receive an incorrect DOS version error message and/or an invalid COMMAND.COM. Did I do something wrong?

The IBM PS/1 has the original DOS on a ROM chip inside the computer. In order to solve this problem, you must disable the ROM DOS by using the CUSTOMIZE utility in the DOS directory. Power down the computer, and hold ALT+PRINT SCREEN while turning the computer back on. This will bypass the ROM chip and allow the computer to boot off the hard drive. Then run **CUSTOMIZ** from the DOS prompt.

Tech Tip: This is a very common problem, and is not limited only to IBM PS/1 computers. It will occur on any computer that has ROM DOS. Some Tandy computers also have this problem.

I have a Compaq computer with DOS 2.11. I'm trying to upgrade to MS-DOS 6.2 and I'm getting the message "Your version of DOS cannot be upgraded with Setup." The Upgrade package says I should be able to upgrade, so what's wrong?

To install MS-DOS 6.0 you need to have MS-DOS version 2.11 or higher. The problem is that Compaq DOS 2.11 is actually based on MS-DOS 2.1 rather than MS-DOS 2.11. Before you can upgrade to MS-DOS 6.*x*, you must upgrade your Compaq DOS 2.11 to MS-DOS 2.11 or later.

Tech Tip: The reason you cannot upgrade from MS-DOS 2.10 or earlier is that Microsoft introduced a change in the structure of the file allocation table (FAT) between MS-DOS 2.10 and 2.11. MS-DOS 6.x uses the new type of FAT and can't work with the old one.

I am having difficulty running DOS 6.*x* on my Hyundai computer. Did I install it incorrectly?

Hyundai machines may have problems with MS-DOS 6.0 due to problems with their internal clock. Contact Hyundai at (800) 234-3553 and request the RTCCLK.SYS clock upgrade that corrects the problem.

How can I find out what's new in MS-DOS 6.2?

After completing setup, type **help whatsnew** at the DOS prompt and press ENTER. All of the new features, and how to use them are covered in MS-DOS Help.

The following features were added to MS-DOS 6.2 or upgraded from MS-DOS 6.0:

- ScanDisk can detect, diagnose, and repair errors in your hard drive and other disks.
- DoubleSpace now includes DoubleGuard, which verifies that your DoubleSpace program is not corrupted in memory.
- HIMEM.SYS now tests your system's memory when you boot your computer.
- SMARTDrive, which sets up a read-only cache by default, will not show the DOS prompt until it has finished writing to your hard drive.
- The MOVE, COPY, and XCOPY commands now prompt you to confirm that you want to replace files with the same names.
- You can now uncompress DoubleSpace drives or remove DoubleSpace from memory completely.
- SMARTDrive can now cache a CD-ROM drive.
- DoubleSpace will automatically mount a compressed floppy disk, or any removable disk or other medium.
- You can now execute one line at a time in any batch file, including the AUTOEXEC.BAT file. You can choose not to execute specific lines while these batch files are running.
- The DISKCOPY command will write the contents of the source disk to your hard drive temporarily, before copying

these contents to the target disk. You will have to exchange disks fewer times, making it faster to copy disks.

■ The Defragmenter now uses extended memory, so that it can defragment larger and fuller disks.

■ DIR, MEM, CHKDSK, and FORMAT commands now display results with commas as thousand separators, making their results easier to read.

The MS-DOS 6.*x* Setup program insists on creating an Uninstall disk in the A drive. How can I get around it?

The Uninstall disk can be created *only* in your A drive. While it is possible to bypass the creation of the Uninstall disk, it is not a good idea. The Uninstall disk is *very* important. Creating this disk lets you return to your old version of DOS if you should have a problem with the new version of DOS. Also, the Uninstall disk can be used to boot your system, making it worth its weight in gold if the hard drive becomes unbootable.

You can start setup by typing **SETUP/G** and pressing ENTER to skip creating the Uninstall disk, but this should only be used as a *last resort.*

How much disk space is required to install DOS 6.0 or 6.2?

The following table shows the disk space requirements needed to install either version of DOS 6. Make sure you have the space required before you use the Setup program.

Type of Setup	MS-DOS 6.0		MS-DOS 6.2	
SETUP /M Minimal installation (Initially requires 512K disk space)	191K	4 files	197K	4 files
SETUP /F - makes a system floppy disk with utilities	1,154K	18 files	1,041K	20 files
SETUP /Q - Manually expands MS-DOS files into the DOS directory	3,233K	96 files	3,013K	93 files

Type of Setup	MS-DOS 6.0		MS-DOS 6.2	
SETUP (DOS only versions of MS Backup, Anti-Virus, Undelete)	4,455K	112 files	4,236K	109 files
SETUP (DOS and Windows versions of utilities)	6,007K	129 files	5,789K	127 files

Tech Tip: You will want some extra free space for temporary files. 512K should be sufficient.

 ## Even with my Uninstall disk I am not able to go back to my old release of DOS. What is wrong?

There are several things which make it impossible to use the Uninstall disk. These are:

- repartitioning or reformatting the hard disk
- deleting or moving the hidden IO.SYS and MSDOS.SYS files
- deleting the OLD_DOS.x directory
- installing DoubleSpace or another disk-compression program

To use your Uninstall disk to revert to your old release of DOS, you need to put the Uninstall disk in drive A while your computer is on, and press CTRL+ALT+DEL. This starts the Uninstall program. Follow the instructions this program provides to revert to your old DOS version.

 ## I was installing DOS 6.x, and got the message "Incompatible hard disk or device driver." Can I install DOS, and if so, how?

This message means that Setup cannot work with your hard disk, or with the partitions that divide your hard disk into logical drives. The solution to this issue depends on what exactly the incompatible disk or driver is. Solutions for some of the problem disks and drivers are given below. If you don't have one of these, you may need to delete a non-DOS partition, or call the equipment manufacturer to see what the problem is.

If you have a problem with	Try this:
Bernoulli drive with disk caching	Enter **REM** before the command line in your CONFIG.SYS or AUTOEXEC.BAT file that installs the disk caching program, restart your computer, install DOS, then remove REM and restart your computer again.
Disk Manager partitions or drivers	Contact Ontrack Computing Systems for a new version of Disk Manager, or, if DOS 4 or later is already on your system, add the DEVICE command for your Disk Manager partition to your CONFIG.SYS file and reboot.
Novell partitions	Start Setup with **A:SETUP /U**.
Prima or Everex partition	Install DOS manually. (See the question "I was told I need to install DOS manually. How do I do this?" earlier in this chapter for steps to do this.)
Syquest removable hard drive	Enter **REM** before the DEVICE=SYQ55.SYS line in your CONFIG.SYS file, restart your system, set up DOS, then remove the REM and restart your system again.
Unix or Xenix partitions	Start Setup with **A:SETUP /U** or install DOS manually. (See the question "I was told I need to install DOS manually. How do I do this?" earlier in this chapter for steps to do this.)
Vfeature Deluxe partitions	Repartition your hard drive with FDISK, or contact Golden Bow Systems.

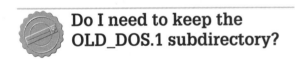

Do I need to keep the OLD_DOS.1 subdirectory?

You should keep the OLD_DOS.1 subdirectory if you think you'll ever want to uninstall DOS 6.*x* on your system. If everything is running properly on your machine, you should have no need to uninstall, therefore you can delete the OLD_DOS.1 directory. Also, if you use DoubleSpace to compress the hard drive, you will not be able to uninstall DOS 6.*x*, and can delete the subdirectory.

To delete the OLD_DOS.1 directory, use the command DELOLDOS.

I heard that I can get a free copy of Stepup for DOS 6.2. What do I need to do?

You can get a free copy of Stepup from Microsoft by downloading it over a modem. The Stepup program will upgrade from MS-DOS 6.0 to MS-DOS 6.2. To download the Stepup program, call Microsoft Product Support Download service, at (206) 936-6735. Set your modem to the following settings to communicate with Microsoft:

Baud rate	1200, 2400, 9600 or 14,400 bps
Parity	none
Data bits	8
Stop bits	1

Tech Tip: The downloading process for Stepup can take up to several hours, depending on the baud rate of your modem transfer.

Why did MS-DOS 6.2 change the Buffers statement in my CONFIG.SYS file to 10,0 during the upgrade?

MS-DOS 6.2 changed the Buffers statement to allow DoubleSpace to make use of the upper memory area. If you use a program that needs Buffers set to the previous setting, you can change the CONFIG.SYS file back to the way it was before the upgrade. However, the only thing that should be affected by the change is that DoubleSpace may take up 10K of your conventional memory.

I'm running Setup and get the "Too Many Primary Partitions" screen. What do I need to do to set up DOS?

If you see either "Too Many Primary Partitions" or "Incompatible Primary DOS Partitions," you should repartition your hard disk before installing DOS 6.*x*. Partitions are created when you have divided your hard drive into several "logical drives" so that you are treating parts of the disk as if they were separate disks. You repartition your hard drive using the FDISK command. After you repartition your hard drive, you can install DOS 6.x. However, after changing the partitions, you need to reformat the new partitions, so you will lose all data in those partitions. Therefore, before you use FDISK, back up your data. Then you can restore your data to the repartitioned hard drive.

Tech Tip: If you need to learn about the Fdisk utility, enter **HELP FDISK** at the DOS prompt and press ENTER. For tips about using FDISK, see Chapter 4, "File and Disk Management, " in this book.

Tech Terror: Repartitioning your hard disk destroys all the data in the partitions you affect. Always back up your data before using FDISK.

I made backups of my MS-DOS Setup disks as soon as I got the program. When I tried reinstalling DOS with those disks, Setup kept asking for the disk I put in the drive, just as if it were the wrong disk. I can read the disks, so they aren't corrupted, but I can't install them. What's wrong?

The Setup program recognizes the different Setup disks by their disk labels. The Setup disks for MS-DOS 5.0 and 6.x disks are each labeled Disk # where # is the disk number and there are six spaces after the word Disk. If the disk labels on your archival copies are not identical, Setup cannot read the disks. You can change the disk label using the LABEL command. You may want to make the archival copies of your DOS disks using DISKCOPY, which copies the disk label as well as the disk contents.

How can I upgrade to DOS 6.0 if the Setup disks won't work in my A drive and I do not have a previous version of DOS installed on my hard disk?

You can:

1. Get the correct size DOS disks for the A drive.

   a. If the disks are the wrong capacity you can order new low-density disks by completing and mailing in the Low-Density Disk Offer coupon in the back of your MS-DOS manual.

   b. If the disks are the wrong size you need to find out if whoever you purchased your upgrade from will exchange it for a copy with the correctly sized disks.

2. Boot the computer from the A drive with a previous version of DOS. Change to the B drive and type **SETUP**.

If this is a new hard drive, you may need to prepare it by using the FDISK and FORMAT commands.

After I start the Setup program, I get a message that says in order to run the single disk upgrade, you must already have MS DOS 6.0 installed.

That's correct—Stepup, the single disk version of Setup, is only for upgrading MS-DOS 6.0 to 6.2. The disk contains files that instruct Setup how to modify the existing 6.0 files to make them into 6.2 files. In other words, Stepup contains only the differences between 6.0 and 6.2, not the entire package. You need to install MS-DOS 6.0 using those Setup disks, then run Stepup. If you don't have MS-DOS 6.0, you'll need to purchase the MS-DOS 6.2 Upgrade, which is the *full* package.

I have a Toshiba machine. When I run MS-DOS 6.2 Stepup, I get an error message saying that Stepup cannot identify the IO.SYS file. What's wrong?

You might not have the original MS-DOS 6.0 IO.SYS file. You can check the size of your IO.SYS file to tell for sure. Type **DIR /AH** at the DOS prompt to show hidden files in the root directory of your hard drive. IO.SYS should be 40470 bytes, and have a date of 3-10-93. This is the size and date of the original MS-DOS 6.0 IO.SYS file, which is the only version of IO.SYS that Stepup is designed to update. Some Toshiba machines have an IO.SYS file that has been modified. Toshiba recommends that you obtain the Toshiba 6.2 Stepup, which will operate properly, and ensure that support for special machine features is retained.

I just ran the MS-DOS 6.2 Stepup program and I now have trouble using any application that needs the EMM386.EXE memory manager. What do I do?

You may encounter this problem if you used a warm boot (pressed CTRL+ALT+DEL) after using the 6.2 Stepup program. Occasionally, areas of memory used by EMM386.EXE or some other programs are not fully re-initialized by a warm boot. Sometimes a cold boot (i.e., restarting the computer with its on/off switch) will solve the problem. Memory errors that can be corrected by doing a cold boot but not a warm boot are rare, but are at least easily fixed.

I just bought a new hard drive for my computer. My version of DOS 6.*x* is labeled as an upgrade. Does this mean I have to install my old version of DOS on this new hard drive before I can install DOS 6.*x*?

Installing an old version of DOS is not necessary. The upgrade disk labeled "Disk 1 - Setup" is a bootable disk which contains working copies of FDISK.EXE and FORMAT.COM, among others, which you can use to partition and format the new drive.

The upgrade only requires that DOS system files be present on the hard drive (they can be from DOS 6.*x*). You can either format the new drive with the /S switch (FORMAT C: /S), or use the SYS command (SYS C:) after formatting to transfer the system files to the hard disk. Once that is done, the upgrade will install properly.

If your DOS 6.*x* disks are for your B floppy drive, you can create a bootable DOS 6.*x* disk to perform the above procedure. Boot your computer using your previous version of DOS, then put the Setup disk in your B floppy drive. Make that drive the current drive and at the B prompt type **SETUP /F**. This creates a DOS 6.*x* disk that you can boot the computer from. It also contains FDISK.EXE and FORMAT.COM.

Tech Tip: You can skip the Uninstall part of the upgrade procedure when starting the Setup program by typing **SETUP /G**. Since this is a new hard drive, there won't be a previous DOS version to uninstall back to.

My hard drive is divided into several 32MB partitions, since I have an old version of DOS. Now that I'm upgrading, is there an easy way to convert the hard drive to a single partition?

There is an easy way to convert to a single partition, but you must back up your data first. After you repartition the hard drive, you will need to restore the data you have backed up. Follow these steps to install DOS and convert the hard drive to a single partition.

1. Install the new DOS on the machine.
2. Create a system disk with the **FORMAT A: /S** command.
3. Copy the FDISK.EXE and FORMAT.COM files from your DOS directory to the system disk.
4. From the system disk, use the FDISK command on the hard disk to delete old partitions and create a single partition.
5. From the system disk, enter **FORMAT C: /S** to reformat the hard drive and copy the system files from the system disk.

6. Create a DOS directory and copy all the necessary files to it, or use Setup, which will automatically handle this.

Note that if you are copying the files, some of the files are compressed and need to be uncompressed with the EXPAND.EXE utility.

Tech Tip: If you back up and restore programs, instead of reinstalling them, they may be looking for files on now nonexistent drives. To correct this, you will need to change the program settings. It may be easier simply to reinstall the programs from the original program disks.

Fast Fixes

Sometimes things can seem pretty hopeless when you encounter a computer problem. If you can't read any of the files from your hard disk or if your system becomes totally unresponsive, you may feel like throwing up your hands and calling it a day. Surprisingly, some problems that seem catastrophic can be fixed quite easily. If you run into what seems like a devastating problem with your computer, this chapter may help. Here you will find some of the common problems encountered by computer users along with some quick fixes that will have you up and running in no time.

My system locked up while running a program. After I rebooted my system, there were no files on drive C except COMMAND.COM. Where are my files?

Don't panic! When the program locked up, it may have caused some file damage, but it's very likely that most, if not all, of your data is still safe inside a hidden file called DBLSPACE.000. Type **DIR /A:H** at the DOS prompt and press ENTER. If you see the files

```
IO.SYS
MSDOS.SYS
DBLSPACE.BIN
DBLSPACE.INI
DBLSPACE.000
```

your problem is that your DoubleSpace host drive is appearing as drive C instead of using the drive letter originally assigned.

To get things running, you need to make DoubleSpace active again. To do this:

1. Make sure you have a blank disk for drive A available.

2. Place Disk 1 of your MS-DOS 6.*x* Setup disks in drive A.

3. Change to drive A by typing **A:** and pressing ENTER.

4. Type **SETUP /F** and press ENTER, then follow the instructions on the screen.

Setup will use your blank disk to create a DOS boot disk containing several key utilities.

5. When Setup is complete, reboot your system using the boot disk you just created.

6. At the DOS prompt, type **DBLSPACE /MOUNT=000** and press ENTER to mount the compressed disk.

Once the DBLSPACE.000 file is mounted, you can reboot your system from the hard drive and things will work normally again. Use CHKDSK in DOS 6.0 or ScanDisk in DOS 6.2 to check for any file and disk corruption that might have resulted from the problem.

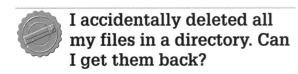

I accidentally deleted all my files in a directory. Can I get them back?

You may be able to recover deleted files if DOS has not placed other data in the same location on the disk as the deleted files. To recover the deleted files, type **UNDELETE** and press ENTER. If DOS can undelete any files, it will prompt you for which ones you want undeleted, as shown in Figure 3-1.

The message you see after entering **UNDELETE** may not exactly match what is shown in Figure 3-1. This is because DOS 6.*x* offers three levels of deletion protection. The message shown in Figure 3-1 would appear if you only had the lowest level of deletion protection.

The higher levels of deletion protection increase your chances of recovering deleted files. You can set which level of deletion protection is in effect on your system for a single session by entering a command at the DOS prompt. To use a higher level

```
C:\WORD\MOUSE>UNDELETE

UNDELETE - A delete protection facility
Copyright (C) 1987-1993 Central Point Software, Inc.
All rights reserved.

Directory: C:\WORD\MOUSE
File Specifications: *.*

    Delete Sentry control file not found.

    Deletion-tracking file not found.

    MS-DOS directory contains   12 deleted files.
    Of those,   12 files may be recovered.

Using the MS-DOS directory method.

     ?OOKS    DOC    36352 12-01-93  2:10p  ...A  Undelete (Y/N)?y
     Please type the first character for ?OOKS    .DOC: b

File successfully undeleted.

     ?US_CARD DOC   573440 12-02-93 12:40p  ...A  Undelete (Y/N)?
```

FIGURE 3-1   Using UNDELETE to restore deleted files

of deletion protection all the time, you need to add a command to your AUTOEXEC.BAT file. For a complete explanation of each of the deletion protection options, see the question "I accidentally deleted a group of files using the DOS Shell. When I used Undelete, I couldn't get them back. Why?" in Chapter 4, "File and Disk Management."

One other thing to consider is that you must provide the correct letter for the first letter of the file. If you don't, you may encounter problems later. For example, if you delete the dictionary file that your word processor uses to check spelling in your document, then undelete it using the wrong first letter, your word processor will not be able to find and open it the next time you want to check your spelling.

I know I saved a file, but I can't remember what directory it's in or what I named it. How do I find it without doing a DIR command in every directory on the system?

You can use the DIR command with the /S switch to search all directories on a disk at once. The /S switch tells DOS to search all subdirectories beneath the current directory for the specified file. You can use any of the other features of the DIR command with this switch. For example, if the program you used to create the missing file assigns a standard extension to all of its files, you can search all of your directories for files with this extension.

Switch to the root directory of the disk to search the entire disk. Then type **DIR *.*EXT* /S** at the DOS prompt and press ENTER, replacing *EXT* with the extension assigned by the program you used to create the missing file. For example, enter **DIR *.DOC /S** to find all documents created with Word or **DIR *.XLS /S** to find all worksheets created with Excel. Figure 3-2 shows a directory listing of all the .PCX files on a disk.

The DIR command in this example also uses the /P switch so that only one screen of files is shown at a time. If you want a printout of all of the files listed by this DIR command, add >PRN at the end of the command. This directs the output of the command to the printer instead of the screen.

Tech Tip: Include /O:D at the end of the DIR command when you want the directory listing sorted by date. This is useful for finding a missing file if you remember which day you worked on it.

```
Volume in drive C is MS-DOS_5
 Volume Serial Number is 1C2D-68CD

Directory of C:\

JILL4B   PCX       585,019 12-30-93   3:58p
JILL3B   PCX       263,378 12-30-93   4:01p
JILL2B   PCX       465,733 12-30-93   4:14p
JILL1B   PCX       261,618 12-30-93   4:31p
         4 file(s)      1,575,748 bytes

Directory of C:\COREL40\PHOTOPNT\CANVAS

GLASS2F  PCX         1,980 07-20-93   12:00a
CEMENT1F PCX         2,179 07-20-93   12:00a
CERAMC2F PCX         2,301 07-20-93   12:00a
CORK1F   PCX         2,130 07-20-93   12:00a
GRASS1F  PCX         1,968 07-20-93   12:00a
PAPER02F PCX         2,168 07-20-93   12:00a
PAPER08F PCX         2,227 07-20-93   12:00a
PAPER20F PCX         2,097 07-20-93   12:00a
STUCCO1F PCX         2,167 07-20-93   12:00a
PAPER14F PCX         2,925 07-20-93   12:00a
Press any key to continue . . .
```

FIGURE 3-2   Listing all .PCX files in all directories

Tech Tip: You aren't limited to searching for files with a specific extension when you use the /S switch. If you remember part of the filename, you can combine the part you remember with wildcard characters to search for filenames that match that pattern. For example, enter **DIR PR*.DOC /S** to search for a Word document file whose name starts with PR.

I can't print. Is it the fault of DOS, my printer, or my program?

Most printer problems have simple solutions. Check to see if any of the following are the cause of your printer's problems:

- Is the printer turned on? This might sound stupid, but turning your printer on solves many printer problems.

- Does the printer have paper? Like the answer above, this seems obvious until you are trying to solve a problem caused by an empty paper tray.

■ Is the printer's online button turned on? Most printers have a button that turns the printer online and offline. Usually, this button has a light or some other indicator telling you that it is on. When the printer is offline, it cannot receive information from the computer.

■ Can the printer print from the DOS prompt? Type **DIR >LPT1** from the DOS prompt and press ENTER. (Replace LPT1 with the name of the port to which your printer is connected; some printers are connected to a COM port.) If the current directory is printed, you know the printing problem is with the program you are trying to use. You should then check the settings that the program is using for printing. If your printer is a page printer (one that waits until it has all the information for a page before it prints any part of the page), you may need to press your printer's online button, its form feed button, and then the online button again. If it still doesn't print, the problem is probably in the connection from the computer to the printer.

■ Are you printing on a network? If so, the problem may relate to the network itself. In this case, you want to contact your network administrator and let that person resolve the difficulty.

I was unable to boot from my hard drive, so I booted from my MS-DOS 5.0 boot disk. Now I don't see any files on my disk. Did I lose all my information?

If you boot up with a DOS 5 boot disk and can't see files on your DOS 6.*x* hard drive, chances are that you're running DoubleSpace. You'll need to reboot using a DOS 6.*x* disk to access your DoubleSpace volume that contains all the files. After doing this, change to the DOS directory on drive C, type **SYS A: H:**, assuming H is the letter of your DoubleSpace host drive, and press ENTER. This command transfers the system files back to the hard drive from the system disk and should allow you to boot normally.

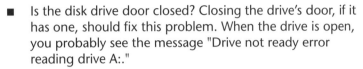

I can't read data from my floppy disks. Where is my data?

Here are some questions you should answer to find the data you have on a disk that DOS cannot read.

- Is the disk drive door closed? Closing the drive's door, if it has one, should fix this problem. When the drive is open, you probably see the message "Drive not ready error reading drive A:."

- Did you put the disk in correctly? It is possible to put 5 1/4" disks in backwards and upside down. Usually, 3 1/2" disks will only fit into the drive one way. Check that the disk is correctly inserted into the drive and try again. When you have this problem, you will probably see the message "General failure error reading drive A:" or "Write protect error writing to drive A:."

- Is the disk formatted? DOS cannot read disks until they are formatted. Disks frequently come unformatted so you can choose how you want the disk formatted. For example, 3 1/2" disks can be formatted to use with either IBM-compatible personal computers or for Apple computers. This problem is indicated by the error message "General failure error reading drive A:."

- How old is the disk? Disks don't always age well. If you are trying to read an old disk, it is possible that the disk is no longer usable and the data is unavailable. That is why you should create backup copies of your important disks. When you have this problem, you will see messages such as "General failure error," "Data error, sector not found," or possibly one of several others.

- Has the disk been abused? Disks do not like magnets, beverages, food, or cigarette smoke. Magnets can rearrange the disk's contents. Beverages, food, and smoke can leave small particles on the disk that prevent the drive from reading it or can scratch the contents of the disk. This problem will cause error messages like "General failure error" and "Data error, sector not found."

I ran out of disk space while running a program. What do I do?

First, you need to save your data. If the program lets you, save your data to a floppy disk. If you are using Windows when you run into this problem, you may be able to start a file management program like Windows' File Manager or utilize a file management feature of the program you are already running to delete files you do not need. The program may also have a feature that lets you go to the DOS prompt so you can delete files that way.

Once you save your data, leave the program and free up more space on your disk. If you only free enough space for saving your data, you will constantly run into this problem. If you are chronically short on disk space, consider buying a larger hard drive, buying a second hard drive, or using DoubleSpace. You may want to check for temporary files that are not deleted when you exit from all running programs. These temporary files include files with a .TMP file extension, or that start with a ~. However, do *not* delete these files while a program is running. These files may represent your data in the program so if you delete them, you may lose your data. Exit all running programs and then delete the temporary files.

I am working with data and my system stopped responding. Do I have to reboot?

Before you reboot a system which has stopped responding, wait. Your computer may be in the middle of performing some task that prevents it from responding to your keystrokes. Some indications that your computer is still working are that the hard drive light is on (or goes off and on) or that your mouse moves on the screen.

If you have waited a while and your computer shows no sign of activity, you may have to reboot. The disadvantage of rebooting is that you will probably lose some of the data you are working with. The amount you lose depends on how long it has been since you saved the data.

I can't boot from my hard disk because one of the lines in CONFIG.SYS or AUTOEXEC.BAT causes the system to freeze. How do I start my computer?

You have three ways to boot your computer when you cannot use the bootup files (CONFIG.SYS and AUTOEXEC.BAT) on your computer's hard drive. These three ways are:

- Boot from drive A using a DOS 6.*x* system disk. Your computer will use the CONFIG.SYS and AUTOEXEC.BAT files, if any, from drive A. You can then change to the C drive, type **EDIT CONFIG.SYS**, and press ENTER to look for and correct the source of the problem.

- Boot your computer without a disk in drive A and press F5 as soon as you see the message "Starting MS-DOS...." Pressing this key bypasses the CONFIG.SYS and AUTOEXEC.BAT files. You can still access your compressed hard disk because the boot process loads DBLSPACE.BIN and DBLSPACE.INI before executing these files.

- Boot your computer without a disk in drive A and press F8 as soon as you see the message "Starting MS-DOS...." Pressing this key lets you select which lines from CONFIG.SYS and AUTOEXEC.BAT you want to perform. After you see the message that DOS will prompt you to confirm each CONFIG.SYS command, you will be prompted to type **Y** or **N** for each line in the CONFIG.SYS file. Then you will be prompted if you want to process AUTOEXEC.BAT. With DOS 6.2, if you type **Y** to this prompt, you will again be prompted to type **Y** or **N** for each line of the AUTOEXEC.BAT file. You can access your compressed hard disk because the boot process loads DBLSPACE.BIN and DBLSPACE.INI before executing CONFIG.SYS. Using F8 is the best method, since you can see exactly which line in CONFIG.SYS or AUTOEXEC.BAT is causing the problem.

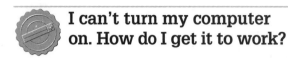

I can't turn my computer on. How do I get it to work?

The first step is to check whether the computer is actually turned on. Sometimes the problem is that the monitor is not displaying information, even though the computer itself is turned on. The easiest way to check this is to listen to your computer carefully. Do you hear a slight whirring sound? If you do, the computer is on and your problem is with the monitor. If you don't hear any sound, either you have a problem with the hardware inside the computer or the computer is not getting electricity.

If your computer is on but your monitor is not showing anything, then your monitor is not turned on, not adjusted correctly, or not receiving a signal from the computer. To determine which, check the following:

- Put your hand on the back of the monitor. Is it warm? If it is, your monitor is turned on. If your monitor is not warm, check that the monitor's power cord is plugged in firmly and that the power strip and outlet it uses are working.

- Next, check that the cable that connects your monitor to your computer is firmly attached at both ends. That cable lets the computer send information to display on the screen. Cleaning the office or moving a few things around on your desk can sometimes jostle this cable loose. Where the monitor cable connects to your computer depends on your computer and monitor.

- Finally, check your monitor's settings. Many of these settings are just like some of the knobs you have on your TV. For example, your monitor may have knobs or another method of setting brightness and contrast on the screen. The brightness and contrast may be turned so low that you cannot see what is on the monitor. Try turning the knobs to see if the text on the screen suddenly appears.

If none of these three steps work, your monitor may be broken. You need to have it checked by a repair person. *Don't* attempt to open the monitor's case. The monitor is the one component of your system that contains dangerously high voltages, even when it is unplugged. Leave this job to the experts!

If your computer is actually turned off, the problem might be that it is not getting electricity. To find out, check the following:

- Is the computer plugged in? Check the power cables from the outlet to the back of the computer. Also check that any power strips the computer uses are turned on.

- Is the outlet working? Test it by plugging another electrical device into the outlet and trying to turn it on.

If these suggestions above do not solve your problem, your computer probably has a hardware problem that needs to be fixed before you can turn your computer on. Contact your system's manufacturer or a computer repair service.

My computer is broken. Did I lose my data?

It depends on the part of the computer that is broken. If your hard disk is broken, you probably have lost your data. If it is a different part of your computer, the repair technician that fixes it can best tell you whether or not your data is damaged.

Tech Tip: If your data is important, back it up. Backing up data as you create it is much easier than re-creating it after losing your hard disk. The MS Backup utility makes backing up your data much easier than before since you no longer have to use complex DOS prompt commands.

I just formatted the wrong floppy disk. Is there any way I can get my data back?

Whether you can retrieve the data on a formatted disk depends on two things.

- First, how did you format it? By default, DOS 6.*x* tries to save information that allows a disk to be unformatted. If you format a disk using the /U switch, however, DOS unconditionally formats the disk and does not save unformat information.

- Second, did you put new data on the disk? If you used the disk to store new data, you may not be able to recover the original data because it was replaced by the new data. The best you can do is copy the new data to another disk, then try to unformat the disk.

To unformat a disk, type **UNFORMAT A:** at the DOS prompt and press ENTER, replacing A with the appropriate drive letter. Next, press ENTER in response to the message. When you type a **Y** to update the system area, you will unformat the disk. Updating the system area removes the information about any new data on the disk.

Why do I get the "Non-system disk or disk error" message when I start my computer?

This message appears because your computer is trying to boot from drive A, but the disk in drive A does not have the system files DOS needs to start. After you turn on your computer, it runs some preliminary tests, then the system's BIOS checks whether there is a disk in drive A. When drive A contains a disk, your computer boots from drive A rather than another location, such as your hard disk. If the disk in drive A does not contain the files needed to boot your computer, you see the "Non-system disk or disk error" message.

To boot your computer, either replace the disk in drive A with a disk containing the system files, or just remove the disk from drive A so your computer will boot from another location such as your hard disk. After replacing or removing the disk, press any key to continue with the boot process.

I was looking at the files on my hard drive and came across a bunch of files with weird looking characters. It says they occupy a few hundred megabytes of disk space. I don't have that much room on my hard drive. I am trying to delete these files but I don't seem to have any luck with the DELETE command. I have also tried Norton's Disk-Doctor. How do I get rid of them?

The files you are seeing are entries in DOS's file allocation table (FAT). These "files" may have actually been files at one time, but their directory entries are severely damaged. Erroneous data has crept into the locations where the file size is stored, resulting in incorrect file sizes. This is a very severe type of disk corruption which can be very tough to eliminate. One DOS command that may be able to remove these corrupt entries is DELTREE. If all of the characters in the filename can be typed from the keyboard (i.e., no graphic blocks or foreign symbols), type **DELTREE** "***filename***" and press ENTER. You *must* include the quotes.

If you're using DOS 6.2, run ScanDisk. ScanDisk may be able to repair the directory structure, but chances are that some data is lost or permanently damaged. If ScanDisk doesn't work, or if there are too many corrupt entries, you should back up the rest of your drive, then reformat the hard disk. This is often the safest, surest, and least tedious method of correcting this type of damage. If you're not sure how the damage occurred, be sure to run the Anti-Virus program to check for viruses.

File and Disk Management

File and disk commands are used more than any other DOS commands because they help you manage the information you have stored on disk. In a short time you are likely to become familiar with the commands you will use most often. You are unlikely to experience problems with those commands. The special switches and commands you use less often, however, are more likely to cause you problems. Look through the tips in the Frustration Busters box that follows for ways to increase your chances of success with options you use infrequently.

FRUSTRATION BUSTERS!

The rules which follow will help you take advantage of commands and options that are unfamiliar:

- You can get complete help on any command by entering **HELP COMMAND** where *COMMAND* is the name of the unfamiliar command. Typing **COMMAND /?** will also give a brief description of most DOS command options.

- Always follow a DOS command entry by a space before entering arguments or switches. Although this is not required for commands such as CD, it is easier to follow a single rule which will work for all commands.

- Separate each argument and switch by a space.

- Use a slash (/) not a backslash (\) before each switch letter and remember that switches are unique to specific commands and will not work with other commands.

- Be cautious with the use of wildcards (* and ?) when deleting or moving files.

- When using a filter such as More, place it at the end of your command entries and separate it from the command with a split vertical bar (|), known as the "pipe" symbol. For example, DIR *.TXT /S |MORE will display files with a .TXT extension from the current directory and its subdirectories, one screen at a time.

- Use the right angle bracket to direct DOS output to a file as in DIR B: > PRINTDIR.TXT.

How can I see if I have any hidden files?

Type **DIR /A:H** at the DOS prompt and press ENTER. This will show all hidden files in the current directory. To see a list of all hidden files anywhere on the drive, change to the root directory of the drive by entering **CD ** and pressing ENTER, then using DIR with the /S parameter, as shown here:

```
DIR /A:H /S
```

What's the difference between the ERASE and DEL commands?

Both commands do the same thing. The ERASE command probably traces its roots to an earlier operating system called CP/M. This was the operating system of choice for many early 8-bit computers, and may have been retained to accommodate users migrating from CP/M to DOS. Although there's no difference in the usage, DEL does save a few keystrokes.

I tried to use MOVE to move a subdirectory on my hard drive to a different parent directory. Why did I get the message "Unable to open source?"

The MOVE command cannot move directories, only normal files. If, while reorganizing your disk or archiving files, you want to copy both the directory and all of its contents while deleting the original, you will have to do it another way.

1. Switch to the new parent directory using the CD command, as in **CD \JFRFILES**.

2. Create a directory with the same name as the one you are going to move. For example, enter **MD TEXTDATA** and press ENTER.

3. You now want to move the entire contents of the old directory to the new directory. For example, you might enter **MOVE \TEXTDATA*.* \JFRFILES\TEXTDATA** to move all of the files in the \TEXTDATA directory to the \JFRFILES\TEXTDATA directory.

If some of the files in the directory use the hidden attribute, they will not be moved. After moving the files, enter **DIR \TEXTDATA /A:H** to see if there are any hidden files in the old directory. If there are, you may need to use the ATTRIB command to change the attributes of these files as in **ATTRIB –H \TEXTDATA*.*.** You can then use MOVE again to move these files. If you still want to keep these files hidden, you may want to note their names on paper, then use ATTRIB to give them this attribute again.

4. After moving all of the files in the original directory into the new directory, delete the original directory, as in **RD \TEXTDATA.** If you receive an error message, it is probably because this directory contains hidden files, or because it has subdirectories.

If the directory you need to move contains subdirectories that also must be moved, there is a quicker way to do this.

1. Use XCOPY to copy the directory, its subdirectories, and the files these directories contain to their new location. You need to make sure that you have enough disk space to copy all of those files before doing so.

2. After copying, delete the original directories and files.

For example:

1. Type **XCOPY \TEXTDATA*.* \JFRFILES\TEXTDATA /S /E** and press ENTER to copy all the files and subdirectories, except for hidden files.

2. Type **DELTREE TEXTDATA** and press ENTER to delete the original directory and all its files and subdirectories.

 I just copied a file into a new directory and accidentally gave it the same name as a file already in that directory. How can I get the original file back?

You can't get the file back. You have overwritten the file and it is gone forever. Your only chance is if you have a recent backup of the file on disk that you can use to restore the file. In DOS 6.2, by default, you should have received a prompt asking you to be sure that you wanted to overwrite the original file. If you didn't see this message, then this prompt has been turned off. To turn it back on, you need to go into your CONFIG.SYS and AUTOEXEC.BAT files to find the line that reads SET COPYCMD=/-Y. When you find this line, delete it, save the file, and restart your system. In the future, you will always get this warning.

How can I delete read-only or hidden files?

There are actually two ways to delete files with the read-only or hidden attribute. Both methods assume that you know the name of the file you want to delete.

Tech Tip: If you think a directory has hidden files in it, but don't know the filenames, type **DIR /A: H** and press ENTER to display a directory listing of only the files in the directory that have the hidden attribute.

1. Use the DELTREE command, making sure to use the exact path to the file; including the drive and directory. For example, you could type **DELTREE C:\IMAGE.IDX** and press ENTER to delete the hidden file, IMAGE.IDX in the root directory. When you are asked to confirm the deletion, be sure the file specified is really the one you want to delete. If you are not sure, respond with **N**.

2. Use the ATTRIB command to remove the attributes, then delete the files normally. For example, you could type **ATTRIB IMAGE.IDX -R -S -H** and press ENTER to remove the read-only, system, and hidden attributes from the IMAGE.IDX file. Then you would type **DEL IMAGE.IDX** and press ENTER to delete the file.

I have several files on my hard drive with a .TMP extension. What are they and can I delete them?

The .TMP files are temporary files created by programs you are running. The .TMP files can be safely deleted once you have exited the program that created them. To delete all of them, change to the directory where the files are located (usually

C:\TEMP or C:\DOS) and type the command: **DEL *.TMP**, then press ENTER.

Tech Tip: Never delete the .TMP files if there is a program still running, or if you find them after restarting your system without exiting all programs. If you delete a .TMP file while a program is still running, and it calls for that file, the program will malfunction and probably stop executing. Some programs also do intermittent backups of data to temporary files. When you restart your computer and reload a program that you didn't first exit (such as when you do a cold boot), some programs can read the temporary files and recover data you might otherwise have lost.

When I ran CHKDSK /F, it found errors and corrected them. Now some of my programs are acting as if files are damaged. Why?

When CHKDSK attempts to correct file structure damage, it may, depending on the type of damage, do so by deleting the data from the damaged location to the end of the file. Consequently, that file cannot function correctly anymore because some of its contents are gone. That is why some of the programs will not work anymore. There are other third-party utilities (Norton Utilities, PC Tools, etc.) that might be able to recover the damaged files, but the success of these utilities depends largely on the type of damage. Once the program files are corrupted, your only real solution is to reinstall the program or restore it from your backups.

What is the difference between RAM and my hard disk space?

Many people confuse RAM and hard disk space because the amounts of both are measured in megabytes (MB). They are quite different though. *RAM, or random access memory*, is memory that your computer can read data from and write data to. RAM, commonly known as "working memory," is the memory that programs are loaded into so they can be executed. RAM is temporary, which means that when your computer's power is turned off, the contents of your RAM are erased.

A *hard disk* is just like a floppy disk except that it stays in your system permanently, instead of being taken in and out of the disk drive. Because the hard disk stays in one location all the time, it is capable of holding much more data than a floppy disk.

A hard disk is the place where programs are stored for later use. Files saved on a hard disk are permanent, at least until they are intentionally erased.

My system has high-density disk drives. Can I format a low-density disk for use on another computer?

Yes. Your high-density disk drives can read and write to low-density disks, and you can format disks as low-density disks so that they can be used on another computer that does not have high-density disk drives. To change the density at which you're formatting, use the Format command with the /F switch. When you use this command, the /F switch is followed by a colon and the capacity the disk will have when formatted. For example, to format a 720K disk in a high-density 3 1/2" disk drive, type **FORMAT A: /F:720** and press ENTER. To format a 5 1/4" floppy disk at low-density simply replace the 720 with 360, the capacity of a low-density 5 1/4" disk.

Tech Tip: Some low-density drives cannot read a disk formatted as low density using a high-density drive. This particular example of incompatibility is rare. However, the sure-fire solution, if you should encounter this problem, is to format disks as low density with a low-density drive instead of with this switch.

I'm trying to rename my \TEXTDATA directory, but I keep getting the messages "Invalid parameter" or "Invalid path or file name." Can't I rename a directory?

The RENAME command can rename files, but not directories, which is why you are getting these error messages. The only way to rename a directory is with the MOVE command. For example, to rename your \TEXTDATA file, you could enter the command **MOVE \TEXTDATA *TEXTFILE*** where *TEXTFILE* is the new name you want for the directory. You will not lose the files in the directory when you move it.

When I enter CHKDSK /F I am asked "Convert to file?" Do I answer Yes or No?

You should answer **No**, then back up your system before running the command again. When CHKDSK asks this question, it has found damage on your hard drive. While converting the files might correct the damage, CHKDSK usually corrects damaged files by deleting the file's contents after the start of the damage, leaving the file's contents incorrect. Backing up your system might let you save the file intact. Do not simply ignore the error. Make sure that you run CHKDSK as soon has you've completed the backup to correct the damage, or you will lose even more data in the future.

If you're using MS-DOS 6.2, the best solution is to run ScanDisk, a new program that can detect file errors, just like CHKDSK, but which is a lot better at correcting them. Run ScanDisk by typing **SCANDISK** and pressing ENTER. Respond to ScanDisk's prompts about scanning your disk and correcting errors.

When I try to delete a file on my hard disk, I get the message "File name is invalid." Why?

Tech Tip: Using quotes to make DOS use an invalid filename only works with the DELTREE command, so do not try this with DEL, ERASE, COPY or any other DOS commands.

Some programs handle writing a file to the disk and updating the file allocation table themselves, instead of letting DOS handle these file management tasks. A few of these programs allow you to use characters in the filename that DOS will not allow. Therefore, you may have created directories or files with names that are invalid according to DOS's filenaming rules. When you try to delete a directory or file with an invalid name, you should use the DELTREE command and enclose the directory or filename in quotes, as in DELTREE "MY FILE." When the quotes are used, DOS recognizes the filename as entered even though it is invalid according to DOS's filenaming rules.

If the illegal file or directory name is the result of directory structure damage, DOS may not be able to delete it, even though you use the quotes. To repair the damage, use MS-DOS 6.2's ScanDisk utility or a third-party disk repair utility.

Somone said that I shouldn't put all of my files and programs in the root directory. Why?

There are two major reasons for not putting all of your files in your root directory.

1. DOS has a limit on how many files and directories can be stored in the root directory of a hard drive. You simply can't have more than 512 entries in the root directory. Since some temporary files may be created in the root directory by programs, you will not want to get too close to this limit. There are no limits, except the available disk space, on the number of files and subdirectories in any other directory.

2. Finding files and programs is *much* easier when they are organized into directories and subdirectories. A hard drive can hold hundreds of megabytes of data, which can include literally thousands of files. Finding a single file out of all of those, if they are not organized, would be a task akin to finding a needle in a haystack.

Whenever I format a disk, DOS asks me if I want to give the disk a volume label. What is a volume and why might it be useful?

The volume label is exactly that, an electronic label saved on the disk. A volume label can contain up to 11 letters, numbers, spaces, or underscores (_). Use the volume label to describe the contents of the disk or its purpose. You can change the label by typing **LABEL** *A:* and pressing ENTER, where *A* is the letter of the drive containing the disk you want to relabel. DOS will display the current label of the disk and prompt you for a new one.

You'll see the label of a disk if you use the VOL or DIR command on the disk.

I accidentally deleted a group of files using the DOS Shell. When I used UNDELETE, I couldn't get them back. Why?

Windows and the DOS Shell do not delete files using standard DOS interrupts. Depending on the level of deletion tracking you are using, DOS may not be able to tell that a file was deleted. In effect, you deleted the files behind DOS's back.

To undelete a file that was deleted in Windows or the DOS Shell, try typing the command **UNDELETE *FILENAME* /DOS**, where *filename* is the name of the file you want to undelete. The /DOS switch recovers only those files that are internally listed as deleted by MS-DOS, prompting you for confirmation on each file. If a deletion-tracking file exists, this switch causes UNDELETE to ignore it.

To avoid this problem in the future, change the level of deletion tracking. DOS 6.*x* offers three levels of deletion tracking: Standard, Delete Tracker, and Delete Sentry. Standard offers the least protection, and Delete Sentry the most. Delete Sentry will always allow you to undelete a file (unless it was wiped from the disk, as when using DELTREE). Standard is the default level of protection, available as soon as you turn your computer on. To enable the Delete Tracker level of deletion tracking, enter **UNDELETE /T**. To enable the Delete Sentry level of deletion tracking, enter **UNDELETE /S**. You can enter these commands at the DOS prompt and press ENTER to use these deletion tracking levels temporarily, or you can include them in your AUTOEXEC.BAT file to always use the selected level of deletion tracking.

Tech Tip: Standard deletion tracking uses no memory or hard disk space. Delete Tracker uses memory, and a small deletion-tracking file. Delete Sentry uses memory, and stores deleted files in a hidden subdirectory for a specified period of time. If you encounter out-of-memory errors while using the Delete Tracker or Delete Sentry level of deletion tracking, you may want to return to the Standard level.

I was taught to park my hard drive heads before turning my computer off. My new computer has MS-DOS 6.*x* and the PARK command doesn't seem to work. How do I park the hard drive heads?

Parking is not needed with modern hard drives because they automatically park their hard drive heads. Therefore, no Park utility is included with DOS 6.*x*. A way to tell if your hard drive heads are being parked automatically is by the sound made by the hard drive when the power is turned off. Many hard drives with "auto head parking" will make a distinctive clicking sound when the power is turned off. If you are unsure about whether your hard drive automatically parks its head, contact the manufacturer of the hard drive or your computer system dealer.

What is a file allocation table?

The file allocation table, often called the FAT, is a map of the physical location of files on a disk. The FAT is located near the beginning of the disk, along with a backup copy of the FAT. Whenever DOS needs to access a file, it looks to the FAT first to find out where the file is physically recorded.

Tech Tip: Errors in your FAT are potentially devastating. Since files are often split into sections and stored on different locations of your disk, due to a lack of contiguous space, the loss of a FAT effectively means that you've lost the files on the disk. Some third-party disk repair utilities will help you reconstruct your FAT if it becomes corrupted.

The online MS-DOS Help says that DOS 6.2's DISKCOPY performs a one-pass DISKCOPY. I get an error message saying "Error creating image file. DISKCOPY will revert to a multiple-pass copy." What's wrong?

Previous versions of DISKCOPY have always read the data from the source disk into conventional memory, which is limited to 640K, then copied it to the target disk. The new DISKCOPY uses free space on the hard disk to temporarily store the data from the source disk. Since the hard disk usually has much more than 640K free, there is usually enough space for DISKCOPY to copy a high-density disk in one pass. The problem you are having concerns *where* on the hard disk DISKCOPY will store the data temporarily. This is determined by the Temp variable, usually found in the AUTOEXEC.BAT file. If the variable is set to an invalid subdirectory, or is not set at all, DISKCOPY may resort to the old method of multiple passes.

To correct the problem, check the following items:

1. Make sure there is enough space free on your hard disk to fit the entire disk being copied. For example, if you are copying a 1.44MB disk, you need at least 1.44MB of free hard disk space.

2. Verify that the Temp variable is valid. To do this, type **SET** at the DOS prompt and press ENTER. If the setting has been defined, you'll see TEMP=*DIRECTORY* along with some other lines of data. *DIRECTORY* represents the directory your Temp variable is set to. Try switching to the directory shown to make sure it actually exists.

For example, when typing **SET** and pressing ENTER, your screen might show the response shown in Figure 4-1.

Try making the Temp directory current by typing **CD\WINDOWS\TEMP** and pressing ENTER. If you receive the error message "Invalid Directory," the Temp variable is set to a directory that doesn't exist. You now need to create it.

If the Temp variable isn't correct or doesn't exist, add the Temp variable to your AUTOEXEC.BAT file and reboot the computer. To do this, use the DOS Editor to add a line such as SET TEMP=C:\DOS to set the temporary file variable to a directory named DOS.

```
COMPSEC=C:\DOS\COMMAND.COM
PROMPT=$P$G
PATH=C:\DOS;C:\WINDOWS;C:\WINWORD;C:\EXCEL
TEMP=C:\WINDOWS\TEMP
WINDIR=C:\WINDOWS
```

FIGURE 4-1   Environmental variable settings

Retry the DISKCOPY command after verifying that there is enough disk space and that the Temp variable is set to an existing directory.

How do I get a large file that will not copy to one floppy disk onto disks?

Use the MS Backup utility. This utility can split the file across as many disks as are needed. It can also provide compression to reduce the number of disks needed. If you are moving the file to another computer, make sure the other computer also has MS-DOS 6.*x*, since the BACKUP command used in previous versions of DOS cannot restore files backed up with MS Backup.

Tech Tip: See Chapter 6 for tips about using the MS Backup utility.

I am trying to clean up my hard disk and I can't delete a directory. What am I doing wrong?

First, you want to check that all of the files in the directory are deleted. To do this quickly, make the directory current, type **DIR**, and press ENTER. If there are any files in the directory type **DEL *.*** and press ENTER.

If you still can't delete the directory, there may be a hidden file in the directory. Type **DIR /A:H** and press ENTER from within the directory to check for hidden files. If the hidden file is not needed, you can either delete it with the DEL command, or you can use the DELTREE command from the directory above the one you want to delete. For example, you could enter:

```
DELTREE C:\JUNK
```

DELTREE removes the directory, and all files and subdirectories beneath it, regardless of file attributes.

How do lost allocation units and cross-linked clusters develop?

The lost allocation units and cross-links are the result of the operating system losing track of information on the hard or floppy disk. There can be any number of reasons why these problems occur, such as:

- Power loss or dips or surges in the computer's power supply
- A failing drive or drive controller
- Rebooting the system while a program is writing to the disk
- Multiple programs writing to same area on the disk when multitasking
- A program that is not functioning correctly
- A program that doesn't work with a compressed disk
- Other hardware or software difficulties

What are the limitations of DOS's FDISK command when used to partition a hard drive?

FDISK can create partitions of up to two gigabytes. You can create up to four partitions on each physical drive. FDISK will recognize up to 1,024 cylinders (tracks on a disk's surface) on the hard disk. If your hard disk has more than 1,024 cylinders, you can partition it with FDISK, but some of the space on the hard disk will be wasted. A third-party partitioning program can be used to access the cylinders above 1,024.

When I run CHKDSK, it reports that my files are using more disk space than when I use DIR and add all of the file sizes together. Why?

MS-DOS writes to disks in clusters of bytes. Therefore, on a computer that uses 2K (2,000 byte) clusters, a file that is 500 bytes will take up the same space, 1 cluster, as a file that is 1,500 bytes. When you use DIR, you see the actual size of the file in bytes, but when you use CHKDSK, the message "*x,xxx,xxx* bytes in user files" reports the space taken up by clusters-in-use. Since some files are smaller than one cluster, this figure is larger. CHKDSK is more accurate because it reports how much actual disk space is being used by your files.

When I use XCOPY to copy a group of files, only a few or no files get copied and the message "Access Denied" appears on the screen. At this point XCOPY terminates and doesn't copy any more files. What is causing this?

This is happening because one of the files being copied currently exists in the destination drive or directory and is a read-only file. You need to remove the read-only attribute and execute the XCOPY command again. To remove the read-only attribute, you use the ATTRIB command, as in **ATTRIB -R**.

Can I copy multiple files from nested subdirectories without using Backup?

You can use XCOPY to copy the files that you mark using ATTRIB.

1. Use ATTRIB to mark all of the files in the nested subdirectory by entering **ATTRIB +A C:*SUBDIR**.* /S** where *SUBDIR* is the name of the highest level directory you want to copy files from. This command sets a "flag," called the archive bit, on all files in the named subdirectory, and all files in subdirectories beneath it.

2. Next, use XCOPY to copy the files by entering **XCOPY C:\\SUBDIR*.* A: /M /S**. This command copies all files and subdirectories beneath the named subdirectory to A. The /M switch tells XCOPY to copy only those files with the archive bit set, and to clear the archive bit on each file once the file is copied to the new disk.

If you need to spread the files across more than one disk, you'll get a "Disk Full" message and the operation will cease. Put in the next disk and issue the XCOPY command again. Only the files not yet copied will be included on the new disk, because those that have already been copied will have the archive bit cleared.

When I use DIR I like it to show the files in a specific way. How can I set the DIR command to always show its results this way?

You can use the *Dircmd* variable to set how the DIR command displays its results. To set the *Dircmd* variable, edit the AUTOEXEC.BAT file and add a line reading **SET DIRCMD=*???*** where *???* would be a parameter specifying how you want the directory to look. Valid values for *???* would be any parameter or combination of parameters you can use together with the DIR command from the DOS prompt. Below is a list of the parameters available for use with the DIR command.

Parameter	Brief Description	
/p	Displays one screen at a time.	
/w	Displays on a wide screen.	
/a[[:]attributes]	Displays only files with specific attributes. The colon is optional.	
	h	Hidden files.
	-h	Files that are not hidden.
	s	System files.
	-s	Non-system files.
	d	Directories only.
	-d	Does not show directories.
	a	Files with the archive bit set (commonly used for backing up).
	-a	Files that do not have the archive bit set.
	r	Read-only files.
	-r	Files that are not read-only.
/o[[:]sortorder]	Used with the following switches to sort the directory listing.	
	n	Alphabetical order by name.

Parameter		Brief Description
	-n	Reverse alphabetical order by name.
	e	Alphabetical order by extension.
	-e	Reverse alphabetical order by extension.
	d	Date and time, earliest first.
	-d	Date and time, latest first.
	s	By size, smallest first.
	-s	By size, largest first.
	g	Directories before files.
	-g	Files before directories.
	/s	Searches the directory and all subdirectories for all occurrences of the specified file(s).
	/b	Shows no summary information and cannot be shown wide. Does not show size or date.
	/l	Uses lowercase letters only.

Can I erase the .CHK files in the root directory of my hard disk?

When CHKDSK or ScanDisk fixes lost allocation units on a hard disk, they save any recovered files in the root directory of the hard disk using a filename like FILE0001.CHK. Any additional files that are recovered are called FILE0002.CHK, FILE0003.CHK, and so on. If these files are text or word processing files, then the information in them may be retrieved by importing them as text files into a word processor. Once the information has been retrieved and resaved under a more meaningful filename, the .CHK files can be deleted. If the files are not text files, such as program or database files, then the information in them will not be recognizable by a program. Because they cannot be retrieved, these files can be deleted. Usually the files CHKDISK or ScanDisk recovers are only a fragment of a larger file, so they aren't usable.

I know I have corrupted files on my disk, but I don't know which ones. How can I find out without reloading all my programs?

To find out which files are corrupted, you need to test them by having DOS carry out an operation using them. To do this, type **COPY *.* NUL** and press ENTER in each directory where you suspect damage. This command copies all of the files to a place that doesn't exist. If a file is misallocated (i.e., corrupted), DOS will give you an error message. If DOS doesn't detect any allocation problems, it will display "1 File(s) Copied."

Use this COPY command before running CHKDSK /F or correcting errors with ScanDisk. These programs will correct the allocation errors, but can't put your corrupted file back together.

Once you have discovered the corrupted files, delete them, then run CHKDSK /F or ScanDisk to fix the allocation table. You will then need to re-create or restore the files that were corrupted. If many files from the same program were corrupted, you may find it easier to reinstall that program.

Do I use FDISK to format my hard disk?

No, FDISK is used to create or delete partitions on the hard disk. The FORMAT command is used to format the hard disk, just as if you were formatting a floppy disk. If the hard disk is brand new, there will not be any partitions defined. If you type **C:** and press ENTER at the DOS prompt and get the message "Invalid drive specification," you need to use FDISK first to set up one or more partitions. After setting up the partitions, use FORMAT to format each of them.

How do I stop the COPY command from prompting before overwriting a file?

Add the /Y parameter to the COPY command. For example, **COPY *.BAT C:\BATCH /Y** will copy all files with the .BAT extension from the current directory to the subdirectory BATCH, and will automatically overwrite any existing files with the same name.

To prevent this prompt from occurring for all COPY, XCOPY, and MOVE commands, insert the command **SET COPYCMD=/-Y** in the AUTOEXEC.BAT file.

How can I remove a directory and all of its files quickly?

DOS 6.*x* includes the new DELTREE command which deletes directories, including all subdirectories and files in the deleted directories. This command also deletes individual files with hidden, system, and read-only attributes, which the DEL command cannot do. Use DELTREE with caution because it is very powerful. You can easily delete something you hadn't intended to delete. You will be asked to confirm your deletion. You may answer No to anything you think you might not want to delete.

For example, assume you have a directory called JUNK, which contains the subdirectory STUFF. These two directories contain many outdated files. You would like to delete JUNK, STUFF, and all the files in these directories. To delete them:

Tech Tip: You don't actually have to use DELTREE from the parent directory. You do, however, have to make sure that you are not in the directory you are trying to delete, or one of its subdirectories.

1. Make JUNK's parent directory (assuming that is the root directory) current by typing **CD ** and pressing ENTER.

2. Type **DELTREE JUNK**, and press ENTER.

3. DELTREE asks if you are sure that you want to delete JUNK and its subdirectories.

4. Type **Y** and press ENTER. JUNK, STUFF, and all files in these directories will be deleted.

I installed a second hard drive and set my old one as my D drive. With FDISK, I see that I have two active partitions, one on each hard drive. Is this dangerous, and, if so, how can I fix it?

There is no danger in having two active partitions. Your computer should function fine. However, a better solution is to set up the partition on the D drive as an extended DOS partition rather than a primary DOS partition. The only way to change this is by repartitioning the disk with FDISK. Since repartitioning the disk would mean losing any files stored there, you may not want to bother.

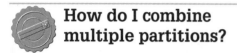

How do I combine multiple partitions?

MS-DOS can only recognize 1,024 hard disk cylinders, so you should make sure that your hard drive does not have more cylinders before attempting to change the partitions with MS-DOS. If you do have more cylinders, you should look into finding a third-party disk partitioning program which can use those other cylinders. While you can use MS-DOS to partition your larger hard disk, those cylinders beyond 1,024 are simply ignored, which means you will get less use out of your hard disk than you could.

There are two easy ways to find out how many cylinders your hard disk has. The easiest, and most accurate, is to check the documentation that came with your computer or hard disk. This documentation should tell you the number of cylinders. You can also call the hardware manufacturer.

Another method is to use MSD (Microsoft Diagnostics utility) to find out how many cylinders your hard drive has. When you use MSD, it checks with your CMOS. The *CMOS* is a section of memory that keeps track of the hardware and operating systems that your computer has. When the hard drive was installed, the CMOS recorded what kind of hard drive it was and the number of cylinders on the disk. The information in CMOS may be incorrect, so this method is not guaranteed to give the correct answer.

To use MSD to find out the number of cylinders on your hard disk:

1. Start MSD by typing **MSD** at the DOS prompt and pressing ENTER.
2. Type **D** or select the Disk Drives button. MSD opens a window displaying the parameters of all of your drives.
3. Look at the text after C: or the letter of your hard drive and note how many cylinders the hard disk has.
4. Press ENTER or ESC to close this dialog box.
5. Exit MSD by pressing F3.

If your hard drive has 1,024 cylinders or less, proceed to repartition the disk using the following steps:

1. Install MS-DOS 6.*x* if you haven't already.

2. Back up all of your data that you want to keep from all drives.

3. Make sure you have a 6.*x* system (bootable) disk for drive A that works without problems.

To check this, actually use it to reboot your computer by putting it in drive A and rebooting.

4. Copy FDISK.EXE, SYS.COM, and FORMAT.EXE from the DOS directory to the system disk.

5. Start the FDISK program by typing **FDISK** and pressing ENTER.

6. Type **4** and press ENTER to choose to display partition information.

7. Note if there is a non-DOS partition or an extended DOS partition. Press ESC to return to the main menu.

8. First delete any non-DOS partitions you may have. If you don't have any, proceed to step 9. To delete a non-DOS partition:

   a. Type **3** and press ENTER to choose to delete partitions.

   b. Type **4** and press ENTER.

   c. Type the number of the partition you want to delete, assuming you have more than one, and press ENTER.

   d. Confirm the deletion by typing **Y** and pressing ENTER.

   e. Press ESC, returning you to the Fdisk Options screen.

   f. Repeat these steps until you have deleted all of your non-DOS partitions.

9. Second, delete any logical drives in the extended DOS partition. If you do not have an extended DOS partition, skip to step 11. To delete the logical drives:

   a. Type **3** and press ENTER to choose to delete partitions.

   b. Type **3** and press ENTER again.

   c. Type the letter of the logical drive you want to delete and press ENTER.

Tech Tip: You can copy the files necessary for repartitioning the hard drive to the system disk by typing **SETUP /F** and pressing ENTER from the drive containing the DOS Setup disks and specifying drive A.

    d. Type **Y** and press ENTER to confirm that you want to delete the drive.

    e. Repeat steps c and d until all the logical drives have been deleted.

    f. Press ESC to return to the Fdisk Options screen.

10. Third, delete the extended DOS partition. If you do not have an extended DOS partition, proceed to step 11. To delete the extended DOS partition:

    a. Type **3** and press ENTER to choose to delete partitions.

    b. Type **2** and press ENTER to delete the extended DOS partition.

    c. Type **Y** and press ENTER to confirm that you want to delete the extended DOS partition.

    d. Press ESC to return to the Fdisk Options screen.

11. Finally, you should delete the primary DOS partition. To do this:

    a. Type **3** and press ENTER.

    b. Type **1** and press ENTER to delete the primary DOS partition.

    c. Press ENTER.

    d. Type the volume label and press ENTER when Fdisk asks you for it. The volume label should appear at the top of the screen.

    e. Type **Y** and press ENTER to confirm that you want to delete the primary DOS partition.

    f. Press ESC to return to the Fdisk Options screen.

12. Having deleted all of your partitions, you now need to create a new primary DOS partition. To create it:

    a. Type **1** and press ENTER to create a new partition.

    b. Type **1** and press ENTER again to create a new primary DOS partition.

    c. Press ENTER to create an active primary DOS partition that uses all available space.

    d. Insert the system or boot disk you created in step 3 into drive A and press a key.

13. At the DOS prompt, type **FORMAT C: /S** and press ENTER. You are formatting the new DOS partition. When asked for a label, you may enter anything up to 11 characters.

14. Reinstall Windows first, if you are using Windows, and then DOS 6.*x*.

Tech Tip: If you have the Stepup program used to upgrade DOS 6.0 to 6.2, you will have to reinstall 6.0 before running Stepup. You are installing Windows before DOS so that you can install the Windows versions of the new DOS utilities.

15. Reinstall all other programs.

16. Restore your backup files. Be careful that you do not overwrite the new C:\CONFIG.SYS, C:\AUTOEXEC.BAT, C:\COMMAND.COM, C:\IO.SYS, or C:\MSDOS.SYS files or any existing files in the C:\DOS directory.

I have about 20 small text files that I want to combine into one big file. Is there a quicker way to combine all the files versus "insert file" with my text editor?

The COPY command can combine any number of files into a single file with its combine feature.

```
COPY FILE1.TXT + FILE2.TXT + FILE3.TXT... FILEX.TXT BIGFILE.TXT
```

The files from FILE1.TXT through FILEX.TXT are the files that are to be combined, and BIGFILE.TXT is the big file that will be created and the other files combined into. This operation leaves the original files intact.

An employee says the files on her floppy disk keep "disappearing" while she's at lunch. She thinks someone may be using her system and deleting the files. What can I do to find out what happened and/or recover the work? HELP!!!

DOS offers you two ways to attempt to recover the lost work, depending on what actually happened. If the files were deleted, you may be able to undelete them. If the disk was reformatted, you may be able to unformat it.

1. To attempt to undelete the files, use the Undelete utility. If you are using the DOS UNDELETE command—rather than the Windows Undelete utility—type **UNDELETE B:**, where B is the drive containing the disk, and press ENTER. Respond to the prompts to undelete the files.

2. To attempt to unformat the disk, type **UNFORMAT B:**, where B is the drive containing the disk, and press ENTER. The UNFORMAT command can recover the lost files and indicate the time and date that the disk was last formatted. You will only recover data if the disk has not been used to save new files.

If the computer has a lock, the employee may consider turning it off and locking it while she is at lunch. You can also check for instructions entered at the DOS prompt if DOSKEY is installed. DOSKEY will allow you to look at the history of commands entered from the DOS prompt to see if anyone is entering DELETE commands. Another suggestion would be to check how she ends her session right before lunch. She may be exiting a program without saving her work.

Other DOS Commands

Although all DOS commands are in some way related to files and disks, the commands discussed in this chapter are not as directly related to specific file and disk commands as those covered in Chapter 4. Problems encountered while executing a command, creating a batch file, and printing are discussed in this chapter.

The time on my computer did not change for daylight saving time. Can I change the time?

You may want to change the time on your computer when daylight saving time begins or ends or when you are using a portable computer in a different time zone. Changing the date or time on your computer will not cause it any damage. However, you won't want to change your date or time randomly. When backing up files or restoring them, it is often useful to know the actual date and time when the different versions of a file were created. To set the time on your computer, enter **TIME *HH:MM:SS*** in which the *HH* represents the hour, *MM* the minutes, and *SS* the seconds. The seconds entry is optional. If you don't enter the seconds, DOS simply starts counting time at the beginning of the minute you specify.

Is there any way to stop a DOS command while it's running?

Stopping a DOS command is only practical if the command takes a while to complete the requested task. Some commands execute so quickly there is no time for you to react. Other commands seem to crank away at completing your request for a period of time. You can attempt to stop these longer running commands by pressing CTRL+C a couple of times. For some commands, DOS will stop the command, displaying ^C where it stops and leaving you at a DOS prompt. For example, if you type **COPY *.* A:** and press ENTER, then realize that you are copying from the wrong directory, you can press CTRL+C. Your screen might look like Figure 5-1. Whether the command will stop when you press CTRL+C depends on the command; some commands ignore your request to stop.

My coworker's DOS prompt shows the directory she is in, but my prompt just shows the active drive. How can I change my prompt?

To change what the DOS prompt shows, you use the PROMPT command. You can change the DOS prompt's contents

```
C:\DOS>COPY *.* A:
DBLSPACE.BIN
EGA.SYS^C

C:\DOS>
```

FIGURE 5-1   Using CTRL+C to stop copying a directory's contents

temporarily by entering the PROMPT command at the DOS PROMPT, or you can set a new default DOS prompt by adding the PROMPT command to your AUTOEXEC.BAT file. To make DOS easier to use, DOS 6.*x*'s default prompt shows the drive and directory. The default prompt is identical to what you would see if you entered **PROMPT PG**. However, when you type **PROMPT** at the DOS prompt and press ENTER, you will see C> just like prior versions of DOS.

The PROMPT command can be used with several different parameters that set what your DOS prompt displays, or you can simply enter text. The symbols you can use are shown below:

This parameter:	Does this in the DOS prompt:
$$	Displays $
$_	Goes to the beginning of the next line
$B	Displays vertical bar (l)
$D	Displays the date
$e	Displays the ANSI escape character code
$G	Displays >
$H	Deletes the previous character in the DOS prompt
$L	Displays <
$N	Displays the current drive
$P	Displays the current path including the drive
$Q	Displays =
$T	Displays the time
$V	Displays the version number for DOS
text	Displays whatever text you typed

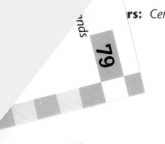
For example, if you want to personalize your DOS prompt, you can type **PROMPT Jane Fox's computer:** and press ENTER. To display the current drive and path, followed by a greater than symbol, you can type **PROMPT PG** and press ENTER. When you first set up DOS, this prompt statement is added to your AUTOEXEC.BAT file, so that it is the most commonly found DOS prompt.

Tech Tip: Changing the DOS prompt does not change how DOS works. All DOS commands will work the same way, no matter what the DOS prompt reads.

How can I tell which version of DOS I currently have installed on my computer?

To determine the version of DOS that is installed on your computer, type **VER** at the DOS prompt and press ENTER. Your current version will be displayed as shown here:

```
C:\>VER

MS-DOS Version 6.20

C:\>
```

I just installed DOS 6.x and when I use the DIR command, I see "Volume in drive C is MS-DOS 5."

The entry at the top of your directory listing is the volume label. This label was probably entered when your drive was first formatted. It really has no bearing on the current version of DOS. If you want, you can change the label of the disk to any name of up to 11 characters using the LABEL command. To do so, type **LABEL *NAME*** at the DOS prompt, where *NAME* represents the new label you want to assign, and press ENTER.

I just tried to copy files with XCOPY and saw the message "Bad command or file name." I've verified that the file exists with the DIR command. What's wrong?

The most likely problem is that DOS can't find the XCOPY command. DOS commands are either internal or external. *Internal commands* are always available when you have DOS loaded. DIR is an internal command. *External commands*, however, are saved in separate files. When you use these commands, DOS must find those files to execute the command. You will get the "Bad command or file name" error message whenever DOS can't find the file for the command you entered.

The most likely solution is to include your DOS directory in your Path statement. The Path statement tells DOS which directories to search when you request a file. If you do not have a Path statement, then DOS will not find the files. To check your Path statement, type **PATH** and press ENTER. If the directory containing your DOS files does not appear in the Path statement, then you'll know the reason you can't copy the file is that DOS can't find the XCOPY command. See "How can I add a new directory to my Path statement?" later in this chapter for details on changing your Path statement so it will include your DOS directory.

How do I find out about the DOS commands? There isn't very much information in the manual.

You can learn more about any DOS command by typing **HELP** at the DOS prompt and pressing ENTER. You should investigate the Notes and Examples sections of Help by highlighting <<Notes>> or <<Examples>> at the top of each help page and pressing ENTER. Quite often, you'll find additional details and explanations there. Figure 5-2 shows the help screen for the INTERLNK command.

What's the difference between the CD and CHDIR commands?

There is no difference in the effect of CD and CHDIR since both commands change the active directory. CHDIR was the command

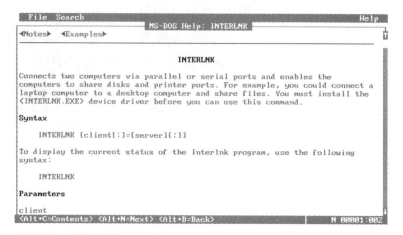

FIGURE 5-2   The MS-DOS online help screen for the INTERLNK command

used in CP/M, the operating system that the first version of DOS was based on. When DOS was first written, CHDIR was kept to make it easier for earlier CP/M users to use. However, for those of us who prefer typing as little as possible, the abbreviation CD was also included to do exactly the same thing. You'll find the same type of holdover in three other commands:

- DEL and ERASE—to delete files
- MD and MKDIR—to create directories
- RD and RMDIR—to remove or delete directories

It doesn't matter which version of these commands you use, since they perform identical tasks. Just use the one you are most comfortable with.

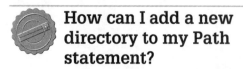

How can I add a new directory to my Path statement?

Your Path statement tells DOS where to look for a file when it cannot locate it in the current directory. Usually, you will have a Path statement in your AUTOEXEC.BAT file, so DOS always knows to search the same directories. Many programs will add their program directories to your Path statement in the AUTOEXEC.BAT file or create a Path statement in this file if there isn't one. This ensures that the programs can always find the files they need to run. You can also change the Path statement for the current DOS session by entering the PATH command at the DOS prompt.

Tech Tip: If you change your Path statement and remove a directory that a program needs to access, you may find yourself receiving messages such as "Cannot find XYZ file" or simply having your program perform incorrectly. Make sure that when you change your Path statement, you do not remove any directories that are needed by a program you use.

To add a directory to your Path statement permanently, you need to edit your AUTOEXEC.BAT file. To do this:

1. Type **COPY AUTOEXEC.BAT AUTOEXEC.OLD** and press ENTER.

This makes a backup copy of your AUTOEXEC.BAT file that you can use if you accidentally make changes to the original that you don't want.

2. Type **EDIT C:\AUTOEXEC.BAT** and press ENTER.

3. Move to the end of the Path statement in this file.

4. Type **;*directory*** where *directory* is the name of the directory you want to add.

5. Select Save from the File menu.

6. Select Exit from the File menu.

Tech Tip: Remember that DOS first searches the current directory for a requested file, then the first directory in the Path statement, then the second, and so on. If the directory you are adding is one you are going to work with frequently, you may want to add it at the beginning of the Path statement.

If you only want to add the directory to your Path statement for the current DOS session, you can simply change the Path statement from the DOS prompt. Be careful to include directories such as \DOS and \WINDOWS or you may have trouble running these programs. Another special feature of the PATH command in a batch file comes into play when you want to add a directory to a previous Path statement. You can type **PATH *new directory*;%PATH%** in the batch file where *new*

directory is the directory or directories you want added to the Path statement. The %PATH% tells DOS to append the existing Path statement to the end of the new Path statement, without your having to retype it.

Tech Tip: Path statements cannot be longer than 127 characters, unless they are in your CONFIG.SYS file. You should avoid Path statements with many directories, however, because long Path statements make DOS a little slower.

Is there any way to print out what DOS displays on my screen, such as the results of my DIR command?

There are several ways to print the information DOS displays on your screen. The first, and easiest, way to print is by using the PRINT SCREEN key. Press PRINT SCREEN or SHIFT+PRINT SCREEN (the PRINT SCREEN key is sometimes labeled Prt Scr or some other abbreviation) to print out whatever you see on the screen at the moment. If your screen is displaying graphics, they will not print properly. When you use PRINT SCREEN, you may need to press the Form Feed button on your printer to have it eject the paper the printout is on. DOS does not send a message to the printer to eject the page once it's finished printing.

If you are working from the DOS prompt, you can print out your entire DOS session by pressing CTRL+PRINT SCREEN. This key combination sends everything you enter or see at the DOS prompt to the printer, until you press CTRL+PRINT SCREEN again to turn it off.

You can also redirect the output of a command, such as the DIR command, for example, to the printer. Instead of seeing the directory listing on the screen, you will have a hard copy of it. To redirect the output of a command to the printer, add > **PRN** at the end of the command, as in **DIR \TEXTDATA >PRN**. The > symbol tells DOS that you are specifying where the output will be sent, and PRN, which stands for printer, tells DOS to send the output to the printer. Instead of PRN, you can use the number of the port your printer is attached to, such as COM2 or LPT1. Usually, PRN is sufficient.

I see CLS in my AUTOEXEC.BAT file. What does that do?

CLS is the command to clear the screen. This command clears the monitor screen and displays the DOS prompt and the cursor in the first line on the screen.

What is a batch file, exactly?

A batch file is just a series of DOS commands saved in a file. Any time you want to execute that series of DOS commands again, you execute the batch file. Batch files can be created in the DOS Editor, or in any text editor or word processing program that can save the file as an ASCII text file. For the most part, you enter the commands in the batch file just as if you were entering them at the DOS prompt.

Batch files also let you do things that you cannot do at the DOS prompt. You can create batch files that display specific messages, or take different actions depending on user input. There are several DOS commands that are only used in batch files, such as PAUSE, CALL, or GOTO. These commands direct the flow of execution in the batch file between different lines. The following is a list of DOS commands that are used exclusively in batch files. Figure 5-3 shows a batch file that uses some of these commands.

@	Prevents the line it begins from echoing to the screen
CALL	Executes a second batch program without stopping the one it is in
CHOICE	Prompts the user to make a choice
ECHO	Sets whether lines in a batch file appear on the screen
GOTO	Tells DOS which line in the batch file to execute next
IF	Tells DOS which line in the batch file to execute next, depending on the results of a calculation or a condition
PAUSE	Pauses execution of a batch file
REM	Prevents the line it begins from being executed
SHIFT	Changes replaceable parameters in a batch file

Creating a batch file is just like creating a program. Many of the same skills and techniques are involved. Essentially, every

```
@ECHO OFF
REM Find out which drive they want to format with.
ECHO You can format a disk in either the 5 1/4" A drive or
ECHO the 3 1/2" B drive.
ECHO Type A to format a 5 1/4" disk or B to format a 3 1/2" disk.
CHOICE /C:AB /T:B,10
IF ERRORLEVEL 2 GOTO B_DRIVE
REM Find out what density they want to format the disk.
ECHO You can format the disk at high density (1.2 MB) or
ECHO low density (360 KB).
ECHO Type H to format the disk at high density or L to
ECHO format the disk at low density.
CHOICE /C:HL /T:H,10
IF ERRORLEVEL 2 GOTO LOW_DENSITY
REM Format A: drive with high density
FORMAT A:
GOTO END
:LOW_DENSITY
REM Format A: drive with low density
FORMAT A: /F:360
GOTO END
:B_DRIVE
REM Find out what density they want to format the disk.
ECHO You can format the disk at high density (1.44 MB) or
ECHO low density (720 KB).
ECHO Type H to format the disk at high density or L to
ECHO format the disk at low density.
CHOICE /C:HL /T:H,10
IF ERRORLEVEL 2 GOTO LO_DENSITY
Rem Format B: drive with high density
FORMAT B:
GOTO END
:LO_DENSITY
REM Format B: drive with low density
FORMAT B: /F:720
:END
```

FIGURE 5-3   A batch file to help users format floppy disks

batch file that you create is a program using the language of DOS commands.

My coworker can make her last command appear by pressing the UP ARROW key. I can't. Why?

Your coworker has DOSKEY loaded. DOSKEY loads a program that remembers the commands you enter. You can use DOSKEY this way to avoid retyping commands. You can type **DOSKEY** at the DOS prompt and press ENTER, or you can add the command to your AUTOEXEC.BAT file so that the program is always loaded when you start your computer.

You can use the following keys to work with DOS commands while DOSKEY is loaded. The template is the last entered DOS command that is saved in memory so you can work with the DOS command entry.

UP ARROW	Displays the DOS command entered before the one displayed
DOWN ARROW	Displays the DOS command entered after the one displayed
PAGE UP	Displays the oldest DOS command entered since DOSKEY was loaded
PAGE DOWN	Displays the newest DOS command entered since DOSKEY was loaded
LEFT ARROW	Moves the cursor left one character in the displayed DOS command
RIGHT ARROW	Moves the cursor right one character in the displayed DOS command
CTRL+LEFT ARROW	Moves the cursor left one word in the displayed DOS command
CTRL+RIGHT ARROW	Moves the cursor right one word in the displayed DOS command
HOME	Moves the cursor to the beginning of the displayed DOS command
END	Moves the cursor to the end of the displayed DOS command
ESC	Clears the currently displayed DOS command
F1	Copies one character from the template
F2	Copies the template up to the character you press after pressing F2
F3	Copies the template from the position where the cursor is in the current DOS command to the end
F4	Deletes all characters from the template starting at the cursor's location to the character you press after pressing F4
F5	Deletes the currently displayed DOS command while copying it into the template
F6	Adds an end-of-line character at the cursor's position
F7	Displays all the commands in memory
ALT+F7	Deletes all the commands in memory
F8	Displays the most recent command that starts with the characters you entered before pressing F8

F9	Displays the command associated with the number you enter when prompted
ALT+F10	Deletes all macro definitions

Tech Tip: The F1, F2, F3, and F4 function keys work as described in the table above, even if DOSKEY is not loaded. However, they can only work with the last command entered.

Can I use the DOS MODE command to redirect my printer ports from LPT1 to LPT2?

Unfortunately, the MODE command does not support redirecting your printer ports to a different parallel port. You can only redirect LPT1 to a serial port, such as COM1. There are, however, public domain utilities that will allow LPT1 to be redirected to LPT2. Two examples of these are SWAPLPT and SWAPPRN. They are usually available through a bulletin board service (BBS) or shareware software distributor.

Is there any way to quickly find out what the contents of a file are from DOS without starting the program I used to create the file?

Assuming that the file is an ASCII file, you can use the TYPE command to look at the file contents. The TYPE command displays the contents of a file in ASCII characters. If the file is coded or formatted heavily, such as a program or spreadsheet file, the ASCII characters that display will be unreadable. For example, Figure 5-4 shows the results of using TYPE with a Microsoft Excel spreadsheet file. However, if the file's contents are primarily ASCII text, as in a batch or word processing file, you may be able to read enough of it to identify the file.

```
C:\MSOFFICE\EXCEL>type timeshet.xls
 ▒ ▫ ♫ ▒ ▫ ✳ ▫ ▫ ► ⁿ⌐±╖MbP?◄ ▫    " ▫   ✳ ▫   ♦ ▫ ▫ _ ▫ ▫ é ▫   Ç        ‰▫♦
MS Sans Serif1▫  á     ∆✳Times New Roman1▫  á ▫   ∆✳Times New Roman¶ ♥ ▫&F§ Page &
Pâ ▫   ä ▫   &     δ?'      δ?(       ≡?)       ≡?M ♀   ▫ ▫ d ⁿ ⁿ í ♀ ▫ d ▫ ▫
 ▫ ▫ ▫ ▫   ∪ ▫ ▲♦
                    General▲♦♦ ▫ ▫▫▲♦ ▫▫♦0.00▲ ▫▫✳#,##0▲♦δ ▫#,##0.00▲♦¶ ▫♦◄#,##
0_):\(#,##0\)▲♦↓ ▫▲_#,##0_);[Red]\(#,##0\)▲♦
C:\MSOFFICE\EXCEL>
```

FIGURE 5-4   Using the TYPE command with a Microsoft Excel spreadsheet file

Tech Tip: Since a file usually includes more information than can fit on a screen, you may want to put **|MORE** at the end of the TYPE command. |MORE feeds information to the screen one screen at a time and pauses. When you press a key, |More will display the next screen of information until the entire file is displayed.

Is there any way to print files without starting a program?

If the files you want to print are text files, yes. You can use DOS's PRINT command to print text files while you continue using DOS. Text files are those that contain only ASCII characters, such as those you create with the DOS Editor. You can also create text files with any word processor that will let you save the file with a text or ASCII format.

To use the PRINT command:

1. Using the CD command, move to the directory containing the text file.

2. Type **PRINT** *FILENAME*, where *FILENAME* is the name of the file to print, and press ENTER.

When I turn my computer on, all the lines in the AUTOEXEC.BAT file appear. Is there anyway to keep them from appearing?

Yes, it is possible to stop the AUTOEXEC.BAT commands from displaying. What your system is doing is "echoing" the commands in your AUTOEXEC.BAT file to the screen. You can turn the echoing feature off for all batch files, or for specific lines in your AUTOEXEC.BAT file.

To turn echoing off for the AUTOEXEC.BAT file and all other batch files, add the command **@ECHO OFF** as the first line in your AUTOEXEC.BAT or batch file. If you need a batch file to echo, or display its lines, while executing, you will need to make **ECHO ON** the first line in that batch file.

To turn off echoing for individual lines in the AUTOEXEC.BAT file, add **@** to the beginning of each line you don't want to appear on the screen while the command is executing.

 **Tech Tip:** In some batch files, you may want to display a message on the screen. This can be done using the ECHO command. Include a line reading **ECHO *MESSAGE*** in which *message* is the message you want to appear. As long as the echoing feature has been turned off with an ECHO OFF entry, this command displays the message. To display a blank line, add the line **ECHO.** with no space between ECHO and the period.

 ## Is there any way to slow down the output of a DOS command like DIR or TYPE?

You can slow down almost all DOS commands by adding I **MORE** at the end of the command. This filter only lets the command display one screen of information at a time. When there is more information than can fit in that one screen, -- More -- appears at the bottom of the screen. You can press any key to make the next screen of information appear. The DIR command has a /P switch you can include in the command that has the same effect. When a DIR command includes /P, DOS automatically stops after each screen.

 ## Is there a faster way to make a bootable DOS disk than the DOS FORMAT /S command?

For a disk to be able to boot your computer, it has to have the system files on it. There are two quick ways to create a bootable, or system, disk.

1. You can use the DOS SYS command to transfer the DOS system files to a formatted disk. For example, you can type **SYS A:** and press ENTER to make a DOS bootable disk in drive A.

2. You can do a quick format if you also want to erase any existing files on the disk. Type **FORMAT A: /Q /S** and press ENTER to perform a quick format and transfer the system files.

I get "Cannot find file QBASIC.EXE" when I attempt to access the online help or edit a file with the EDIT command. What is wrong?

The QBASIC.EXE file is needed in order to execute the HELP command or for the Editor to function properly. Both the online DOS Help and the DOS Editor actually use the editor from QBASIC to display the Help information or to let you edit text files.

Can I include lines that do not execute in my batch file so that I can explain to other users what the executing lines do?

It is a good idea to add explanatory lines to batch files. Any line in a batch file that starts with REM is not executed. REM, which is short for Remark, effectively tells DOS to ignore the remainder of that line. You can use REM to include documentation for a batch file as part of a batch file, as you can see in Figure 5-3. You can also use it to disable a specific line in the batch file. For example, you might disable a specific device driver by adding REM at the beginning of the line in your CONFIG.SYS file that loads that device driver, then rebooting your system.

Is there a screen saver utility that comes with DOS?

No, but you can create a batch file that will emulate a screen saver. Make sure you place this file in a directory listed in your Path statement (usually found in your AUTOEXEC.BAT file) so it is readily available from any subdirectory. At the DOS prompt type **EDIT B.BAT** and press ENTER to open the DOS Editor. Then type the following lines, pressing ENTER after each line:

```
@ECHO OFF
CLS
PAUSE > NUL
```

After the last line, press ALT+F to open the File menu, and select Exit by pressing X. When prompted to save, select Yes. That's it! This only works from a DOS prompt, not within an application. Whenever you want to blank the screen, simply type **B** and press ENTER. Pressing any key will "wake up" the screen.

I have problems reading the screen in DOS because of bad eyesight. Is there anything I can do?

You can display the screen text in a larger font. At the DOS prompt, type **MODE CO40**, then press ENTER. Your screen will look like Figure 5-5. To return the screen to normal type **MODE CO80** and press ENTER. The MODE command changes the video display mode. Keep in mind that many programs set the screen mode as they execute, so this setting will only affect the command-line programs that don't set up their own screens.

```
C:\>cd \msoffice\excel

C:\MSOFFICE\EXCEL>dir

 Volume in drive C is N
 Volume Serial Number is 19D0-2069
 Directory of C:\MSOFFICE\EXCEL

.              <DIR>        12-13-93    11:21a
..             <DIR>        12-13-93    11:21a
XLCALL   DLL      2048      10-28-93    12:00a
XLREADME HLP     58426      10-28-93    12:00a
PSS      HLP     46180      10-28-93    12:00a
EXCEL    EXE   2766592      10-28-93    12:00a
LIBRARY        <DIR>        12-13-93    11:24a
EXAMPLES       <DIR>        12-13-93    11:24a
EXCELHLP HLP   1433495      10-28-93    12:00a
XLSTART        <DIR>        12-13-93    11:53a
CHKLIST  MS         54      12-16-93     1:49p
TIMESHET XLS     14385      01-06-94     8:43a
       12 file(s)       4321180 bytes
                       85229568 bytes free

C:\MSOFFICE\EXCEL>
```

FIGURE 5-5   Displaying larger text for easier reading

Is there any way to make DOS execute a batch file one line at a time?

In MS-DOS 6.2, you can execute a batch file one line at a time. To do this, type **COMMAND /Y /C BATCH.BAT**, in which *Batch.bat* is the name of your batch file and press ENTER. Stepping through a batch file one line at a time lets you debug it by letting you isolate which lines contain errors. The following shows how a batch file runs one line at a time:

```
C:\JUNK>command /y /c mydisk.bat
mydisk.bat [Y/N]?Y
ECHO OFF [Y/N]?Y
REM Find out which drive they want to format with. [Y/N]?Y
ECHO You can format a disk in either the 5 1/4" A drive or the
3 1/2" B drive. [Y/N]?Y
You can format a disk in either the 5 1/4" A drive or the 3 1/2"
B drive.
ECHO Type A to format a 5 1/4" drive or B to format a 3 1/2" drive.
[Y/N]?
```

How can I tell a batch file to execute different commands depending on the outcome of a CHKDSK?

You can create a batch program that takes different actions depending on the result of a CHKDSK operation by using an Errorlevel parameter. The CHKDSK command returns an error-level value to the DOS prompt as it completes. This value will be zero if it found no errors on the drive, or 255 if it found errors. In the batch file shown in Figure 5-6, if CHKDSK finds no errors, the screen clears; if errors are detected, an error message appears.

I need to write some batch files that get user input to choose from a menu. Is there a way to do this?

The CHOICE command in a batch file allows you to get user input and make decisions based on that input. After the CHOICE

```
CHKDSK
IF ERRORLEVEL 0 GOTO END
ECHO Errors were detected!
PAUSE
:END
CLS
```

FIGURE 5-6   A batch file using the CHKDSK result to determine its actions

command runs, it sets an errorlevel value that can be used in an If statement.

The basic format of the CHOICE command is: CHOICE /C:*keys text*. The parameter /C:*keys* is optional. Without this parameter the CHOICE statement only responds to Y and N. For example, the command **CHOICE Do you want to continue?** returns either errorlevel equalling 1 for Y or 2 for N. You can customize the menu selections. The /C:*keys* parameter tells CHOICE what input to select: For example,

```
CHOICE /C:ABC Choose Apples, Bananas or Cherries:
```

will display:

```
Choose Apples, Bananas or Cherries: [A,B,C]?
```

Typing **A** returns errorlevel 1, **B** returns errorlevel 2, and **C** returns errorlevel 3.

Tech Tip: There are additional switches that customize how CHOICE works. The /S switch makes CHOICE case sensitive. The /N switch suppresses the display of the prompt, though the choices selected still apply. You can also use the /T switch to specify a default selection and limit the amount of time allowed before selecting the default.

How can I create the escape character when trying to use ANSI escape sequences?

The escape character is used most often to send ANSI escape sequences to the ANSI.SYS device driver. These escape sequences, when used in the PROMPT command, can do things like change the color of the screen and the characters on it. You can create the escape character by typing **PROMPT $e.**

95

Chapter 5 *Other DOS Commands*

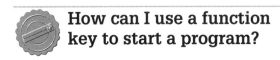

How can I use a function key to start a program?

You can use ANSI.SYS, the device driver for your keyboard and monitor, to redirect the function key to have it start a program or batch file. In order to do this, you must add the line **DEVICE=C:\DOS\ANSI.SYS** to your CONFIG.SYS file to load ANSI.SYS when you start your system. After loading ANSI.SYS, you need to tell it what you want to happen when you press that function key. To indicate this, you enter an ANSI escape sequence. ANSI escape sequences always start by entering the ASCII escape character. The syntax for the ANSI function key redirection escape sequence will be:

```
Esc[code;stringp
```

Esc, the ASCII escape character, can be entered by typing **PROMPT $e**. In the syntax, *code* is the code for the key or key combination you want to use. You may also use the key itself in quotation marks. For example, after you enter **PROMPT $e["D";"F"** at the DOS prompt and press ENTER, the letter *F* would appear every time you press the D key. The *string* would be either the characters in quotes or the key codes for the key strokes you want to be processed when the *code* key is pressed. When you enter **PROMPT $e[0;59;"C:\DOCS\MENU\MENU1";13p**, for example, at the DOS prompt and press ENTER, the F1 key will execute the file MENU1.BAT in the C:\DOCS\MENU subdirectory.

Notice that the 13 is added at the end of the string part of the escape sequence. This is the ASCII code for the ENTER key. If it were not there you would have to actually press ENTER to execute the command supplied by the reassigned key. After you reassign the keys, you should type **PROMPT PG** at the DOS prompt and press ENTER. This returns the prompt to showing the drive and directory after the escape sequence is entered. If you do not enter the last PROMPT command, no characters will display for the DOS prompt after this command is executed.

For more information on the ANSI escape codes for the keys available for remapping, type **HELP ANSI.SYS** at the DOS prompt and press ENTER. Scroll down to the bottom of the online MS-DOS Help screen to see the other ways you can use ANSI.SYS.

Utilities

MS-DOS utilities provide features beyond the basic DOS commands. They are generally thought of as those extra programs supplied with MS-DOS that have their own menu structure. MS-DOS 6.x includes several utilities: MS Backup, Undelete, Defragmenter (also called Defrag), Anti-Virus, DOS Editor, and DoubleSpace. This chapter contains questions on all of these utilities except DoubleSpace. Because of the large number of questions about DoubleSpace, Chapter 8 is dedicated solely to DoubleSpace questions and answers.

You may not be using all of the Microsoft utilities, either because you don't have a need for them, or because you are using one of the many third-party utilities that offer the same features. The MS-DOS utilities are described in the box below. Some popular third-party utilities that offer some of the same functions as the MS-DOS utilities are: Norton Utilities, Norton AntiVirus, Stacker, and Fastback. Since Microsoft does not create these utilities, DOS is not designed with an eye toward the features and requirements of these utilities. If you want to continue using the third-party utilities you are familiar with, you may need to contact the company that creates them to get an upgraded version that maintains full compatibility with new versions of DOS.

FRUSTRATION BUSTERS!

MS-DOS 6.*x* provides several utilities that make working with DOS easier. These MS-DOS utilities and the functions they provide are:

- **Anti-Virus:** Checks your disks for viruses that can damage your data and tie up your computer's resources. DOS has one version of this utility to run from the DOS prompt and another to run from within Windows.

- **Backup:** Backs up data from your hard disk to floppy disks, compressing your data to save space. Later, you can use Backup to restore the data from the backup disks. DOS has two versions of this utility, one which runs from the DOS prompt and another which runs from within Windows.

- **Defragmenter:** Rearranges files on a disk so they are stored contiguously. Your computer can read contiguous files more quickly than fragmented files, so this utility should speed up your hard drive.

- **DOS Editor:** Lets you create and modify text files, such as AUTOEXEC.BAT and CONFIG.SYS.

- **DoubleSpace:** Compresses your data on a disk so you can fit more data on it.

- **Undelete:** Recovers files that you have deleted. Files can be undeleted if DOS has not written another file to the same location. DOS has two versions of this utility, one which runs from the DOS prompt and another which runs from within Windows.

Do I have to format disks before using them as backup disks?

It is not necessary to format disks before using them to back up data if you are using MS-DOS 6.*x*. MS Backup, the new backup utility in MS-DOS 6.*x*, automatically formats disks during the backup procedure.

Are the old BACKUP and RESTORE commands compatible with the new MS Backup utility?

The old BACKUP and RESTORE commands are not compatible with the new MS Backup utility. MS Backup writes the data in an entirely different format than the old BACKUP command used. It also does "on-the-fly" compression of the data to reduce the number of disks required for the backup process. The RESTORE command is included with MS-DOS 6.*x* to retain compatibility with old backup disks you may have archived. You can also set up the old BACKUP to work with MS-DOS 6.*x*, or obtain the MS-DOS supplemental disk from Microsoft, which will contain a copy of BACKUP. To order this disk, use the order form from the back of your MS-DOS 6.*x* documentation.

Why do I need to run the compatibility test before using MS Backup for the first time?

The compatibility test ensures that the timing is correct between the computer and the floppy disk drives. This allows MS Backup to use the high-speed transfer process when writing backup data to the floppy disks you are backing up onto.

How do DOS 6's deletion protection levels work?

Undelete for MS-DOS 6.*x* offers you three levels of deletion protection. You can choose which level to use—Standard, Delete Tracker, or Delete Sentry—based on your needs or limitations. The level you choose should depend on how frequently you accidentally delete the wrong file and how much of a safety net you want.

Standard This is the level of protection you get automatically when you turn on your computer. It uses no memory or disk space. However, it also offers you the least amount of protection. With Standard protection, you can undelete a file if DOS has not used that file's disk location to store another file. The fewer things you do between deleting the file and attempting to undelete it, the more likely you are to recover the file intact.

   Standard deletion tracking does not keep a record of deleted files, so it may look like it cannot undelete files at all. After all, how would it know where to find them? This level of deletion tracking depends on a quirk in how DOS deletes files. DOS maintains a record of what files are on your disk, and where they are located on that disk, in the *file allocation table* (FAT). When you delete a file, DOS marks the space it used as empty in the FAT, but leaves the filename in the FAT, changing the first letter in the filename to a σ. If you try undeleting the file, Undelete looks for files in the FAT that have σ as the first character in their names. If the space that file used has not been overwritten by another file, the file can be undeleted by substituting a valid filename character for the first letter. You will be prompted for this character.

   The names of the deleted files are deleted from the FAT when another file uses the space that used to be assigned to the deleted file. Therefore, you should undelete the file as soon as you realize your mistake. Simply adding one file to the disk may make it impossible to undelete the file you want.

Delete Tracker Delete Tracker provides slightly better deletion protection than the Standard option. It requires a small amount of disk space and about 13.5K of memory. Delete Tracker maintains a file called PCTRACKR.DEL, which records the location of every file that is deleted. You can recover a file if no other file has been written to that location.

   Delete Tracker is more effective than the Standard deletion protection because you have a consistent record of deleted files. With Standard protection, any new file may remove all record of the deleted file from the FAT. With Delete Tracker, you still have a record of the file and its location. Even if part of the file is overwritten, Delete Tracker may make it possible to recover the remainder of the file.

To set up Delete Tracker level of deletion protection, enter **UNDELETE /TC-300** at the DOS prompt and press ENTER. In this command, the /T switch enables Delete Tracker. The C is the letter of the drive for which you want to enable Delete Tracker. The -300 indicates the maximum number of entries to appear in the PCTRACKER.DEL file. You can specify any number of files between 1 and 999; the default size for hard drives larger than 32MB is 303, which creates a PCTRACKR.DEL file of 55K. If you always want to use Delete Tracker level of protection, include this command in your AUTOEXEC.BAT file.

Delete Sentry   Delete Sentry offers the greatest level of deletion protection. Delete Sentry requires 13.5K of memory and up to 7 percent of your hard disk space. Delete Sentry creates a hidden \SENTRY directory. Deleted files are copied to this directory and the FAT is not told that the space the file used is available for use. When a deleted file causes the \SENTRY directory to use more than 7 percent of your hard disk space, the oldest file in the directory is deleted from this directory, and the FAT is told that the space that file used is available for use. With Delete Sentry, you won't have to worry about new files overwriting a recently deleted file.

To enable the Delete Sentry level of deletion protection, enter **UNDELETE /SC** at the DOS prompt and press ENTER. /S is the switch which enables Delete Sentry and C is the letter of the drive for which you want to enable Delete Sentry.

What does Defrag actually do to my disk and why do I want to use it?

Defrag is a utility which reorganizes the contents of your disk. When you save or copy files to a disk, DOS stores them in whatever locations are available. If the file is large or your disk is very full, DOS may have to break the file into several parts and store them in separate locations. The physical locations of the files on your disk are stored in the FAT.

Where your files are actually stored on the disk doesn't matter. DOS can find and reassemble the file for you, so you don't need to worry about its location. However, when you have a large disk, such as your hard disk, and many of the files on it are fragmented, it takes longer for each file to be opened or resaved because the read head of your drive needs to move around more. Also, greatly fragmented files are more susceptible to errors that creep into the FAT because there are more pieces of information to keep track of as the file is reassembled.

Defrag moves the files around on your disk so that each file is stored in one contiguous location. This way, files can be retrieved quicker since they are all together. Also, you are less likely to develop file allocation errors, because DOS has less information to track for each file.

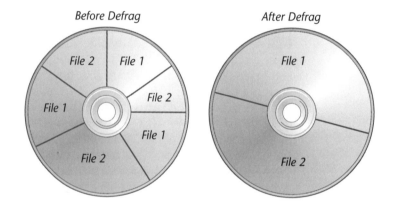

Before Defrag

After Defrag

 I installed DOS 6.x. Now when I type BACKUP and press ENTER I get the message "Incorrect DOS version." How do I back up my files?

BACKUP is not included with MS-DOS 6.x. MS-DOS 6.x ships with two new backup programs, MSBACKUP.EXE for DOS and MWBACKUP.EXE for Windows. If there is a BACKUP.EXE file in your DOS directory, it came from an earlier version of DOS. If you want to use the older BACKUP command, you need to use SETVER to include it in the SETVER version table before you can use it with MS-DOS 6.x. For example, you can type **SETVER BACKUP.EXE 5.00** and press ENTER, assuming that your copy of BACKUP came from MS-DOS version 5.0. This will add BACKUP to the SETVER table and allow it to work with DOS 6.x. You will also need SETVER loaded in CONFIG.SYS.

What exactly are viruses and why are they a problem?

A virus is a program that is designed to hide within another file and to re-create itself automatically. Even if they don't do anything to your system other than exist, they are using disk space that you could be using. Also, the techniques viruses use to hide themselves can lead to errors in your FAT.

The biggest reason for not wanting viruses on your disks is that many of them were created for destructive purposes. Some viruses have been deliberately designed to destroy the data on hard drives. Other viruses are unwittingly destructive. For example, a new programmer who is trying to write a virus simply to learn about them may accidentally include commands which can be destructive in the context of certain hardware or software combinations.

Therefore, you should take precautions against virus infections. You can do this by using MS-DOS 6.*x*'s new Anti-Virus utility or employing third-party anti-virus utilities. You can also limit your system's exposure to viruses by avoiding using non-professional or illegally copied software, sharing disks with other users, and connecting with public bulletin boards or computer networks.

Can the new Anti-Virus program protect me from all viruses?

There is no anti-virus program which can guarantee protection against all viruses. The Anti-Virus utility included with MS-DOS 6.*x* has a database of hundreds of known viruses which the utility can detect. However, new viruses are being written and discovered all the time, so this database cannot give Anti-Virus the ability to protect you against all possible viruses. To increase the protection that Anti-Virus can give you, you should order the Virus Protection updates available through Microsoft. These updates include the data on hundreds of new viruses that you might encounter. You can order these updates at a discount, using the Virus Protection Update Order Form in the back of your DOS documentation.

Before investing in updated virus protection, you may want to consider just how likely you are to suffer a virus infection. The most common sources of viruses are:

- Public computer bulletin boards or networks such as the Internet.

- Disks loaned by friends or coworkers, especially those who use bulletin boards or computer networks.

- Shareware or non-professionally created software.

If you have no contact with any of these sources, you are less likely to get a virus on your computer. However, even if you do not put your computer at risk, running an anti-virus program at least occasionally reduces the risk of damage by a virus.

Tech Terror: Most software produced by professional companies is safe from viruses because they rigorously check their disks for viruses. However, even this is not a surety against infection. Viruses are designed to be sneaky and hard to find, so there is still a remote possibility that, despite all of your precautions, a virus will infect your system.

I copy all the files in my \WORKING directory to a backup disk each day. Is there a way to copy only the files that have changed since yesterday?

Copying only the files that have changed is a good idea since it protects your most recent work with a minimal investment in time. If you use the REPLACE and XCOPY commands, you can limit your copy procedure to those files that changed since the last backup. The REPLACE command can either replace files in the destination directory with files of the same name from the source directory, or add only new files to the destination directory. You need to do two things to back up your \WORKING directory properly: add new files to the backup disks and replace files that have changed.

To copy newly created files to the destination disk and to update those files that have changed since you last backed up, you need to use REPLACE, XCOPY, and ATTRIB. For example, to back up the contents of your \WORKING directory, you can use the commands:

```
REPLACE \WORKING B:\ /A
XCOPY \WORKING B:\ /A
ATTRIB \WORKING\*.* -A
```

Entering the REPLACE command with the /A switch tells DOS to copy only the files from the source directory that do not already exist in the destination directory. This command will copy all new files in the \WORKING directory to the disk in the B drive, because those files do not already exist on the B drive disk. The second command tells DOS to copy those files from the source directory that already exist in the destination directory, but which have the archive bit turned on. This bit is turned on every time you modify the file. Therefore, only the files that have changed since you last backed up the \WORKING directory are copied to the backup disk. The last command turns the archive attribute off for all files in the directory so you will not back up unchanged files the next time. The last two commands can be replaced with **REPLACE \WORKING B:\ /U** to replace files only when the version on the destination disk is older than the version you are copying. However, some programs do not always update the file's time and date when they change it, but they have to turn on the archive bit. You can put these three commands in a batch file to run every time you want to back up your computer.

The scroll bars in the DOS Editor disappeared. What can I do to get them back?

The scroll bars are a feature that can be turned on or off as shown in the screen in Figure 6-1. If they don't appear, either you accidentally turned the scroll bars off or someone else may have used your system and turned them off. To turn them back on:

1. Open the Options menu by pressing ALT+O.

2. Choose Display by highlighting it and pressing ENTER or by pressing D.

3. Make sure an X appears between the brackets before Scroll Bars, as in the dialog box shown in Figure 6-2. You can make the X appear by clicking on the box, or by moving the cursor to it and pressing SPACEBAR.

4. Select OK by highlighting it and pressing ENTER, or clicking it with the mouse.

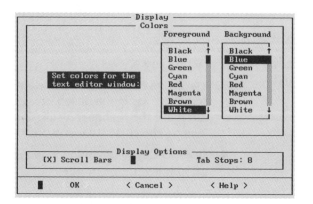

```
    File  Edit  Search  Options                                      Help
                          ┌FORMAT.BAT┐
@ECHO OFF
REM Find out which drive they want to format with.
ECHO You can format a disk in either the 5 1/4" A drive or the 3 1/2" B drive.
CHOICE /C:AB /T:B,10
IF ERRORLEVEL 1 GOTO A_DRIVE
REM Find out what density they want to format at.
ECHO You can format the disk at high density (1.44 MB) or low density (720 KB)
CHOICE /C:HL /T:H,10
IF ERRORLEVEL 2 GOTO LO_DENSITY
Rem Format B: drive with high density
FORMAT B:
:LO_DENSITY
REM Format B: drive with low density
FORMAT B: /F:720
:A_DRIVE
REM Find out what density they want to format at.
ECHO You can format the disk at high density (1.2 MB) or low density (360 KB).
CHOICE /C:HL /T:H,10
IF ERRORLEVEL 2 GOTO LOW_DENSITY
REM Format A: drive with high density
FORMAT A:
:LOW_DENSITY
MS-DOS Editor  <F1=Help> Press ALT to activate menus          00004:001
```

FIGURE 6-1   The DOS Editor without scroll bars

I got an "out of memory" message when I tried to open a document in the DOS Editor. Why?

The most likely reason for your "out of memory" message is a file that is too large. The largest file that the DOS Editor can read is the size of the amount of free conventional memory minus 289K. For example, if you have 509K free memory after loading the DOS Editor, the largest file you can open is 220K. If your document is larger than that, or if you add enough text so that your document becomes larger than that, you will receive an "out of memory" message. To avoid this message, use a word processor which can handle larger files, or divide your file into several smaller files.

```
                 ┌─ Display ─────────────────────┐
                 │ ┌─ Colors ───────────────────┐ │
                 │         Foreground  Background  │
                 │         ┌─────────┐ ┌─────────┐ │
                 │         │ Black  ↑│ │ Black  ↑│ │
                 │         │ Blue    │ │ Blue    │ │
 ┌─────────────┐ │         │ Green   │ │ Green   │ │
 │Set colors for the│      │ Cyan    │ │ Cyan    │ │
 │text editor window:│     │ Red     │ │ Red     │ │
 └─────────────┘ │         │ Magenta │ │ Magenta │ │
                 │         │ Brown   │ │ Brown   │ │
                 │         │ White  ↓│ │ White  ↓│ │
                 │         └─────────┘ └─────────┘ │
                 │ ┌─ Display Options ───────────┐ │
                 │ │ [X] Scroll Bars    Tab Stops: 8│ │
                 │ └───────────────────────────┘ │
                 │   ■  OK    < Cancel >   < Help > │
                 └───────────────────────────────┘
```

FIGURE 6-2   The Display dialog box in DOS Editor

Can you set margins in the DOS Editor?

You cannot change the margin settings in the DOS Editor. The DOS Editor is designed to create plain text files called ASCII text files. *ASCII (American Standard for Computer Information Interchange)* refers to the limited set of characters that can appear in an ASCII text file. DOS batch files and files like CONFIG.SYS must be in ASCII text format, without margins or special formatting codes. If you want to change margins for your document, use a word processing program.

I used the Comp utility to verify the integrity of files after saving them to floppy disks. Why do I get the message "Bad command or file name" with DOS 6.x?

The Comp utility is no longer included with MS-DOS 6.x. If you still want to use this utility, you can either use the COMP.EXE file from your previous version of DOS, or get the MS-DOS 6.x supplemental disk from Microsoft by ordering it with the coupon in the back of the manual that came with your package of MS-DOS 6.x. The supplemental disk's version of Comp is ready to run with MS-DOS 6.x.

To use your old Comp utility, copy the file from your earlier DOS Setup disks into the C:\DOS subdirectory. If you're working from MS-DOS 5.0 disks, use the Expand utility rather than just copying the file. For example, type **EXPAND A:\COMP.EX_ C:\DOS\COMP.EXE** and press ENTER to uncompress the COMP.EXE file and place it in the DOS subdirectory.

Next, you'll need to add Comp to the SETVER version table. Type **SETVER COMP.EXE 5.00** and press ENTER to tell MS-DOS 6.x that the COMP.EXE file came from DOS 5.00. Check your CONFIG.SYS file to see that SETVER is installed. The line will look like this:

```
DEVICE=C:\DOS\SETVER.EXE
```

Reboot your computer and test the Comp utility.

...s the difference ...en MSAV and Vsafe, the two virus utilities that came with MS-DOS 6.*x*?

MSAV and the Windows Anti-Virus utility can scan your disks for viruses. You can choose what these programs are supposed to do if they detect viruses—either note them and alert you, or attempt to remove them. While these utilities can help you recover from a virus infection, they cannot prevent you from getting viruses.

Vsafe is a memory resident program. As long as it is in memory, Vsafe looks out for virus-like activity. When it detects virus-like activity, Vsafe either stops the activity, or alerts you to it. Vsafe tries to prevent you from getting a virus, then tries to prevent an existing virus from doing damage when it activates.

Why does RESTORE tell me I have no files to restore, when I can see the backup files on the disks when I use the DIR command?

RESTORE restores the backed up files to the directory that they were backed up from. If RESTORE does not find that directory or the file itself on the disk you are trying to restore to, it will report that there were no files found to restore. You can work around this problem by specifying that you want to restore the entire backup and to create the file or directory if it doesn't already exist on the disk you are restoring to. Do this by entering **RESTORE B: D:*.* /S** and pressing ENTER. In this command, B is the drive the backup disks are in, and D is the drive you want to restore the files onto.

You can also restore only the files that are no longer on the computer, leaving the existing files alone. This is accomplished in much the same way that you restore all files. The only difference is an additional switch on the RESTORE command line, as in **RESTORE A: C:*.* /S /N**. The /N switch, which tells RESTORE not to overwrite files that already exist, is the only difference between this command and the previous one which restored all files. A is the drive containing the backup disks and C is the drive you want to restore to.

If you want to restore only one directory and its files from the backup disks, but you do not remember the exact directory name, enter this line: **RESTORE A: C:*.* /S /D**. The /D switch

displays a directory of the backup disks without actually
restoring files, so you can note the exact directory name.

I used the RESTORE command, but none of the files from my second or later disks were restored. What can I do?

To restore files on later disks when the
RESTORE command only restores
those on the first disk, you need to
reenter the RESTORE command, using
the syntax **RESTORE A: C:*.* /S /N**.
This command will restore all the files
from the backup disks in the A drive to
the C drive. The /S switch tells DOS to re-create subdirectories, if
needed, to restore the files. The /N switch tells DOS to restore
only those files that do not already exist on the drive you are
restoring to.

 If RESTORE cannot continue, but you have disks left to restore,
enter the RESTORE command again using the same syntax. This
time, put the next disk in the drive. When RESTORE returns a
"Disk out of sequence" error message to you, choose to
Continue. RESTORE should pick up where it left off.

When I run the Backup utility in Windows, it works up to a point and then my computer just stops responding. What is going on?

Something loading in your AUTOEXEC.BAT or CONFIG.SYS file is
conflicting with Windows or the Backup utility. To check if this is
actually the problem, try booting your computer using the
minimum you need for Windows. To do this:

1. Reboot your computer with CTRL+ALT+DEL, or by turning it
   off and then on again.

2. The instant you see the message "Starting MS-DOS,"
   press F8. DOS will display the message "MS-DOS will
   prompt you to confirm each CONFIG.SYS command."

3. Press **Y** to only the four lines which start or set:

   - HIMEM.SYS

   - FILES

- BUFFERS
- SHELL

My computer cannot pass MS Backup's compatibility test when I'm in Windows' Enhanced Mode, but passes with no problem in DOS or in Windows' Standard Mode. Why?

If you are having problems with MS Backup's compatibility test in Windows' Enhanced mode, the most likely cause of your problem is the presence of a conflicting device driver installed by another application in Windows. The Windows software for some tape backup units commonly installs a virtual device driver that conflicts with VFINTD.386, the virtual device driver used by the Windows version of MS Backup.

I backed up my entire hard drive, then installed a new hard drive with MS-DOS 6.x already on it. How do I restore the data I backed up with MS-DOS 5.0's BACKUP command?

MS-DOS 6.x not only includes the MS Backup utility, which both backs up and restores data, it also has the same RESTORE command used in older versions of DOS. To restore your data, type **RESTORE B: C:*.* /S** and press ENTER.

ScanDisk reported that it fixed my file errors, but I still can't run some of my programs. Why?

ScanDisk attempts to correct the file structure errors. Sometimes, this means sacrificing file contents in order to correct the structure damage. While the file's structure may be repaired, the data inside the file may not be complete or correct. If the program was having problems before ScanDisk found errors in its files, the program may continue to have problems until the files are recopied from a backup disk or reinstalled from the original program disks.

I need to make backup copies of some important files, but I only want to copy files made since Monday. Can I do it?

The XCOPY command can copy files with dates after a specified d For example, you can type **XCOI A: /D:1/17/94** at the DOS prompt and press ENTER where 1/17/94 is Monday's date. The /D switch tells XCOPY to only copy those files with a date later than the one you specify. Add the /S switch if the files are in subdirectories, since this switch tells XCOPY to copy from subdirectories as well as the parent directory specified.

I backed up my hard drive with MS Backup, reformatted it, and reinstalled DOS 6.*x*. Now I can't restore my files. How do I get my files back?

You are having difficulty restoring your data because a necessary file was destroyed when you reformatted the hard disk. MS Backup stores information about each backup you do in a backup catalog. Ordinarily, the backup catalog files are stored in the DOS directory. To restore your files you'll need to:

1. Start MS Backup and rerun the compatibility test.
2. Choose Restore.
3. Select Catalog, then Retrieve.
4. Insert the last disk in the backup set into a floppy drive and select that drive.

The last disk of the backup set also contains the backup catalog. MS Backup now retrieves the catalog from the backup disk and places it in your DOS directory.

After retrieving the catalog file from the backup disk, you can load that catalog to restore your files. Choose Select Files, then select the files you want to restore. You do not have to restore your DOS directory since you reinstalled DOS.

I program in Assembly language and use EXE2BIN.EXE to convert my Assembly programs to .COM files. I can't find this utility with MS-DOS 6.*x*. How do I create my .COM files?

EXE2BIN.EXE does not come with MS-DOS 6.*x*. However, you can use the EXE2BIN.EXE file provided with MS-DOS 5 to continue creating .COM files if you add EXE2BIN.EXE to the SETVER table. To do this:

1. Copy the EXE2BIN.EXE file from your old MS-DOS 5 Setup disks or the OLD_DOS.x directory into the DOS directory.

2. Check your CONFIG.SYS file to ensure that it installs SETVER. The line installing SETVER will look like **DEVICE=C:\DOS\SETVER.EXE.**

3. Add the EXE2BIN.EXE file to the SETVER table. For example, you might type **SETVER EXE2BIN.EXE 5.00** at the DOS prompt and press ENTER.

Can I use the MS-DOS 6.*x* utilities with other versions of DOS?

Some of the new utilities, such as MS Backup and Anti-Virus, can run with older versions of DOS. However, doing so isn't recommended. Microsoft does not support using these utilities with older versions of DOS because they have not been fully tested on older DOS versions and could create errors if used with them. If you try using them with older DOS versions, do so at your own risk! After all, if you have the new utilities, you have a copy of MS-DOS 6.*x* and might as well use the updated features it offers.

How do I get MS Backup to put the catalogs into a different directory?

To set the directory where MS Backup stores catalog files, add an environment variable to your AUTOEXEC.BAT file. The line setting up this environmental variable reads **SET**

MSDOSDATA=C:\DOS if you want the catalogs stored in the C:\DOS directory. MS Backup for both DOS and Windows will now use the directory specified by MSDOSDATA for the catalogs. Move the present catalogs to this directory so that they can be accessed.

The DOS version of MS Backup will also use this directory as the new location for storing the MSBACKUP.INI file. The Windows version of MS Backup stores the equivalent file, MWBACKUP.INI, in the location specified with the WINDIR environment variable.

How often should I run Defrag?

How often you run Defrag depends on how much you use your hard disk. If you delete or move files around a lot, particularly if those files are large, you may need to run Defrag once a week. When you run Defrag, it shows you how fragmented your drive is before beginning the process. Run Defrag when the drive is less than 95 percent unfragmented. For an average user, running Defrag once a month should be sufficient.

I keep getting "Insufficient memory" messages when trying to run Defrag on my 2GB external hard drive. What's wrong?

Your insufficient memory problem is not caused by the size of the drive you're trying to defragment, but by the number of files on that drive. Generally, this problem shows up when the number of files on the hard disk you are attempting to defragment approaches 10,000. Of course, very few systems actually have this many files on one partition.

There are several things you can do which may alleviate this problem.

- MS-DOS 6.0 Defrag uses conventional and upper memory for holding directory structure. You can free conventional memory by using EMM386.EXE with the NOEMS parameter, and loading no other items into upper memory.

- You can also start Defrag with the /G0 switch to force it into Text mode. In Text mode, Defrag itself uses less memory.

- If the memory problem persists, you'll have to temporarily reduce the number of files on the drive. To do this, back up some files onto floppy disks, delete them from the drive, then run Defrag again. Once Defrag is finished, restore the backed up files. They will be saved contiguously.

MS-DOS 6.2 can use up to 384K of extended memory for its Defrag directory structure, making this problem extremely rare with this version of DOS.

DOS Shell

DOS Shell is a program that helps you use your programs and manage your files. It can display the contents of your disks as well as list programs that you can run. The commands available in DOS Shell provide the most popularly used file management features. With DOS Shell, instead of entering all the necessary information at a DOS prompt, you enter it in dialog boxes that prompt you for the information. DOS Shell is not provided with DOS 6.2, but you can get it from Microsoft by ordering the supplemental disks. DOS Shell is included on the Setup disks for DOS 6.0.

FRUSTRATION BUSTERS!

DOS Shell is a good way to work with the files and programs on your computer. You can also use other programs such as Windows and Norton's Commander to provide a similar interface. The tasks that you can perform from DOS Shell include:

- Copying, moving, deleting, and renaming files.

- Looking at the contents of a disk and its directories.

- Running programs you have installed as well as DOS utilities.

- Using more than one program at a time when you enable task swapping.

How can I set up DOS Shell to open Windows?

This is not recommended. Since Windows is an entire operating environment of its own, starting it from a shell program like DOS Shell can cause conflicts within Windows. Windows is only designed to run from the DOS prompt, with no other DOS programs running at the time. If you really want to use both DOS Shell and Windows, start Windows first, then open a DOS Prompt window and run DOS Shell from this window.

I don't have a mouse cursor in DOS Shell, but I do have one in my DOS applications. Why?

The mouse driver on your system is not compatible with DOS Shell. The mouse driver is the program in your computer that handles communications between your mouse, DOS, and other programs. Some of the special features of DOS Shell will not operate properly with an older mouse driver, even though other programs work correctly. You need to install a newer version of the driver that is compatible with DOS Shell. To do so, contact your mouse manufacturer. When the new mouse driver is installed, DOS Shell will detect the new driver and use it. You do not actually need to buy a new mouse itself, since the problem is occurring with the file, not with the actual mouse.

Tech Tip: If you are using a Mouse Systems mouse in DOS Shell, you may find that the mouse pointer isn't visible but the mouse still works when you click or drag. You need to upgrade the mouse driver. Contact Mouse Systems for an updated mouse driver.

How can I get DOS Shell to work with my mouse?

The first time you ran DOS Shell, it displayed a dialog box asking if you wanted to use a mouse. Your response was recorded in the DOSSHELL.INI file. You can edit the DOSSHELL.INI file to change your response and make the mouse available. The line where your response was recorded appears as:

```
mouseinfo = 6.02, disable
```

6.02 is the version number of the mouse DOS Shell detects on your system. Since you chose to disable the mouse for DOS Shell, "disable" appears after the comma. Now that you want to use the mouse, change "disable" to "ignore." You can use the DOS Editor to edit the DOSSHELL.INI file.

I use DOS Shell and I have noticed that when I restart my computer, I have new batch files in my DOS directory. What is creating these files and can I safely delete them?

These batch files are created by DOS Shell when task swapping is enabled, and are deleted when you exit DOS Shell properly. If your computer is restarted or stops responding before you have properly exited from DOS Shell, these files will not be deleted. The three proper ways to exit DOS Shell are to:

1. Select Exit from the File menu.

2. Press ALT+F4.

3. Press F3.

A good test to see if DOS Shell is still running is to type **EXIT** at the DOS prompt and press ENTER.

- If you see another DOS prompt, then DOS Shell is not running, and it is safe to turn off your computer.

- If you return to DOS Shell after pressing ENTER, you then need to exit DOS Shell using one of the ways described above.

- If multiple copies of DOS Shell are running, you may have to repeat the process of typing **EXIT** and pressing ENTER to exit DOS Shell several times.

Once you have exited from DOS Shell properly, you can delete the stray batch files that appeared in your DOS directory.

Tech Tip: You may see .TMP files in your DOS directory, as well as the .BAT files. These may be created by Windows or another program. These files are placed in the directory set by the Temp variable.

Why is my AUTOEXEC.BAT file deleted when I delete files from a subdirectory with DOS Shell? I'm not deleting from the root directory and the file I intended to delete is not named AUTOEXEC.BAT.

The most likely solution is that the Select Across Directories option is enabled. This option allows you to select files in several different directories, and then carry out an operation on all of them at once. Disable this option and the confusion of accidentally deleting the AUTOEXEC.BAT file will be resolved. AUTOEXEC.BAT is probably the first file alphabetically in your root directory, so it might be accidentally selected. To disable this option, select the Select Across Directories command in the Options menu.

When I start DOS Shell, I don't see the display I'm used to seeing. What could be causing this and how do I fix it?

DOS Shell has several different view options, and yours was changed. To restore the familiar view, you need to reselect it. To do so, select Display from the Options menu. If you do not know which of the displays you have used before, you will need to try each of them. If the colors were changed along with the screen display mode, you will also need to select Colors from the Options menu and select the color scheme you prefer.

Another reason your DOS Shell window may look different is that one of the options in the View menu may be selected to display different information. The top part of the View menu selects what appears in DOS Shell. The View menu has the following options:

- Single File List: Displays the directory tree on the left and a list of files on the right.

- Dual File Lists: Displays two directory tree and file list combinations, each for a different drive and directory. Figure 7-1 shows this type of display.

- All Files: Displays file information for the highlighted file on the left and all of the files on the currently selected drive on the right. Figure 7-2 shows this type of display.

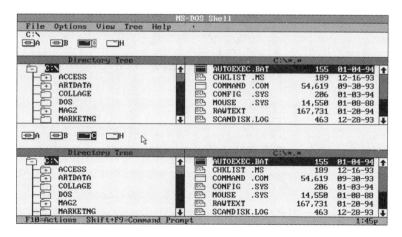

FIGURE 7-1   Dual File Lists displayed in DOS Shell

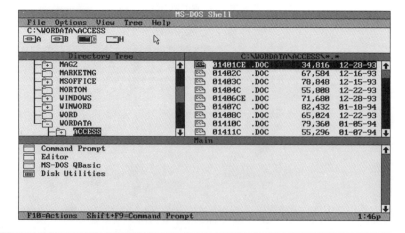

```
                          MS-DOS Shell
 File  Options  View  Tree  Help
 C:\WORDATA\ACCESS
 ⊟]A   ⊟]B   ■]C   □]H        ⅍
                                            *.*
                        ▤ 01401CE .DOC    34,816  12-28-93  10:38a ↑
 File                   ▤ 01402C  .DOC    67,584  12-16-93  10:44a
    Name : 01401CE.DOC  ▤ 01403C  .DOC    78,848  12-15-93   3:55p
    Attr : ...a         ▤ 01404C  .DOC    55,808  12-22-93   2:27p
 Selected         C     ▤ 01406CE .DOC    71,680  12-28-93  11:16a
    Number:       1     ▤ 01407C  .DOC    82,432  01-18-94   8:14p
    Size :      155     ▤ 01408C  .DOC    65,024  12-22-93   6:21p
 Directory              ▤ 01410C  .DOC    79,360  01-05-94  11:32a
    Name : ACCESS       ▤ 01411C  .DOC    55,296  01-07-94   3:44p
    Size :    1,214,464 ▤ 01412C  .DOC    67,072  12-23-93   3:39p
    Files :          27 ▤ 01413C  .DOC    39,424  12-17-93   1:08p
 Disk                   ▤ 01414C  .DOC    43,520  01-05-94  11:32a
    Name : MSDOS6_2     ▤ 01418C  .DOC    41,472  01-07-94   3:44p
    Size :  190,562,304 ▤ 01419C  .DOC    75,264  01-12-94   4:34p
    Avail :  81,641,472 ▤ 01420C  .DOC    20,992  12-22-93   3:28p
    Files :       1,417 ▤ 01421C  .DOC    65,536  01-18-94   4:49p
    Dirs :           58 ▤ 014ABC  .DOC    17,920  01-07-94   4:08p
                        ▤ 014AC   .DOC     7,168  01-18-94   4:34p ↓
 F10=Actions   Shift+F9=Command Prompt                         1:45p
```

FIGURE 7-2   List of all files displayed in DOS Shell

- Program/File Lists: Displays the directory tree on the left and a list of files on the right for one drive and directory combination at the top of the screen and the program items in a program group at the bottom. Figure 7-3 shows this type of display.

- Program List: Displays a list of program items in a program group.

```
                          MS-DOS Shell
 File  Options  View  Tree  Help
 C:\WORDATA\ACCESS
 ⊟]A   ⊟]B   ■]C   □]H        ⅍
         Directory Tree              C:\WORDATA\ACCESS\*.*
      ┌─▢ MAG2          ↑   ▤ 01401CE .DOC    34,816  12-28-93 ↑
      ├─▢ MARKETNG          ▤ 01402C  .DOC    67,584  12-16-93
      ├─▢ MSOFFICE          ▤ 01403C  .DOC    78,848  12-15-93
      ├─▢ NORTON            ▤ 01404C  .DOC    55,808  12-22-93
      ├─▢ WINDOWS           ▤ 01406CE .DOC    71,680  12-28-93
      ├─▢ WINWORD           ▤ 01407C  .DOC    82,432  01-18-94
      ├─▢ WORD              ▤ 01408C  .DOC    65,024  12-22-93
      └─▢ WORDATA           ▤ 01410C  .DOC    79,360  01-05-94
          └─▢ ACCESS    ↓   ▤ 01411C  .DOC    55,296  01-07-94 ↓
                                  Main
  ▯ Command Prompt                                              ↑
  ▯ Editor
  ▯ MS-DOS QBasic
  ▦ Disk Utilities



                                                               ↓
 F10=Actions   Shift+F9=Command Prompt                         1:46p
```

FIGURE 7-3   Program List and File List displayed in DOS Shell

Tech Tip: All of the settings you create for DOS Shell, including program groups, display modes, and color schemes, are stored in a file called DOSSHELL.INI, which should be in your DOS directory. If this file is damaged, deleted, or moved to a directory that is not in the Path statement, DOS Shell cannot find it when starting, and will revert to the default settings.

Is there any way to prevent DOS Shell from reading all the files and directories on my disk while starting?

No, you cannot prevent DOS Shell from reading the files and directories on your disk. However, as soon as you see the DOS Shell screen, you can start working with it. You do not have to wait until DOS Shell finishes reading your disk.

Every time I leave DOS Shell I get the error message "Unable to update DOSSHELL.INI." Why?

DOSSHELL.INI is the file that contains all of your settings in DOS Shell, including display modes, program groups, and other customizable options. DOS Shell updates this file each time you exit, so that it contains the most up-to-date settings. This error message is most commonly caused by one of two reasons:

1. The DOSSHELL.INI file has the Read-Only attribute set or is on a write-protected disk.

2. The PATH command in your AUTOEXEC.BAT file is incorrect. The DOS directory may be omitted or it may read C:DOS instead of C:\DOS. If the directory containing the DOSSHELL.INI file is not in the Path statement, or is not entered correctly, DOS cannot find the DOSSHELL.INI file.

Every time I try to use the Command Prompt item from my Main group I get the message "Bad command or file name" and never get to the DOS prompt. What's wrong?

Check the Temp variable in your AUTOEXEC.BAT file. It should read something like SET TEMP=C:\DOS using any drive and directory path. Delete this line from your AUTOEXEC.BAT file and retype it. Make sure that you do not put an extra space at the end of the line. This error will occur if there is a trailing space at the end of this line in your AUTOEXEC.BAT file.

I load DOS Shell in my AUTOEXEC.BAT file. Every time, it immediately switches to the DOS prompt. Why?

Most likely, you are logging onto your network in your AUTOEXEC.BAT file before starting DOS Shell and starting DOS Shell with the Program List view as the default. DOS Shell is immediately executing whatever item is highlighted on the list, which seems to be the Command Prompt item. This problem only occurs when DOS Shell is loaded in the AUTOEXEC.BAT file after AUTOEXEC.BAT first loads IPX and NETX and logs into the network. The cause of the problem is an extra ENTER after the system login script, the user login script, or the login batch file. DOS Shell registers the ENTER just as if you had pressed ENTER while in DOS Shell and starts the highlighted program item. Remove the extra ENTER to solve the problem.

When I try to switch between programs, DOS Shell just stops functioning, and I need to reboot my computer. Why?

Check the documentation on the programs you are switching between to find out if they can use expanded memory. DOS Shell's Task Swapper may hang when you switch between applications that cannot use expanded memory. If that is what is happening, you should reinstall DOS Shell's grabber (.GRB) file from the Setup disks. The .GRB filename reflects the kind of video you have on your system. Some names you may find are: MONO, CGA, EGA, EGAMONO, VGA, VGAMONO, and HERC. You must use the EXPAND command provided by DOS to decompress the

.GRB files. For example, if you have a VGA monitor, you should type **EXPAND A:\VGA.IN_ C:\DOS\DOSSHELL.GRB** and press ENTER.

I added all my frequently used DOS programs to the Main group in DOS Shell. Everything is OK for a while, then some or all of my program items disappear. What's wrong?

DOS Shell doesn't warn you when another copy of DOS Shell is already running on your system. Since it is a shell, it's possible to switch to a DOS prompt to do something, then type **DOSSHELL** and press ENTER again, starting a second copy of DOS Shell with the first one still open. If you do this two or three times in succession, the final result is often a corrupt DOSSHELL.INI file. The DOSSHELL.INI file contains all of the settings for program groups in DOS Shell. With several different copies of DOS Shell writing changes to it, this files ends up with conflicting entries, corrupting it.

To keep this from happening in the future, make sure you type **EXIT** and press ENTER to switch back to DOS Shell after running a DOS program or executing a DOS command. This will return you to DOS Shell instead of starting a new copy of DOS Shell.

Look for this question earlier in this chapter: "I use DOS Shell and I have noticed that when I restart my computer, I have new batch files in my DOS directory. What is creating these files and can I safely delete them?" This question explains the three ways to properly exit DOS Shell.

I tried to get into DOS Shell after installing MS-DOS 6.2 and it wasn't there. What happened?

MS-DOS 6.2 doesn't come with DOS Shell. If you want to continue using DOS Shell, you need to use one from an earlier version. If you upgraded from an earlier version of DOS that had DOS Shell, you can use that copy. Alternatively, you can contact Microsoft about getting a supplemental disk that includes DOS Shell files. If you have access to a modem, you can also download the DOS62SP.EXE file from the Microsoft Download Service (MSDL). The file is a compressed file containing the same files that are on the supplemental disks. It will automatically uncompress when you try to execute it. The file is also available through CompuServe and other online services.

To use a copy of DOS Shell from an earlier version of DOS, you first need to move the files from the OLD_DOS.x directory to the new DOS directory. Then, you may need to update your SETVER table for this program. For example, if you were using DOS Shell previously, DOS Shell program files will be in the OLD_DOS.x directory, which contains the files from your old version of DOS that are not used by DOS 6.2.

1. Switch to the OLD_DOS.x directory.

2. Type **COPY DOSSHELL.* \DOS** and press ENTER to copy all DOS Shell files to the DOS directory.

3. Type **SETVER DOSSHELL.EXE 5.00** at the DOS prompt and press ENTER to add the DOS Shell file to the SETVER table. 5.00 is the version number of your old DOS version.

4. Reboot your computer by turning it off and on or by pressing CTRL+ALT+DEL to make the change effective. You should now be able to use DOS Shell.

If you have no version of DOS Shell available, you can order the supplemental disks, which include DOS Shell. You can order these supplemental disks from Microsoft using the card in the back of your MS-DOS 6.2 manual or by calling Microsoft Consumer Sales at (800) 426-9400.

I heard I can start a program from DOS Shell by selecting the data I want to use. How do I do it?

DOS Shell lets you create associations between specific file extensions and a program. Associating a file provides yet another way to start an application from DOS Shell. Once you create an association, you can select a file with an association's extensions, and DOS Shell will first open the associated program, then open the selected data file in the program. For example, you could create an association between files with a .DOC extension and Word for DOS. When you select a file with the .DOC extension in DOS Shell, it automatically opens Word for DOS, with the selected document open. To

associate specific extensions with a program using a version of
DOS Shell from MS-DOS version 5.0 or earlier:

1. Highlight the program file in the File List.
2. Select Associate from the File menu.
3. Enter the extensions you want to associate with the
   program.

Tech Note: For an association to work, the program must accept a data file
as a command line parameter. To test this, go to the DOS prompt, and type
the command that starts the program, a space, then the name of a file with
the correct extension, then press ENTER. If this does not start the program
and open the data file, neither will selecting an associated data file in DOS
Shell. Also, the program you are associating with must be in a directory
included in the Path statement, or be in the same directory as the data file.

When entering the extension, don't include the period before
the file extension, only the characters that appear after the
period. For example, if you want to associate the current
program file with files that have a .DOC extension, type **DOC**. If
you want to associate multiple extensions, put a space between
each extension.

Tech Tip: You can
enter a period, with
no text after it, to
associate all files
that do not have
extensions.

4. Select OK.

If you are using a version of DOS Shell that comes with
MS-DOS 6.0:

1. Highlight the data file in the File List.
2. Select Associate from the File menu.
3. Enter the program you want to associate with the
   extension of the currently selected data file. The program
   must be able to accept the data file as a command line
   parameter, and either be in a directory listed in the Path
   statement or be in the same directory as the data file.
4. Select OK.

To start a program using a file with an associated file extension:

1. Highlight the file with the data you want to use.

2. Select Open from the File menu, or double-click on the file, or press ENTER.

How do I add my own programs to the Program List?

The initial entries in the Program List are only a starting point for the programs that are listed. You can add your own entries for the programs you have installed on your computer.

1. Switch to the program group you want to add a program item to.

2. Select New from the File menu.

3. Select Program Item and OK.

4. Make the following entries in the Add Program dialog box which you can see in Figure 7-4.

   a. Type the text to appear in the Program List in the Program Title text box.

   b. Type the DOS command or commands to perform when the program item is selected in the Commands text box. If you want multiple commands, separate them with a space and a semicolon. If you want to be prompted for an entry when you select the program item, mark where the entry's contents are placed in the commands with %1 through %9. For example, the Editor program item has the entry of EDIT %1. When you select the Editor program item, DOS Shell will prompt for a filename to edit and use your entry in place of the %1. EDIT will open this file for you in the DOS Editor.

```
┌──────────────────────────── Add Program ────────────────────────────┐
│                                                                      │
│  Program Title . . . . [                                          ]  │
│                                                                      │
│  Commands  . . . . . . [                                          ]  │
│                                                                      │
│  Startup Directory . . [                                          ]  │
│                                                                      │
│  Application Shortcut Key        [                      ]            │
│                                                                      │
│  [X] Pause after exit        Password . .  [              ]          │
│    (    OK    )   ( Cancel )   (  Help  )   ( Advanced... )           │
└──────────────────────────────────────────────────────────────────────┘
```

FIGURE 7-4   Program items are added in the Add Program dialog box

    c. In the Startup Directory text box, type the directory where the data files to use with the program are stored.

    d. Set any options for the program item. For example, you can assign a key combination to start the program while in another part of DOS Shell.

5. Select OK.
When you select OK, dialog boxes will appear for each of the replacement parameters in the Commands text box. The replacement parameters are %1 through %9. In this dialog box, you can enter the information to prompt the user for the text to use in place of the replacement parameter when opening the program item. You can enter the title of the dialog box that prompts the user, the text that appears at the top of the dialog box which explains what the user should enter, and the text that appears next to the text box that the user types the replacement text in. You can also type an entry for DOS Shell to use as the default entry for the replacement parameter. Select OK when you finish making the entries in this dialog box. If you have more than one replacement parameter in the Commands dialog box, you will see another dialog box for the next replacement parameter, until you have entered the necessary information for all of the replacement parameters you used.

At this point, you have added the program item. You can now start the program item by highlighting it and pressing ENTER, or by double-clicking it. If your program item doesn't start the program, highlight the program item, select Properties in the File menu, and adjust the entries in the dialog box.

I noticed that I have both a DOSSHELL.COM and a DOSSHELL.EXE file in my DOS directory. Why?

DOS 5.0 and 6.0 both include a DOSSHELL.COM and a DOSSHELL.EXE file. The .COM file takes precedence over the .EXE file, so when you type **DOSSHELL** and press ENTER, the .COM file is loaded first and then it calls the .EXE file. A .COMfile contains a single segment for its code and data and is only 64K. .EXE files have many code and data segments. Since the .COM file is smaller it loads faster. The .COM file's code is also in the .EXE file.

When I try to start a program from DOS Shell, I get the error message "Unable to load COMMAND.COM or DOSSWAP.EXE." Why?

This error message usually indicates that the DOSSHELL.INI file is corrupt. This file is the one that contains all of the settings for DOS Shell. To correct this problem, expand the DOSSHELL.INI file from the DOS Setup disk again. The three compressed files that contain the DOSSHELL.INI file are: MONO.IN_, CGA.IN_, and EGA.IN_. Choose the appropriate one for your monitor and expand it. For VGA systems, expand EGA.IN_. To expand these files and copy them to your hard disk, use the DOS EXPAND command. For example, type **EXPAND A:\EGA.IN_ C:\DOS\DOSSHELL.INI** and press ENTER if you have an EGA monitor and stored your DOS files in the C:\DOS directory.

Tech Tip: Re-expanding the DOSSHELL.INI file from the DOS Setup disks will overwrite any custom settings you may have added since you installed DOS Shell. You could also restore the DOSSHELL.INI file from a recent backup, which would preserve the custom settings.

Task swapping isn't working with some of the programs I use with DOS Shell. Am I setting something wrong?

Task swapping is the feature that allows you to run multiple programs from DOS Shell at once and to switch between them without having to exit. DOS Shell will task swap most programs, but there are some that either require too much memory or take full control of the memory. Because of this, these programs cannot be task swapped. For example, Windows, as an operating environment, takes complete control of memory, so it cannot be task swapped within DOS Shell.

Tech Terror: Don't run Windows from DOS Shell. Because Windows is an operating environment that tries to take full control of the system, it can conflict with its operation when started from DOS Shell. DOS Shell is not designed to cope with these conflicts. You can, however, run DOS Shell within Windows without difficulty.

How can I speed up task swapping with DOS Shell?

In order to speed up task swapping, you will need expanded or extended memory.

1. Change your CONFIG.SYS file to create a RAM drive, by putting DEVICE=C:\DOS\RAMDRIVE.SYS /E 1024 after the command for the extended memory manager (usually DEVICE=C:\DOS\HIMEM.SYS). A 1MB RAM drive is more than adequate.

2. Add the following lines to the AUTOEXEC.BAT file:

```
MD D:\TEMP
SET TEMP=D:\TEMP
```

These lines create a directory in the RAM drive (assuming it is drive D) and set programs such as DOS Shell to put its temporary files into the \TEMP directory on this drive. When task swapping is enabled in DOS Shell, the RAM drive will be used for temporary files. Since it is faster to write to and read from RAM than from your hard disk, your task swapping will go faster. However, if your programs use extended memory, you are better off using the extended memory for the programs rather than for temporary files. If you have Windows, use it to switch between tasks and do not create a RAM drive.

Is there a way to switch the mouse buttons in DOS Shell?

Whether or not you can switch mouse buttons mostly depends on the mouse driver you are using. The MS Mouse driver version 9.0, for example, allows swapping of mouse buttons. There are a very few types of mouse that switch buttons by some type of mechanical switch. Logitech drivers allow swapping mouse buttons, but you must have a terminate-and-stay-resident program (TSR) loaded. To find out if you can swap mouse buttons, check the documentation that came with your mouse. Swapping the left and right mouse buttons often makes the mouse easier to use if you are left-handed.

DoubleSpace

When you first purchased your computer, your hard disk probably seemed to provide all the storage space you'd ever need. Now that you've been using your system for a while, you are probably considering removing a program or some old data to make room for something else. You can solve your disk space problems by buying a second hard drive or you can utilize the DoubleSpace utility provided with DOS 6.*x* to increase the available space on your existing hard disk. The amount of extra space you gain by running DoubleSpace depends on the type of files on your disk and whether they are stored in regular or compressed format.

DoubleSpace is a program which compresses your data to store it in a smaller area on your disk. If you have ever worked with zipped or archived files, you may be familiar with the idea of a program squeezing your data to store it in less space. DoubleSpace is like the file compression programs except it works "in the background" with the data on an entire disk. You don't need to specify which files to expand and compress; DoubleSpace stores *all* of the data in a compressed format. When you work with a file, DoubleSpace expands the data. When you save a file, DoubleSpace automatically compresses its contents as it stores the file.

DoubleSpace creates a compressed volume file (CVF) for each compressed "drive." This "drive" is actually just a large file but DoubleSpace convinces applications to treat it as another drive.

When you create a compressed drive with DoubleSpace, you also have an uncompressed drive called a *host drive*. You store files that you do not want compressed on the host drive. Uncompressed files must include the system files your computer needs to start. Your host drive also contains two files called DBLSPACE.INI, which contains the initial settings to use

131

for the compressed drive, and DBLSPACE.BIN, which contains the instructions that tell your computer how to read the compressed drive. Other files such as 386SPART.PAR, a permanent swap file for Windows, are stored on the host drive because they will not function correctly if compressed.

The advantage of using DoubleSpace is the ability to store more information without investing in additional hardware. The disadvantage is a slight performance decline with some applications. This performance loss is caused by the resources DoubleSpace uses when compressing and expanding your data.

The Frustration Busters box that follows highlights some of the problems with DoubleSpace in DOS 6.0. Using DoubleSpace in DOS 6.2 solves these problems.

FRUSTRATION BUSTERS!

You may have heard about problems with DoubleSpace in DOS 6.0. DoubleSpace in DOS 6.2 has several features to prevent problems. These include a ScanDisk feature, which checks the integrity of the drive, and DoubleGuard, which prevents other programs from corrupting the memory that DoubleSpace uses. However, the way DoubleSpace performs the compression process has not changed. The problem with DoubleSpace in DOS 6.0 was that these protection features were missing. When something went wrong in DOS 6.0, data was frequently lost. Most of the problems that users experienced with DoubleSpace in DOS 6.0 can be traced to one of the following causes:

- **Older BIOS:** The system BIOS (Basic Input/Output System) communicates with DOS to handle requests for data from the hard disk. Because of the way DoubleSpace works with the disk, a recent version of the BIOS is required. This is still true with DOS 6.2. If you are having problems with data loss with DOS 6.0 DoubleSpace and your machine is more than three years old, contact the manufacturer to see if a BIOS upgrade is available.

■ **Older hard drive or controller:** There are a few known compatibility problems with specific hardware models.

■ **"Misbehaving" applications:** Programmers often employ "tricks" to speed up disk access or to work with memory while their program is running. DoubleSpace is designed to work with programs that "follow the rules" when it comes to disk access. If you experience data loss only when using a certain program, contact the program's manufacturer to see if they recommend installing the software on uncompressed disk space. DOS 6.2 now includes the DoubleGuard feature to help protect the DoubleSpace program from being overwritten by misbehaving programs while DoubleSpace is loaded in memory.

■ **Damaged hard drives:** When you install DoubleSpace, you generally use the entire free space on the hard drive to set up the compressed volume file. This often involves using areas of the drive that have never been used before. If the drive has a bad sector located in this previously unused space, problems can start to appear after installing DoubleSpace. DOS 6.2 includes the ScanDisk utility to check for drive problems and DoubleSpace runs ScanDisk automatically during setup. After discovering bad sectors, ScanDisk tells DOS and DoubleSpace not to use them.

■ **No backup:** A good, up-to-date backup is the best defense against unforeseen problems such as a power failure while DoubleSpace is compressing your files. DOS 6.2 DoubleSpace reminds you to make a backup, explains the importance of having a backup, then offers an opportunity to exit DoubleSpace and create a backup before installing.

I have Stacker but I want to use DoubleSpace. How can I convert?

First, check which version of Stacker you have. If you have version *2.x* or 3.0, contact Microsoft Consumer Sales at (800) 426-9400 to obtain the Stacker-to-DoubleSpace conversion disk. Make sure you use the proper conversion disk for your version of MS-DOS—either 6.0 or 6.2.

If you have a disk compressed with Stacker 3.1, follow these steps:

1. Unstack your Stacker drives using the UNSTACK command. You should also unstack floppy disks. If the floppy disks are configured using Stacker's StackerAnywhere feature, you do not need to change the disk.

2. Type the following commands (assuming the drive is C) and press ENTER at the end of each line:

```
ATTRIB -R -H -S STACKER.INI
ATTRIB -R -H -S DBLSPACE.BIN
DEL STACKER.INI
DEL DBLSPACE.BIN
```

3. Restart your computer.

4. Type **DBLSPACE** and press ENTER to compress the disk.

If you have Stacker version *2.x* or 3.0 and do not want to wait for a conversion disk, back up your files from your Stacker compressed disk. Next, reformat the disk and restore your files following these steps:

1. Back up all data on the hard drive.

2. Boot the system with an MS-DOS 6.*x* boot disk that contains a copy of FORMAT.EXE. Press F5 when you see "Starting MS-DOS...."

Your files are not visible at this point. The drive now appearing as drive C is your Stacker host drive.

3. Type **FORMAT C: /S** and press ENTER. You must respond to the other prompts for this command.

4. Once the drive is reformatted, you should re-install MS-DOS 6.*x*, then restore your data.

How do I change from XtraDrive disk compression to DoubleSpace disk compression?

To change from XtraDrive disk compression to DoubleSpace, run the XtraDrive uninstallation program to remove the compression. After you remove the old compression you can install DoubleSpace.

I have DoubleSpace on my machine. I am installing a new program. Do I run DoubleSpace again to compress this program?

No, it is not necessary to run DoubleSpace to compress each new program. Once DoubleSpace is installed, files are compressed as they are copied to the hard drive. Additionally, the files are decompressed as you copy them from the hard drive to a floppy disk unless you are copying to a compressed floppy disk.

Do I need to back up the host drive for my DoubleSpace compressed drive to completely back up the hard drive?

It may not be necessary to back up the host drive each time you run a backup. A backup of the DoubleSpace compressed drive is sufficient, unless you have installed applications or stored other files on the host drive that are not on the compressed drive. By default, there are several hidden DOS system files (IO.SYS, MSDOS.SYS, and DBLSPACE.*) on the host drive that you do not need to back up.

Can I use DoubleSpace on my floppy disks?

Yes, you can use DoubleSpace with floppy disks. However, you cannot compress 360K disks. When you compress a disk, you will need at least 65K of free space on the disk. DOS 6.2 has Automount, which automatically mounts compressed drives and makes them available for use when you put a floppy disk in a drive.

A point to consider is that only DOS 6 can use compressed floppy disks. If you plan to use the disks with computers using earlier DOS releases, do not compress them. For example, when you use the ATTRIB command in DOS 5 to look at the contents of a disk compressed with DOS 6, you might see something like this:

```
C:\>ATTRIB  A:
     SHR     A:\IO.SYS
     SHR     A:\MSDOS.SYS
     A       A:\READTHIS.TXT
     SHR     A:\DBLSPACE.000
     SHR     A:\DBLSPACE.BIN
       R     A:\COMMAND.COM

C:\>
```

DBLSPACE.000 is the compressed file that contains all files stored on the floppy disk. DOS 5 cannot read the files from the compressed disk.

 **Tech Tip:** When you compress a floppy disk, it has files in both the compressed and uncompressed parts of the disk. To look at files on the uncompressed part of the floppy disk, you need to use the letter for the host drive of the disk. For example, if the disk in drive A is compressed, you can look at its uncompressed files by specifying drive F, the host drive for drive A.

 ## How can I compress a floppy drive and not compress my hard drive?

To compress floppy disks without compressing your hard drive, you must first run DoubleSpace on your hard drive to compress a small part of unused space. When DoubleSpace is finished, you can have DoubleSpace delete the new drive it created. Once the compressed drive is deleted, you can start compressing floppies while leaving the hard drive uncompressed. These are the steps you will follow:

1. Type **DBLSPACE** and press ENTER at the DOS prompt to start DoubleSpace.

2. Choose Custom Setup.

3. Choose Create a new empty compressed drive from the Custom Setup menu.

   You will see a listing of the amount of free space on your drive. Note the current free space on the drive.

4. Press ENTER to select the drive.

   You will see a prompt for the size of the new drive. Select the amount of free space to leave on the host drive and change it to equal the total free space minus one megabyte. Also, note the drive letter that DoubleSpace will assign to the new drive.

5. Press ENTER after selecting Continue to create the compressed drive.

6. Exit DoubleSpace when it is finished creating the new drive.

7. Type **DBLSPACE /DELETE** *drive:* and press ENTER at the DOS prompt to delete the new drive. *Drive:* is the drive letter DoubleSpace assigned to the new drive.

8. Type **y** for confirmation and DoubleSpace deletes the compressed drive.

You can now run DoubleSpace to compress floppy disks and the one megabyte of disk space previously used by the compressed hard disk drive is returned to drive C. Be aware, however, that the DoubleSpace program will load into memory each time you start your computer, which takes 38K to 53K of RAM.

Tech Tip: You need to have the floppy you want to compress in the drive before you select Compress Existing Drive in DoubleSpace. If you do not have a disk in the drive, DoubleSpace will not see the drive as a compressible drive.

Are there any special steps I need to take when I copy a file from my hard drive to a floppy disk after running DoubleSpace?

No, the DoubleSpace "compression engine" handles the entire process of compressing/decompressing everything going into and out of the DoubleSpaced drive.

DoubleSpace broke my hard drive. What happened?

Software never breaks hardware. Your hard disk may have had an undetected bad area before installing DoubleSpace as described in the following scenario. Before compression, data is stored on the hard disk on a cluster-by-cluster basis. (A *cluster* is simply a logical unit of space on the hard drive made up of smaller logical units called *sectors*.) Often, some of the sectors are unused and one or more of those sectors may be physically defective. Compression saves information on a sector-by-sector basis rather than by clusters. All sectors are used with this method, including the bad ones. As a result of this change, it might appear as if the compression broke the hardware, when, in fact, the increased efficiency of the compression simply found problems that existed all along.

Under DOS 6.2, the ScanDisk utility locates the physical problems with the disk before running DoubleSpace. ScanDisk finds the areas that are bad and tells the operating system not to use them. Most hard drives have a few bad clusters. When you format a disk, part of the procedure checks for these bad areas and insures that they are not used later for data storage.

When I start DoubleSpace, I see the message "Your computer might be running software that is incompatible with DoubleSpace." How do I run DoubleSpace?

The most likely culprit is the line containing SMARTDRV in your AUTOEXEC.BAT or CONFIG.SYS file. Prior versions of SMARTDrive are not designed to work with DoubleSpace compressed disks. Change the line containing SMARTDRV to refer to the SMARTDRV.EXE file in the DOS directory containing your DOS 6 files. If SMARTDRV is not the problem, another program that is loaded as CONFIG.SYS or AUTOEXEC.BAT is processed at startup might be at fault. Reboot your computer and press F5 when you see "Starting MS-DOS...." This will bypass your startup files and allow DoubleSpace to run.

Why, since I ran DoubleSpace, do I receive the error message "You must specify the host drive for a DoubleSpace drive" every time the computer boots up?

This error is coming from SMARTDrive. The problem is the SMARTDRV.EXE line in the AUTOEXEC.BAT file that starts SMARTDrive. This line may instruct SMARTDrive to cache a DoubleSpace compressed drive. Instead, you want SMARTDrive to cache the host drive (the physical uncompressed drive containing the CVF file that represents the compressed drive). To resolve the problem, edit the AUTOEXEC.BAT file and change the drive letter specified on the SMARTDRV.EXE line to reference the host drive. To find which drive letter is the host drive for drive C, type **DBLSPACE /LIST** and press ENTER while at a DOS prompt. DoubleSpace lists the drive letters and their status as you can see here:

```
C:\>DBLSPACE /LIST
Drive  Type                    Total Free  Total Size  CVF Filename
-----  ----------------------  ----------  ----------  ---------------
  A    Removable-media drive   No disk in drive
  B    Removable-media drive   No disk in drive
  C    Compressed hard drive    80.23 MB    179.99 MB   H:\DBLSPACE.000
  D    Available for DoubleSpace
  E    Available for DoubleSpace     Compressed drive
  F    Available for DoubleSpace
  G    Available for DoubleSpace                     CVF file stored in
  H    Local hard drive         2.34 MB    118.63 MB     host drive

DoubleGuard safety checking is enabled.            Host drive
Automounting is enabled for drive(s) AB

C:\ >
```

Tech Tip: You must restart the computer after making these changes to put them in effect.

You can also remove all drive letters from the SMARTDRV line and, by default, SMARTDrive automatically caches the host drives for all compressed DoubleSpace drives. For example, when the DoubleSpace drive is drive C and the host drive is H, the line: C:\DOS\SMARTDRV.EXE C instructs SMARTDrive to cache the compressed drive C. This line causes the error message. The modified line C:\DOS\SMARTDRV.EXE H instructs SMARTDrive to cache drive H (which in this example is the host drive for C). If you remove all drive letters, the line would read C:\DOS\SMARTDRV.EXE and SMARTDrive automatically caches drive H. To find the current drive-caching status of SMARTDrive, simply type **SMARTDRV** at the DOS prompt and press ENTER.

How do I get my disk that I compressed with DoubleSpace back the way it was?

The steps for uncompressing a disk compressed with DoubleSpace differ for DOS 6.0 and 6.2. If you are using MS-DOS 6.2, type **DBLSPACE /UNCOMPRESS** at the DOS prompt and press ENTER. This is the same as selecting Uncompress from the Tools menu in the DoubleSpace utility.

There is no automatic decompression utility for DoubleSpace in MS-DOS 6.0. When using MS-DOS 6.0, you must remove DoubleSpace manually. You can back up your data and reformat the host drive as described earlier in the chapter under the question "I have Stacker but I want to use DoubleSpace. How can I convert?" Another option is to move all files from your compressed drive to its host drive following these steps:

1. Use the MOVE command to move files from the compressed to the uncompressed disk. You will need to move a few files at a time since the uncompressed drive will not be able hold all of the files from the compressed drive at the same time.

2. Resize the compressed disk by starting DoubleSpace, selecting Change Size from the Drive menu, and entering a smaller number for the remaining free space on the uncompressed drive.

3. Repeat steps 1 and 2 until all of your data is off the compressed drive.

4. Delete the compressed drive by selecting Delete from the Drive menu in the DoubleSpace utility.

Are the files put into a DoubleSpaced drive compressed as you load them?

Yes. You do not need to run DoubleSpace again. By the same token, files saved to an uncompressed drive, such as a floppy disk, are uncompressed.

Can I store more information on backup disks if I first DoubleSpace the disks and then back up to those disks using MS Backup?

No, the MS Backup utility automatically compresses data while backing up. Using compressed disks will not yield any additional compression. DoubleSpace compression is not utilized even if it is available when MS Backup writes to the disks with its high-speed transfer process.

My buddy and I each have the same computer with the same size hard drive. We both have roughly the same amount of data, yet he got more free space when he ran DBLSPACE than I did. Why?

The amount of compression depends on the type of data on the compressed disk. Your friend's data was simply more compressible. Program files and files that are already compressed will not compress very much. Text files and certain types of graphics files (such as .TIF files) compress substantially.

I tried to uncompress using the command "DBLSPACE /UNCOMPRESS C:" and received a message that there were files in the root directory of both the compressed drive and the host drive with identical names. The uncompress process said that it couldn't continue until there were no common names. Now what?

Use the TYPE command to look at the DBLSPACE.LOG file on the host drive. That file will tell you what files are common to the root directories of both drives. Remove or rename one of each of the duplicate files, or move one of the files with the same name from the root directory of either the compressed or host drive.

Can I use DoubleSpace if I am part of a network?

If you normally attach to a Novell NetWare network, it is important to log into the network before compressing your hard drive using DoubleSpace. This prevents confusion with drive letters. DoubleSpace initially sets the compressed drive to use the fifth letter following the last local drive for the host or uncompressed drive. This drive will conflict with the drives Novell uses if you run DoubleSpace before you log into the network. If you normally log in with a NetWare server mapped at F but are not logged in when you run DoubleSpace, DoubleSpace will reserve F. When you next log into the network, the server is mapped to I instead (the next letter available after H). Although you can usually change drive mappings later, it is easier to set them beforehand. If you use DoubleSpace after logging into the network to compress one of your drives (not the network's), DoubleSpace will not use letters that cause conflicts. DoubleSpace leaves your mappings, such as F, intact and reserves other letters.

I just put some files in my compressed drive. The files must take up more room than their size since I have a lot less free space. What happened?

Some files do not compress as well as others. For example, when you copy files with a .ZIP file extension, they do not compress well since they are already compressed. When you copy these files to a compressed disk, free space decreases by more than the file size.

Can I make my compressed drive larger so I can put more data there?

You can make your compressed drive larger but you will be making the host drive smaller. You may be willing to sacrifice space on the host drive when your compressed disk becomes full. To enlarge the compressed drive, follow these steps:

1. Type **DBLSPACE** at the DOS prompt and press ENTER to start the DoubleSpace program.

2. Highlight the compressed drive you want to enlarge, and then select Change Size from the Drive menu.

   The Change Size dialog box appears. The New Free Space line shows how much free space the compressed and uncompressed drives will have if you choose OK.

3. Type a smaller number for New Free Space on the uncompressed drive. Notice that as you change this number, DoubleSpace adjusts the New Free Space amount for the compressed drive.

4. Select OK to change the drive.

Tech Tip: You may free space on an extremely fragmented compressed drive by defragmenting it. Information on defragmenting compressed drives is available under the question "Does the Defrag utility work on compressed drives?"

I tried to change the size of my compressed drive but was told that it is too fragmented. I ran Defrag but I still get the same message. Why?

When DoubleSpace resizes a compressed drive, it reassigns a block of hard disk space from the compressed drive to the uncompressed drive, or the reverse. If files on the drives are too fragmented, there is not a contiguous block of disk space that is large enough to allow DoubleSpace to transfer in this way. The DoubleSpace program suggests defragmenting the drive and trying the operation again. The Microsoft Defrag program tries to re-save all files on one end of a drive and, in the process, create a large block of unused space at the other end. DoubleSpace can transfer this unused space from one drive to another when you resize drives.

Microsoft Defrag cannot move and re-save hidden, read-only, or system files. These files may be scattered throughout the drive, thereby preventing DoubleSpace from resizing the compressed disk. To fix the problem, unhide the files, run Defrag, and then hide the files again (they were probably hidden for a reason).

To view hidden files on a drive, type the following, pressing ENTER after each line:

```
CD \
DIR /AH /S /P
```

Make a note of the filenames. To view the system, hidden, and read-only attributes on a file, type **ATTRIB *filename,*** where *filename* is the name of the file, and press ENTER. To remove these attributes, type **ATTRIB *filename* -S -H -R** and press ENTER. Remove all the attributes from the hidden files that you found on your drive except the IO.SYS and MSDOS.SYS files. These two are part of the MS-DOS system that is currently running and cannot be modified.

For example, if you find a system, hidden, read-only file called IMAGE.IDX on the root directory of drive C, type **ATTRIB C:\IMAGE.IDX -S -H -R** and press ENTER to remove these attributes.

At this point, run the Defrag program. When the program is finished running, reassign the attributes to the files by typing **ATTRIB *filename* +S +H +R** and pressing ENTER. You can then change the size of your compressed drive successfully.

If this process is unsuccessful, the hidden MSDOS.SYS file must be preventing the drive from being resized. You will need to boot your computer from a floppy disk to remove the hidden file attribute from this file. Then run Defrag and restore the attributes of this file.

Does the Defrag utility work on compressed drives?

Defrag will defragment the file containing the compressed drive but it does not defragment the contents of the compressed drive. To defragment the contents of a compressed drive, the Defrag program automatically starts the DoubleSpace program with the /Defrag switch. You will see DoubleSpace Defrag start to slowly count the percentage completed after the main defragmentation is finished. You can also defragment your DoubleSpace compressed drive by typing **DBLSPACE /DEFRAG** at the DOS prompt and pressing ENTER.

Tech Tip: Defragmenting can take an hour or longer. You may want to start the process at the end of the day and let it run overnight.

How do I know which disk is my compressed disk?

When you start DoubleSpace in DOS 6.2, the screen displays the mounted compressed drives as shown here:

Drive	Description	Free Space (MB)	Total Space (MB)
C	Compressed hard drive	80.27	179.91

If you think you have another compressed drive that is not mounted, select Mount from the Drive menu and DoubleSpace lists available unmounted compressed disks. You can also see a report from the DOS prompt by typing **DBLSPACE /LIST** and pressing ENTER.

Tech Tip: DBLSPACE /LIST is also good for finding RAM drives, floppy drives, and other types of drives.

I just ran DoubleSpace, but now I need to free up more room on my uncompressed drive. What can I do?

Type **DBLSPACE** at the DOS prompt and press ENTER. If you have more than one compressed drive, select the one associated with the uncompressed drive that you want to modify. Enlarging the uncompressed drive will shrink the size of the compressed drive. From the menu, select Drive, then select Change Size. Increase the New Free Space entry for your uncompressed drive and press ENTER.

DBLSPACE /CHKDSK reports that it found no errors, but some of the programs are acting as if files are damaged (program hangs, data error, etc.). Why am I having this problem?

The DBLSPACE /CHKDSK routine only checks for file structure abnormalities, not for file content. The program files might not contain the correct information to operate properly. Other third-party utilities such as Norton Utilities and PC Tools may be better at recovering the damaged files. Successful recovery depends on the type of damage. Try re-installing the programs, or recover the files from your backups if other approaches fail.

Tech Tip: If you have this problem more than once, run ScanDisk to check for disk problems.

I want to format my hard drive and have it compressed with DoubleSpace. When I type FORMAT C:, DOS displays the message "You must use DBLSPACE /FORMAT C: to format that drive." When I type DBLSPACE /FORMAT C:, it doesn't work either. How can I format my hard drive without removing DoubleSpace?

You can format the host drive with the standard FORMAT command, but when you reboot, DoubleSpace will no longer be in effect. The DoubleSpace utility will not allow you to format your boot drive. The solution is to boot with a floppy disk that contains the DBLSPACE.EXE utility. You can then type

DBLSPACE /FORMAT C: from the A: DOS prompt. When you reboot, you will still have your host drive, and drive C will be empty (*and* compressed!).

Every time I boot my machine, it goes into DoubleSpace. Why?

This indicates that DoubleSpace did not successfully compress drive C. Before DoubleSpace compresses drive C, it renames your existing AUTOEXEC.BAT to AUTOEXEC.000, then creates its own AUTOEXEC.BAT. If there is some type of difficulty, such as a power failure, the compression process is interrupted. This leaves the DoubleSpace AUTOEXEC.BAT in effect, because DoubleSpace did not complete the process and remove the file. When the computer is restarted, DoubleSpace will continue the compression process.

I have a large 1Gb hard drive. I just ran DoubleSpace but it only gave me a 512MB DoubleSpaced drive. I expected to get 2Gb. What went wrong?

DoubleSpace compressed volume files have a limit of 256MB. This yields a theoretical maximum size DoubleSpace drive of 512MB. If you have a large hard drive, you have two options:

1. Compress existing free space on the large drive by 256MB at a time, thereby creating several 512MB DoubleSpace drives on one host drive.
2. Repartition the large drive with FDISK into smaller partitions of 256MB (or slightly larger) in order to better manage the DoubleSpace size limitation.

I have DOS 6.0 and I used DoubleSpace on some floppy disks. I can't access the data on the disks while in Windows. For each floppy disk, I must exit Windows, manually mount the disk, and then restart Windows. What am I doing wrong?

You are not doing anything wrong. MS-DOS 6.0 does not automatically mount floppies. The only way to use a DoubleSpaced floppy from Windows is to mount the floppy before starting Windows. If you use DoubleSpaced floppies often, upgrade to DOS 6.2 since it automatically mounts floppies, even in Windows!

I added a second hard drive and my DoubleSpaced drive C is now drive D. However, I cannot see any of my files on drive D. How can I regain access to my files?

As long as you have the same version of DOS on your new drive C, you can access your files by following these steps:

1. Type the following commands at the DOS prompt, pressing ENTER after each one, to copy the DBLSPACE.INI file from the root directory on drive D to the root directory of drive C.

```
ATTRIB D:\DBLSPACE.INI -S -H
COPY D:\DBLSPACE.INI C:\
```

The DBLSPACE.INI file has read-only, system, and hidden attributes set on it. These commands remove these attributes and copy the file to drive C.

2. Type **EDIT C:\DBLSPACE.INI** and press ENTER to edit the C:\DBLSPACE.INI file to reflect the change in the drive assignments.

The line you should change is the ActivateDrive line. This line will read ActivateDrive=?,C0 where ? is the letter used by the host drive. This is not important because you do not change this letter.

3. Change the letter C in the ActivateDrive line to the letter *D*. The changed line reads as ActivateDrive=?,D0.

4. Save the file and exit from the editor.

5. Type **ATTRIB C:\DBLSPACE.INI +R +S +H** and press ENTER to add the read-only, system, and hidden file attributes to this copy of the file.

6. Reboot the machine. Drive D should mount, using the drive represented by ? in step 3 as its host.

Why is my system running slower after installing DoubleSpace?

Compression software inherently slows down your system's performance because that program is constantly running "in the background" to decompress and compress the data. On most systems, the performance loss is negligible. You can enhance your system's performance by loading SMARTDrive. Make sure your AUTOEXEC.BAT file includes the line:

    C:\DOS\SMARTDRV.EXE

I just got a DoubleGuard Alarm message. Is something wrong with my disk?

When a DoubleGuard Alarm message appears, DoubleGuard has detected that an application damaged memory that DoubleSpace was using. This is not a normal occurrence since each program has its own section of memory and does not use memory used by another program. When this problem occurs, DoubleGuard immediately shuts down your computer to minimize the chance of data loss. If you receive a DoubleGuard Alarm message, do the following:

1. Remember which application you were using and the activity you were performing when you saw this message. This may help you identify the cause of the problem.

2. Turn your computer off and then on again.

3. Type **SCANDISK /ALL** at the DOS prompt and press ENTER. ScanDisk checks all of your drives to detect and correct any problems caused by the program that violated DoubleSpace's memory.

Tech Tip: If you have this problem more than once with the same program, contact the program's manufacturer to see if they know of any problems caused by running their program with DoubleSpace.

I just got the message "Compressed drive C is currently too fragmented to mount." How do I use this drive's data?

This message as well as the message "The C:\DBLSPACE.nnn file is too fragmented to mount" indicate that DoubleSpace in DOS 6.2 cannot mount the drive because its compressed volume file is stored in too many fragments on your hard disk.

To correct this problem, increase the MaxFileFragments setting in your DBLSPACE.INI file. MaxFileFragments sets the number of file fragments a compressed volume file can have. You can increase the number to access your compressed data by following these steps:

1. Type **TYPE H:\DBLSPACE.INI** and press ENTER, replacing the *H* with the letter of the host drive if another drive letter is appropriate.

2. Look at the number after MaxFileFragments =.

3. Type **DBLSPACE /MAXFILEFRAGMENTS=128** and press ENTER. If the number after MaxFileFragments is already 128 or higher, replace the 128 with a higher number, such as 200.

4. Restart your computer. DoubleSpace should now be able to mount the drive. At this point, you want to use Defrag and Dblspace /Defrag to reduce the number of disk fragments, as described under the question "Does the Defrag utility work on compressed drives?".

If DoubleSpace still cannot mount the drive, follow these steps:

1. Type **SCANDISK /ALL /SURFACE** at the DOS prompt and press ENTER to check the reliability of your hard disk.

2. Restart your computer. If DoubleSpace still cannot mount the drive, proceed to step 3.

3. Type **ATTRIB H:\DBLSPACE.000 -R -S -H** and press ENTER. This example assumes the host drive is drive H and you only have one compressed drive. This command removes the read-only, system, and hidden file attributes on the compressed volume file.

4. Type **DEFRAG** at the DOS prompt and press ENTER to defragment the disk.

5. Type **ATTRIB** *filename* **+R +S +H** and press ENTER. Replace *filename* with the name of the file used in step 3. This command returns the read-only, system, and hidden file attributes on the compressed volume file.

6. Restart your computer again. DoubleSpace should now be able to mount the compressed drive.

I just saw the message "DoubleSpace could not mount drive C due to problems with the drive." What is wrong?

This message indicates internal organization problems that prevent the drive from being used. The problem is in the compressed volume file (CVF) that stores the contents of a compressed disk. This message also includes the name of the CVF that is causing the problem. To use the compressed drive again, you need to run ScanDisk on the drive's CVF, and then restart your system. If the CVF is for the compressed disk you use for booting, you should use a different procedure, which is described below. With either procedure, however, if ScanDisk displays a dialog box describing a problem, choose the Fix It button.

If this problem occurs for a compressed drive other than your boot drive, type **SCANDISK** *filename* and press ENTER. *Filename* is the same filename that you initially saw in the error message. If you see the message "Bad command or filename," follow the next procedure.

If this problem occurs for a compressed boot drive or if DOS cannot find the SCANDISK program, follow these steps:

1. Insert Setup Disk 1 for DOS in drive A (or B) of your computer.

2. Change to the drive that contains Setup Disk 1.

3. Type **ScanDisk C:***filename* and press ENTER. *Filename* is the same filename that you initially saw in the error message.

4. Remove the floppy disk and restart your computer when ScanDisk has finished.

Can I change the level of compression used by DoubleSpace to make more space available?

No, you cannot change the actual amount of compression applied to your files, but you can change the estimated compression ratio (ECR). ECR estimates the free space on the compressed drive. Ordinarily, making this change is not advisable; since DoubleSpace adjusts this ratio based on the compression of existing compressed files. If you have a large, highly compressible file (such as a 3MB text file) and only 2.3MB of space free, adjusting the ECR may let you save the file. This same operation may not work if you are trying to save 3MB of program files, since programs do not compress as well as text. To change the ECR, type **DBLSPACE /RATIO=*x.x***, where *x.x* is a compression ratio between 1.0 and 16.0, and press ENTER.

I installed DOS 6.2 on an older machine (8088/286) with 512K of total RAM. Why can't I run DoubleSpace?

Your computer needs 500K of conventional memory to install DoubleSpace. In addition, once installed, DoubleSpace uses about 43K to 53K of memory, which can cause problems for other programs on a machine with only 512K. In this case, increase RAM to 640K or higher before you use DoubleSpace.

Why does DoubleSpace use more memory under MS-DOS 6.2 than it did under MS-DOS 6.0?

Since DoubleSpace in DOS 6.2 has additional features, the DoubleSpace program for DOS 6.2 is larger than the one for DOS 6.0. However, one of the new features is the ability to load part of DoubleSpace into the high memory area (HMA). This is the same area that MS-DOS uses if you specify DOS=HIGH in CONFIG.SYS. If enough of the HMA is available, part of DoubleSpace automatically loads there, leaving around 38K in conventional or upper memory. This is actually smaller than the original DoubleSpace, which took 43K.

The other item that uses the HMA is the BUFFERS= line in CONFIG.SYS. If more than 10 buffers are specified, the buffers use too much of the HMA and force DoubleSpace to load into conventional memory. Try setting BUFFERS= to 10 to maximize conventional memory.

You can also disable the Automount feature of DoubleSpace under DOS 6.2, to save about 1K. However, if DoubleSpace loads part of itself into the HMA, the extra RAM will show up in the HMA, *not* in conventional or upper memory.

When I try to shrink the size of my compressed drive, DoubleSpace gives me a maximum free space on the uncompressed drive that I can change, but it is not enough. I deleted some files from the compressed drive but the maximum size for the uncompressed drive still did not change. Why?

DoubleSpace calculates the allowable space on the uncompressed drive based on the free space at the end of the compressed drive. Deleting files does not necessarily delete the files located at the end of the compressed drive. Use DBLSPACE /DEFRAG to re-order the files so that the gaps from the deleted files are filled, and the ending portion of the DBLSPACE volume contains the additional space freed by the deleted files. Then, DoubleSpace will recognize the additional free space when you resize the uncompressed drive.

I think my application doesn't like DoubleSpace. How can I check?

If you think your program does not work with DoubleSpace, you should first check Table 8-1. This table lists many programs that cause problems when used with DoubleSpace. Usually, these programs perform disk writes using BIOS rather than DOS. When a program does not work well with DoubleSpace, problems including locking the system, corrupting the program's own data, and corrupting system files may occur.

To find out if your problems are caused by a program's interaction with DoubleSpace or by another source, you need to test how the program functions without DoubleSpace installed. To test this, install the program on the uncompressed drive, temporarily disable DoubleSpace, and then try running the program. If the program functions correctly without DoubleSpace, then DoubleSpace is the problem. Otherwise, the difficulty is with the program itself.

The process of disabling DoubleSpace in order to check how your program runs without it is different for MS-DOS 6.0 and 6.2. If you are using MS-DOS 6.2, follow these steps:

1. Determine which drive is the uncompressed host drive by typing **DBLSPACE /INFO** at the DOS prompt and pressing ENTER.

2. Switch to the host drive by typing **H:**, assuming H is the host drive, and pressing ENTER.

3. Type **DIR** and press ENTER. At the end of the directory listing, you will see how much space is free on the uncompressed drive. Check this against the space required by your program to ensure that the uncompressed drive has enough room to install the program.

4. If there is not enough space on the uncompressed drive to contain the application, you need to create the free space. To do this:

    a. Type **DBLSPACE** at the DOS prompt and press ENTER.

    b. Press ALT+D to open the Drive menu.

    c. Select Change Size by pressing C.

    d. Enter a new amount of free space for the host drive.

    e. Select OK.

    f. Select Exit from the File menu.

5. Install the program, following the directions provided with its documentation.

6. Copy CONFIG.SYS and AUTOEXEC.BAT from the compressed drive to the uncompressed drive along with any files that they execute or reference. Be sure to put them in the appropriate directories.

7. Reboot your system.

8. Press CTRL+F8 when you see the phrase "Starting MS-DOS..." to disable DoubleSpace.

9. Respond as appropriate when prompted about whether to execute the various lines of the CONFIG.SYS file.

Program	Problem	Fixes
Argus Financial Software	Does not run from a compressed drive because the copy protection key cannot be compressed	Reinstall to the original disks then install on your host drive
Complete Communicator with voice files	Voices do not work when voice files are stored on a compressed drive	Install voice files on your host drive
Empire Deluxe	Prompts for a password every time it is loaded because the configuration file cannot be read when it is installed on a compressed drive	Install on your host drive
Zone 66 and Labyrinth	Does not run from a compressed drive	Install on your host drive, and start only after clean boots (they are sensitive to memory managers and TSRs)
Informix	Produces errors if run from a compressed drive since the .EXE files are affected by being compressed	Install on your host drive
Links and Links 386	Freezes your computer after DoubleSpace is installed since Links cannot interpret DoubleSpace's compression of already compressed files	Reinstall on the compressed drive
Lotus 1-2-3, version 2.01	Displays a message indicating that 1-2-3 has been uninstalled because the copy protection does not work with DoubleSpace	Get the Lotus Value Pack to run the program to remove copy protection
Movie Master 4.0	Does not run from the compressed drive since the copy protection's authorization code must be executed from an uncompressed drive	Install on your host drive
MultiMate 3.3 and 4.0	Produces errors such as "Divide overflow" if run from a compressed drive	Install on your host drive
Quicken for DOS	Does not run from a compressed drive	Install on your host drive
Tony La Russa Baseball II	Does not run from a compressed drive	Install on your host drive and run only after booting without installing EMM386 with the RAM or NOEMS parameter
Zsoft PhotoFinish	Does not run from a compressed drive when the virtual memory option is enabled	Install on your host drive

TABLE 8-1   Programs known to have problems with DoubleSpace

10. Start the program and see how it runs on the uncompressed drive.

Disabling DoubleSpace requires a different procedure in MS-DOS 6.0. To test the source of your problems with the program in MS-DOS 6.0, do this:

1. Install the program in question on the uncompressed drive following steps 1 through 4 above.

2. Create a boot disk for the A drive that does not enable DoubleSpace. To do this:

   a. Put a blank disk in the A drive.

   b. Type **FORMAT A: /S** at the DOS prompt and press ENTER.

   c. Type **DELTREE A:\DBLSPACE.BIN** at the DOS prompt and press ENTER to remove this file from your boot disk. Be *very* certain you do not delete the DBLSPACE.BIN file on your host drive. If you do, you will lose the contents of your compressed drive.

   d. Copy the CONFIG.SYS and AUTOEXEC.BAT files onto the boot disk.

   e. Make sure that any files called for or executed by CONFIG.SYS or AUTOEXEC.BAT are in the appropriate directories on the host drive.

   f. Reboot your system with the boot disk you just created in the A drive.

   g. Press F8 when you see the "Starting MS-DOS..." message.

   h. Respond Yes or No when prompted about executing each line of CONFIG.SYS.

3. Start your application and test it to see if it now functions correctly. Again, if it does respond correctly, your problem is that it cannot work with DoubleSpace. If it does not respond correctly, your problem is with the program itself.

In either case, if the application works, the program may not be compatible with DoubleSpace, or the program may not have enough memory to function while DoubleSpace is in memory at the same time. You may want to contact the software manufacturer to learn how you can use the software with DoubleSpace.

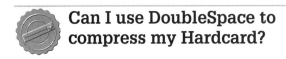

Can I use DoubleSpace to compress my Hardcard?

You can use DoubleSpace to compress a Hardcard, but the drive is not automatically mounted. This is a problem if your Hardcard is also your boot drive. A Hardcard is not mounted automatically because the DoubleSpace program (DBLSPACE.BIN) loads before CONFIG.SYS is processed. CONFIG.SYS must be processed before you can access your Hardcard. If your Hardcard is *not* the boot drive, you can mount the Hardcard in AUTOEXEC.BAT by adding this line:

```
DBLSPACE /MOUNT
```

When you reboot, your Hardcard is mounted during the startup process.

If your Hardcard is the boot drive, you have two choices:

1. Use the DoubleSpace Custom setup, and choose to create a new drive from the existing free space on C. Make the drive size as large as you can by using all but 2MB of the current free space on drive C. Once you create the new compressed drive, you can move files there and resize the compressed drive to make it larger (taking up the space you freed by moving files from C to the new drive). This is less work than the next option, but also less convenient.

2. To have your compressed drive show up as drive C, set up the host drive to contain all the files needed to boot your computer. Copy the MS-DOS system files (the two hidden files in your root directory), DBLSPACE.EXE (which mounts compressed drives), AUTOEXEC.BAT and CONFIG.SYS, and any other item that loads from AUTOEXEC.BAT and CONFIG.SYS into the host drive after compressing your original drive C. The AUTOEXEC.BAT should contain the DBLSPACE /MOUNT command as above. Assuming that drive H is the host drive for drive C, which is compressed, enter the following commands, pressing ENTER after each one:

```
SYS H:
COPY C:\AUTOEXEC.BAT H:
COPY C:\CONFIG.SYS H:
COPY C:\directory\system files H:
```

Repeat the last command for the different files used by AUTOEXEC.BAT and CONFIG.SYS.

How do I change the letter of my compressed disk?

By default, DoubleSpace reserves four free drive letters between the compressed drive (usually C) and the host drive. For example, if you compress C, then DoubleSpace reserves D, E, F, and G. The host drive (the drive that contains the compressed volume file for drive C) will be H. Installing DoubleSpace sets the compressed drive five letters after the last local drive, by default. You can change the letters, although the steps are different for DOS 6.0 and DOS 6.2.

In DOS 6.0, follow these steps:

1. Change to the host drive (usually H).

2. Type **ATTRIB -R -S -H DBLSPACE.INI** and press ENTER to clear all the attributes from the hidden file DBLSPACE.INI. This file stores the initial settings for DoubleSpace.

3. Type **EDIT DBLSPACE.INI** and press ENTER to modify this file. This file contains a line like the one shown below that sets the letters for the compressed and host drives.

```
ActivateDrive=H,C0
```

4. Edit the ActivateDrive line in DBLSPACE.INI. Change the letter after the = to the letter for the host drive and change the letter after the comma to the letter for the compressed drive. Do not change the number at the end of the line.

5. Change the LastDrive= letter to match your new host drive.

6. Select Exit from the File menu and select Yes when prompted if you want to save the file.

7. Type **ATTRIB +R +S +H DBLSPACE.INI** and press ENTER to return all the attributes to the file DBLSPACE.INI.

Use the above steps with caution! Setting a line incorrectly can cause you to lose access to your data.
For MS-DOS 6.2:

■ Type **DBLSPACE /HOST=*drive letter***, where *drive letter* is the letter for the host drive and press ENTER. This changes the letter of the host drive. If you want to change the letter of the compressed drive, you should follow the same steps you use in DOS 6.0.

For either version of DOS, the changes you make will not take effect until you restart your computer.

Memory

Memory is essential to everything you want to do with your computer. It is where your computer stores the instructions for tasks it is performing. Part of its memory is used to store some of the DOS commands that are used frequently. If you are using Windows, additional memory is needed for that operating environment. Also, any applications programs and the data you are currently using with them are assigned a section of memory.

To make using memory easier, DOS 6.*x* has a MemMaker utility. MemMaker optimizes how your computer uses its memory. With MemMaker, you can have an optimal memory arrangement without devoting the time to configure memory allocation manually.

MemMaker optimizes memory on systems with an 80386 or higher processor. To optimize memory, it transfers programs and device drivers out of conventional memory and into other memory your computer has. MemMaker does this by modifying your CONFIG.SYS and AUTOEXEC.BAT files. If you ever want to return to your prior CONFIG.SYS and AUTOEXEC.BAT files, you can; the old files are renamed CONFIG.UMB and AUTOEXEC.UMB and stored in your DOS directory.

FRUSTRATION BUSTERS!

It can be frustrating when you don't know what type of memory you need to make a program run. At minimum, your computer has conventional memory, but it probably has several other types as well. Following is a list of the different types of memory and what they are used for:

- **Read-only memory (ROM)**: Read-only memory contains vital information that is needed during the boot operation for your computer. Because this information is essential, it is stored in ROM where it cannot be overwritten. ROM does not require power to store information, so ROM programs are available the instant the computer is turned on. All PCs have ROM memory.

- **Conventional memory**: All personal computers have conventional memory. This is the starting point for counting the memory on your system. Most programs use conventional memory. The disadvantage of conventional memory is that DOS can only use 640K of it.

- **Reserved memory**: If your computer has more than 640K of memory, the next 384K is reserved memory (also called the upper memory area). Prior to DOS 5, this memory was strictly reserved for hardware addressing, page handlers for expanded memory, and copies of your ROM BIOS and Video ROM BIOS. DOS 5 and later versions let you use the remaining part of this memory as upper memory blocks (UMBs). Not everything can be put here but several of the device drivers in your CONFIG.SYS files can. Device drivers loaded by the CONFIG.SYS file are loaded with the commands that start DEVICE= or DEVICEHIGH=. It's important to understand that some of this area is used by the computer's hardware and cannot be used for loading device drivers. This means that the amount of upper memory blocks available will vary, depending on the hardware installed in the system.

- **High memory area (HMA)**: This is the first 64K of extended memory.

If you use the DOS=HIGH command in CONFIG.SYS, DOS will load a large portion of itself (40K or more) into the HMA, leaving only 15-20K in conventional memory. The exact sizes will vary, depending upon the number of files, buffers, stacks, and environment space you set aside in CONFIG.SYS. If you have DOS 6.2 and use DoubleSpace, any remaining HMA space will be used to load a portion of the DBLSPACE.BIN program.

■ **Extended memory**: This is the memory above 1MB. When people talk about how many megabytes of RAM their computer has, that number minus one (for conventional and reserved memory) is the amount of extended memory. Newer machines are built to handle several megabytes of this type of memory. Earlier computers did not have this type of memory.

■ **Expanded memory (EMS)**: This is memory stored separately from your computer's RAM. Expanded memory was the first solution to the problem of insufficient memory when programs started needing more space than conventional memory can provide. Expanded memory can only hold the data you are using but not the programs you are running. Access to expanded memory is not as fast as to extended memory and requires that the programs that use this memory be specifically designed to use it. Expanded memory is designed to meet a set of specifications, usually LIM 3.2 or LIM 4.0. When you use expanded memory, your computer sets up page frames in reserved memory to handle the data in the expanded memory. If your computer (like most newer computers) has only extended memory, an expanded memory emulator (like EMM386.EXE, included with DOS) can be used to convert extended memory into expanded memory for programs that require it.

These different types of memory are diagrammed in Figure 9-1.

RAM

Extended Memory

1088K ....

High Memory Area

1024K

Reserved Memory

640K

Conventional Memory

0K

Expanded Memory

FIGURE 9-1   Different types of memory in a computer

What is the difference between RAM and ROM?

RAM stands for random access memory. The computer can both read and write to RAM. RAM is your computer's working memory. It is where programs are loaded when they are read from a storage device, such as a disk. When someone asks how much memory a computer has, they are talking about RAM.

ROM stands for read-only memory. The computer can read from ROM but cannot write to it. ROM can store small programs or instructions permanently on computer chips, such as ROM BIOS. These chips contain the main logic instructions, which govern the functioning of the computer or of a device such as a drive or a mouse.

Tech Tip: If your computer has a "shadow RAM" feature enabled, your computer will copy the contents of ROM into RAM in the reserved memory section when you boot up. The basic routines stored in ROM can be executed faster from RAM.

The games I used in DOS 5 worked fine in DOS 6 until I installed DoubleSpace. Why am I getting an "Insufficient memory" error message?

DoubleSpace consumes between 38K and 52K of memory, depending on your configuration. For memory-hungry applications (and games can be very memory-hungry), that loss of conventional memory can cause real problems. This is especially true when your computer has attachments such as a CD-ROM drive, a sound card, a SCSI drive, and a fax modem card, all of which may require device drivers to be loaded into memory. Try disabling drivers for anything not needed for the game, such as the fax and CD-ROM drivers. You may even want to create a multiple configuration menu (a new feature in DOS 6.0) so that when you boot your computer, you can configure your computer to disable the drivers for other attachments so you can run games, or to load all the device drivers without leaving enough memory for your games. For more information on multiple configuration menus, see this question in Chapter 10: "I want to use different CONFIG.SYS and AUTOEXEC.BAT files. Do I need to create separate boot disks for each set of CONFIG.SYS and AUTOEXEC.BAT files?"

How do I know what kind of memory I have on my computer?

For a quick look at memory statistics, type **MEM** at the DOS prompt and press ENTER. For more detailed information, Microsoft has included a Microsoft Diagnostic program with DOS 6.*x* that can report on your computer's components. Some of this information is very useful when you are trying to isolate a problem caused by hardware, software, or a combination of both. This Microsoft Diagnostic program can report on the memory your computer is using. To see this report, type **MSD** at the DOS prompt and press ENTER. After Microsoft Diagnostic evaluates your computer, you will see a main screen for selecting the type of information you want to see. Type **M** for Memory and Microsoft Diagnostic will display a screen like the one shown in Figure 9-2. The information on the right half of the dialog box lists the conventional memory, reserved memory, extended memory, and expanded memory your computer is using. You can also print this information by pressing ALT+F for the File menu and typing **P** for Print. When you select OK, you will print a report on your computer's components.

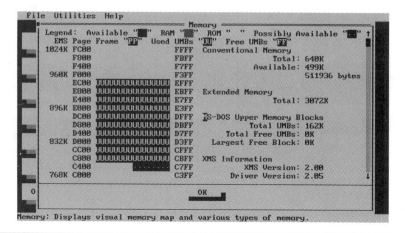

FIGURE 9-2   Dialog box showing information about memory

The message "Expanded memory services unavailable" displays when I start my computer. How can I use some of my upper memory?

You probably can. As long as you have these lines:

```
DEVICE=C:\DOS\HIMEM.SYS
DEVICE=C:\DOS\EMM386.EXE
```

and either one of these lines

```
DOS=UMB
DOS=HIGH,UMB
```

you should have upper memory available. If you get the above message, *and* no other error messages about expanded memory, you probably have the NOEMS parameter specified for EMM386.EXE. No expanded memory is provided by EMM386.EXE. If you need expanded memory as well as upper memory, remove the NOEMS parameter and replace it with either the word RAM or a number representing the amount of EMS in kilobytes that you want, as shown here:

```
DEVICE=C:\DOS\EMM386.EXE RAM
DEVICE=C:\DOS\EMM386.EXE 2048
```

The second example makes 2MB available as expanded memory, but does not allow upper memory block usage.

Tech Tip: The DOS MEM command will display the memory your computer is ready to use. When you type **MEM** at the DOS prompt and press ENTER, DOS displays a report of the available memory as shown in Figure 9-3.

 When I ran MemMaker, I chose to not set aside any EMS memory for my applications. How can I reconfigure my memory to include EMS memory for an application that requires it?

You can re-run MemMaker and choose to have EMS memory. Re-running MemMaker is the easiest way to set up your memory configuration for EMS. However, you can also accomplish this by

```
Memory Type        Total  =   Used   -    Free
----------------   -------    -------     -------
Conventional        640K       101K       539K
Upper                 0K         0K         0K
Reserved            384K       384K         0K
Extended (XMS)*   3,072K     1,504K     1,568K
----------------   -------    -------     -------
Total memory      4,096K     1,989K     2,107K

Total under 1 MB    640K       101K       539K

Total Expanded (EMS)                3,392K (3,473,408 bytes)
Free Expanded (EMS)*                1,808K (1,851,392 bytes)

* EMM386 is using XMS memory to simulate EMS memory as needed.
  Free EMS memory may change as free XMS memory changes.

Largest executable program size     539K (551,648 bytes)
Largest free upper memory block       0K       (0 bytes)
MS-DOS is resident in the high memory area.
```

FIGURE 9-3   Report created with the MEM command

editing your CONFIG.SYS file. In this file, you can change the line that contains the device driver EMM386.EXE. The line will look something like:

```
DEVICE=C:\DOS\EMM386.EXE NOEMS
```

Change this line to:

```
DEVICE=C:\DOS\EMM386.EXE RAM
```

How can I increase the 640K memory limit I have on my computer? Can running a DOS utility, adding more memory, or buying a newer computer help?

All computers have a limit of 640K of conventional memory when running DOS. Running a DOS utility, adding more memory, or buying a new computer will not change this limitation of DOS. This is because DOS is a 16-bit operating system and can only reference a maximum of 1,024K of memory, of which 640K is reserved for programs (conventional memory), and 384K for hardware use (reserved memory).

DOS 5 and above have made some of the reserved memory available to load additional programs that are otherwise placed into conventional memory. The EMM386.EXE memory manager, which comes with DOS, can convert any unused parts of this 384K area for use as upper memory blocks (UMBs), and can use extended memory to simulate expanded memory for programs that can use it. You can load device drivers and some memory-resident programs into UMBs instead of conventional memory. Putting both HIMEM.SYS and EMM386.EXE in the CONFIG.SYS file can usually provide you with an additional 100K or so in which to load programs. UMBs are a good place to load mouse and CD-ROM drivers, saving you valuable conventional memory space. To take advantage of the UMB, add the following lines to CONFIG.SYS before using any DEVICEHIGH and LOADHIGH commands:

```
DEVICE=C:\DOS\HIMEM.SYS
DEVICE=C:\DOS\EMM386.EXE
DOS=UMB
```

You will need to add NOEMS or RAM at the end of the second line to select whether you want any expanded memory.

Tech Tip: To use upper memory blocks, you must have a 386 or higher computer as well as the lines in your CONFIG.SYS file.

Every time I boot my machine it goes into MemMaker. What's wrong?

If MemMaker starts every time you boot your machine, it indicates that MemMaker did not successfully complete the memory optimization. When MemMaker starts, it adds lines to the CONFIG.SYS and AUTOEXEC.BAT files. These lines are removed when MemMaker finishes the memory optimization process. If MemMaker runs into some type of conflict, it may not complete this process. This leaves the lines in the CONFIG.SYS and AUTOEXEC.BAT files. Usually, this problem is caused by a line in the AUTOEXEC.BAT that, when executed, does not immediately return control of the system. Examples of these types of programs are menus, Windows, and other programs that you use to work with your data.

To fix the problem, exit to the DOS prompt, then edit the AUTOEXEC.BAT file. Type **REM** and a space at the beginning of any line that executes menus or other programs. Save the file and exit, then reboot. If your machine reboots directly to a DOS prompt after executing the AUTOEXEC.BAT file, then you are ready to run MemMaker. After MemMaker is complete, you can remove those REM (remark) statements.

My CONFIG.SYS file has DOS=HIGH, yet when I turn my computer on, I see the message "HMA not available; Loading DOS low." How do I get DOS to load high?

DOS cannot load itself into the high memory area if it does not exist or if the extended memory manager is not loaded. If your computer has extended memory, you have a high memory area. If you see this message, either your XMS manager (such as HIMEM.SYS) is not in the CONFIG.SYS, or it failed to load properly.

I get the message "EMM386 Exception Error #6" when I try to run an application. The application ran fine the last time I used it. What does this message mean?

Tech Tip: Remember that you can selectively execute lines in your CONFIG.SYS file instead of editing this file. Just press F8 when you see "Starting MS-DOS...," then type **y** or **n** to select which lines you want to execute.

EMM386 Exception #6 means "Invalid Opcode" or invalid instructions were sent to the processor. This error is usually caused by a corrupt file. If the application ran fine before and suddenly refuses to work correctly, this probably indicates that one or more of the files the application uses have become corrupted. The first thing to try is to re-install the application and try it. If the problem goes away, the application's files were probably in poor condition.

If the problem persists after reinstalling, you have a loaded TSR or RAM-resident program that is causing the trouble. You can edit the CONFIG.SYS and AUTOEXEC.BAT files and add REM followed by a space to lines for drivers and TSR programs that are not necessary to access the hardware. Reboot the computer and try the application again. If it works, remove REM and the space from one line at a time, rebooting and retrying the application after each line has been put back to original condition. When the message reappears, you will have determined what is at fault. Try putting a new copy of the driver or program on the hard drive and retrying the application. You may need to load the offending driver or program into conventional memory instead.

I ran DoubleSpace on my 286 computer with 2MB of RAM, now I get "Insufficient memory" messages from other applications. Why don't I have enough memory?

On a 80386 or higher processor, the EMM386.EXE driver can load other programs into upper memory. However, EMM386.EXE does not work on 286 computers. Since the DoubleSpace program takes 38K to 51K of memory, you may need a third-party program for the 286 to use memory above 640K, so DoubleSpace can be loaded outside of conventional memory.

What is the difference between the EMM386.EXE options, RAM, and NOEMS?

EMM386.EXE is a device driver for 80386 and higher computers. It has two primary functions. First, EMM386.EXE can simulate expanded memory using extended memory. Second, EMM386.EXE can manage the upper memory blocks when used in combination with DOS=UMB in the CONFIG.SYS file so device drivers or programs can be loaded high. These device drivers or programs are loaded high with the DEVICEHIGH instruction found in the CONFIG.SYS file and with the LOADHIGH instruction typically found in the AUTOEXEC.BAT file. By loading these various items high, your computer has more conventional memory left available for DOS-based applications.

The two options RAM and NOEMS are called *switches*. The RAM switch instructs EMM386.EXE to set up expanded memory as well as to manage upper memory blocks. EMM386.EXE uses room in the upper memory blocks to manage the expanded memory so less space is available to load programs into the UMA. The NOEMS switch enables the management of the upper memory area, but does not set up expanded memory. The advantage to using NOEMS is that more memory is free in the upper memory block area for programs to be loaded high.

I have 8MB of RAM on my computer. How do I tell MemMaker to use all of my RAM?

MemMaker does not optimize the use of all the system RAM, just the upper memory blocks. This stays the same no matter how much RAM your system has. Most DOS programs, however, need a certain amount of conventional memory (the memory below 640K), so MemMaker is useful for freeing up conventional memory. Running MemMaker automatically inserts all of the needed lines in CONFIG.SYS.

How can I tell if DOS loaded into the high memory area?

You can use the MEM command to display what is loaded into memory. Type **MEM** and press ENTER from a DOS prompt. This command displays a report like the one shown in Figure 9-3. This command's output tells you if MS-DOS is loaded into the high memory area. If MS-DOS cannot load into high memory, one of the following messages is displayed: "The high memory area is available" or "High memory area is in use."

After upgrading to DOS 6.x, CTRL-ALT-DEL does not reboot my machine. How do I get this key combination to work?

On your machine, EMM386.EXE is not monitoring and intercepting when you press CTRL+ALT+DEL. To get this key combination to work, you need to add ALTBOOT to the EMM386.EXE line in the CONFIG.SYS file, as shown here:

```
DEVICE=C:\DOS\EMM386.EXE NOEMS ALTBOOT
```

I have DOS=HIGH in my CONFIG.SYS file, but none of my terminate-and-stay-resident (TSR) programs seem to be loading into high memory. What am I doing wrong?

The command DOS=HIGH instructs DOS to load itself into the high memory area. It does *not* enable access to the upper memory blocks. Add DOS=UMB to the CONFIG.SYS file to enable this functionality. However, before your computer can load TSR programs into upper memory using the DEVICEHIGH and LOADHIGH (also abbreviated as LH) commands, you must add the following lines to the CONFIG.SYS file:

```
DEVICE=C:\DOS\HIMEM.SYS
DEVICE=C:\DOS\EMM386.EXE NOEMS
DOS=UMB
```

The second line can also be DEVICE=C:\DOS\EMM386.EXE RAM. These lines assume EMM386.ESE is installed in your DOS directory on drive C.

Please note:

- The HIMEM.SYS line must appear *before* the line for EMM386.EXE.

- You must provide the complete path for your memory drivers. For example, DEVICE=C:\DOS\HIMEM.SYS is acceptable but DEVICE=HIMEM.SYS may not be.

- You must use either the NOEMS or RAM switch on the EMM386 line in order to use the UMBs. The RAM switch instructs EMM386.EXE to set up expanded memory when an application needs it. The NOEMS switch instructs EMM386.EXE not to provide expanded memory.

- If you want to load part of DOS into the high memory area and also enable the UMBs, you can combine the two lines into one as shown here:

```
DOS=HIGH,UMB
```

My computer has a 512K cache and a 1MB video RAM. Why doesn't this memory get included by the MEM command?

Cache memory and video RAM are separate from your computer's RAM. Cache memory and video RAM are dedicated for specific purposes. Cache memory temporarily stores data that will be used by your computer and is faster than your computer's regular memory. Video memory is specifically built to handle sending and receiving information simultaneously to improve your computer screen's appearance. Both of these types of memory are not included in the MEM command's output.

What does the HIGHSCAN parameter on the EMM386.EXE line in my CONFIG.SYS file do?

The HIGHSCAN parameter tells EMM386.EXE to scan the upper region in the upper memory area (addresses F000-FFFF) for free blocks of memory that might be usable for upper memory blocks (UMB). Using this parameter may yield slightly more upper memory for loading device drivers and TSRs into the UMB. On some systems, using this area of memory can cause problems, so if you experience lockups or error messages relating to memory, try removing the HIGHSCAN parameter.

When I boot, I get the error message "Size of expanded memory pool adjusted. Press any key when ready...", but then it says "EMM386 successfully installed." I am specifying 8MB of expanded memory and I know that I have 8MB in my machine. Am I getting expanded memory or not?

The message you are getting is not an error, but a notification. If your machine has 8MB of RAM, you typically only have a maximum of 7MB available for expanded memory. The first megabyte is reserved for conventional memory and reserved memory. Also, if you load DOS high, you lose another 64K to DOS. EMM386.EXE realizes that you have less memory available for expanded memory than what you are asking for, so it displays this message to let you know that it is using as much as it can allocate.

Additionally, you will also get this message depending on the size of expanded memory you ask for. EMM386 sets up expanded memory in 16K pages, so if you are asking for an amount of expanded memory that is not a multiple of 16, EMM386.EXE adjusts to the next lowest multiple of 16, and gives you the message to let you know it has done so.

Anytime you are not sure how much expanded memory you have, you can type **EMM386** at the DOS prompt and press ENTER to display information as shown in the illustration on the next page.

```
MICROSOFT Expanded Memory Manager 386   Version 4.48
Copyright Microsoft Corporation 1986, 1993

  Available expanded memory . . . . . . . .   3008 KB

  LIM/EMS version . . . . . . . . . . . . .    4.0
  Total expanded memory pages . . . . . . .    212
  Available expanded memory pages . . . . .    188
  Total handles . . . . . . . . . . . . .       64
  Active handles  . . . . . . . . . . . . .      1
  Page frame segment  . . . . . . . . . . .   E000 H

  Total upper memory available  . . . . . .      0 KB
  Largest Upper Memory Block available  . .      0 KB
  Upper memory starting address . . . . . .   C800 H

EMM386 Active.
```

Since running MemMaker I have been receiving a parity error on my computer. How can I get rid of this error?

A parity error is generated by the hardware. The system constantly checks data going into and out of RAM to make sure that the memory remains reliable. When a RAM chip becomes faulty, the parity chip sends a signal to the central processing unit (CPU) telling it to halt the system (most of the time) and displays the message you see on your screen.

You are seeing this error now since MemMaker provided access to memory that you were not using. To resolve the issue, note the entire error message and contact a local hardware repair person so the faulty memory can be tested and replaced. A temporary solution is to boot your system and press F5 to do a clean boot, or press F8 to boot your computer and select which commands from CONFIG.SYS and AUTOEXEC.BAT are performed. If you press F8, skip the commands that operate on high memory. You will not be able to use the higher memory until you get the hardware problem resolved.

How do I find out what is using my computer's conventional memory?

You can list the programs in conventional and reserved memory and the memory these programs use by typing **MEM /C** (the C is short for Classify) and pressing ENTER. When you enter this command, DOS displays information like that shown in Figure 9-4. You can see which programs are loaded into conventional and reserved memory as well as their sizes. The report is usually larger than one screen, so you can also add the /P switch to generate the report one screen at a time as in Figure 9-4.

```
Modules using memory below 1 MB:

  Name           Total      =   Conventional  +   Upper Memory
  --------    ----------------    ----------------    ----------------
  MSDOS        19,053   (19K)     19,053   (19K)          0   (0K)
  HIMEM         1,104    (1K)      1,104    (1K)          0   (0K)
  EMM386        4,144    (4K)      4,144    (4K)          0   (0K)
  COMMAND       2,928    (3K)      2,928    (3K)          0   (0K)
  SNAP        105,952  (103K)    105,952  (103K)          0   (0K)
  SETVER          832    (1K)          0    (0K)        832   (1K)
  ANSI          4,240    (4K)          0    (0K)      4,240   (4K)
  SMARTDRV     27,488   (27K)          0    (0K)     27,488  (27K)
  SHARE        25,936   (25K)          0    (0K)     25,936  (25K)
  DOSKEY        4,144    (4K)          0    (0K)      4,144   (4K)
  MOUSE        17,296   (17K)          0    (0K)     17,296  (17K)
  Free        600,656  (587K)    522,000  (510K)     78,656  (77K)

Memory Summary:

  Type of Memory       Total    =    Used    +    Free
  ----------------    ----------    ----------    ----------
  Conventional        655,360       133,360       522,000
  Upper               158,592        79,936        78,656
Press any key to continue . . .
```

FIGURE 9-4   Report created with **MEM /C/P**

After upgrading my Packard Bell computer to DOS 6.x, Microsoft Windows will not run in 386 Enhanced mode. I am using the new version of EMM386.EXE. Windows ran fine with my previous version of DOS. What happened?

Windows stopped working because Packard Bell's version of Microsoft Windows 3.1 (an OEM version of Microsoft Windows) typically installs Windows to use the Packard Bell video display driver HTVDD.386. This driver uses the same memory addresses as EMM386.EXE—C600-C7FF. To correct the problem, simply use the DOS Editor to add a memory address exclusion to the EMM386.EXE line of the CONFIG.SYS file and exclude this address.

Before the exclusion, the line may look like this:

```
DEVICE=C:\DOS\EMM386.EXE RAM
```

After the exclusion, it looks like this:

```
DEVICE=C:\DOS\EMM386.EXE RAM X=C600-C7FF
```

You can also correct the problem by using a standard Microsoft Windows 3.1 video display driver instead of Packard Bell's HTVDD.386.

Tech Tip: This problem also occurs with Packard Bell Windows 3.0 and EMM386.EXE. If you are running DOS 6 with Windows 3.0, add the X=C600-C7FF line to the EMM386.EXE line in CONFIG.SYS.

Why did MemMaker put DOS=UMB and DOS=HIGH on separate lines?

While DOS=UMB and DOS=HIGH can be combined as in DOS=UMB,HIGH, you do not have to combine them. MemMaker uses the separate line method since not every system will have the DOS=HIGH setting activated. Having MemMaker insert two separate lines was a simpler method to implement while writing the program. There is no functional difference between having the two items together or apart, since both commands are processed at the start of CONFIG.SYS regardless of their actual location in the file.

I just added more memory to my 486 EISA computer so now I have more than 16MB total RAM. I am using DOS's HIMEM.SYS for my extended memory manager. However, DOS's MEM command only reports 16MB. Why doesn't MEM show all of the memory?

EISA computer systems require a special switch for HIMEM.SYS to recognize more than 16MB of memory installed. If your computer's CMOS settings are correct for the new amount of total memory, adding the /EISA switch to the HIMEM.SYS device line in your CONFIG.SYS file will correct the problem. For example, the line may originally look like this:

```
DEVICE=C:\DOS\HIMEM.SYS
```

After adding the switch, the line would look like this:

```
DEVICE=C:\DOS\HIMEM.SYS /EISA
```

I get the error message "Bad or missing *file name*" listed for EMM386.EXE and HIMEM.SYS every time I boot up. I am running Stacker on my computer. Doesn't Stacker work with high memory?

Stacker maintains a separate copy of your CONFIG.SYS and AUTOEXEC.BAT files on its host drive, which is usually drive D. When you first turn your computer on, the only drive recognized is the host drive, which at that time is labeled as drive C. Since HIMEM.SYS and EMM386.EXE usually load early in the CONFIG.SYS file, before Stacker activates, DOS is trying to find those files on the Stacker host drive. Copy HIMEM.SYS and

EMM386.EXE to the host drive, then check the copy of
CONFIG.SYS on the host drive to see that the files are being
loaded from the proper place.

Tech Tip: If any line in your CONFIG.SYS or AUTOEXEC.BAT file displays
the "Bad command or file name" message, check that you have
supplied the correct location for the file.

When running a program, my computer displays the message "EMM386 DMA buffer is too small." What is causing this and how can I prevent it?

The program that displays this message probably performs
something called direct memory access (DMA), which is a fast
method of moving data directly to RAM without going through
your computer's processor. This program needs a different
memory configuration containing a larger DMA buffer to work
properly. Edit your CONFIG.SYS file and add "D=48" to the end
of the line containing EMM386.EXE. For example, before
editing, the line would look like this:

```
DEVICE=C:\DOS\EMM386.EXE RAM
```

After editing, it would look like this:

```
DEVICE=C:\DOS\EMM386.EXE RAM D=48
```

Save the changes, reboot, and then try the program again.
MemMaker may also produce this error if Quarterdeck's
QEMM is being used instead of DOS memory managers. The
solution is to first get rid of QEMM and use HIMEM.SYS and
EMM386.EXE and also add "D=48" to EMM386.

Tech Tip: If Windows 3.1 is the only application displaying
this message, you can also solve this problem by editing
the \WINDOWS\SYSTEM.INI file. In the [Enh386] section,
change the number after DMABUFFERSIZE= to 48.

Can I manually optimize and improve on MemMaker's UMB configuration?

If you are willing to spend the time, you can probably improve on MemMaker's configuration for UMB. At best, MemMaker and other memory management products can only make a "best guess" based on information that is contained as part of the product. You, on the other hand, can experiment with a wider range of combinations and verify with better accuracy how well those combinations function on your system. You can change the order of the different components of the CONFIG.SYS and AUTOEXEC.BAT files loading into the UMA, which might yield better management of the available space in the UMA. Loading larger components first, and then working your way down will usually fit more components into the UMA, because the UMA will have contiguous space. To load a driver in the UMA, a large enough UMB (which is a contiguous block in the UMA) must be available. You can also map out available space more aggressively in the UMA than some of the memory managers. Be prepared to spend a good amount of time doing this—it requires a lot of trial-and-error testing, and will never be as fast as MemMaker!

Why does EMM386.EXE tell me "Cannot establish page frame"?

EMM386.EXE displays this message when it cannot create the page frames needed to establish expanded memory. For EMM386.EXE to establish page frames for expanded memory, your computer must meet the following four requirements:

1. A 386 or higher processor.

2. Sufficient extended memory (typically 384K in addition to reserved memory).

3. Either the line "DOS=UMB" or "DOS=HIGH,UMB" in CONFIG.SYS.

4. The RAM switch, AUTO switch, or a number specifying the amount of EMS you require on the EMM386.EXE line in the CONFIG.SYS.

After those requirements have been met, check for the following:

■ Is the A20 handler enabled? The A20 handler gives your computer access to the high memory area. Check for a message from the HIMEM.SYS driver during the bootup process that indicates that this handler is disabled. When the A20 handler is enabled, typing **MEM** at the DOS prompt and pressing ENTER will show DOS resident in the high memory area, assuming you are loading DOS into high memory in the CONFIG.SYS file.

■ Are there network cards, modems, scanners, or other cards installed in upper memory blocks? Remember, they occupy the same area of memory where the page frame resides. Use Microsoft Diagnostic's memory option to see if a contiguous block of the UMA is available. To do this, type **MSD** at the DOS prompt and press ENTER, then select Memory. MSD displays a report of your computer's memory like the one shown in Figure 9-2 earlier in this chapter. You can also see where the different programs loaded into memory reside by selecting Memory Block Display from the Utilities menu in MSD. By moving up and down through the list of allocated memory you can see the blocks that each loaded item occupies (conventional memory ends at address A000 and reserved memory ends at F000). Figure 9-5 shows the dialog box this command displays. The |---| represents the block filled by MOUSE.COM and the U's represent other UMBs. You may need to modify memory settings for your computer's hardware to move the address range for other programs loaded in the UMBs in order to make room for a larger page frame area. If your application supports LIM 4.0 specifications you can use the Pn parameter to set up your page frame. For example, you can change the EMM386.EXE line in your CONFIG.SYS file to look like this:

Tech Tip: A message indicating that the A20 handler has been enabled is a good indication that HIMEM.SYS is functioning properly. If HIMEM.SYS isn't working correctly, EMM386 probably won't either.

```
DEVICE=C:\DOS\EMM386.EXE p0=c400 p1=d000 p2=d400 p3=e000
```

This example breaks the page into four smaller 16K segments. Note that applications that are designed for LIM 3.2 specifications cannot work with this type of page frame.

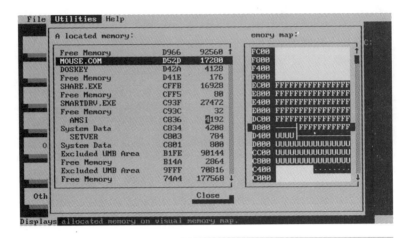

FIGURE 9-5   MSD displaying the sections of memory programs use

I have already optimized my memory but I need "just a little more." How can I get it?

You can tweak a little more memory by following these steps:

- Remove the device drivers you do not need. Go through CONFIG.SYS and AUTOEXEC.BAT and remark out anything that you do not absolutely *need*. Some examples are: DEVICE=C:\DOS\ANSI.SYS, if you are not planning on using different screen colors while at the DOS prompt, or DEVICE=C:\DOS\SETVER.EXE, if you don't need any old files or programs that are only compatible with older versions of DOS. DOSKEY is another possibility if you are willing to forgo its convenience.

- Reduce the space DOS sets up to handle your open files. In CONFIG.SYS, set the "Files=XX" line to the minimum number that is required. Each file that is allocated takes 100 bytes of conventional RAM. If you're not sure, set it to a lower number and reboot. If you run your programs and you get a message that says "Not enough file handles," the number is too low. A good starting point is "Files=35" if you have Windows and "Files=30" if you don't.

- Reduce the space DOS sets up for buffers. Each buffer takes 512 bytes plus a small amount of overhead (usually about 20 bytes) for a total of 532 bytes. For example, decreasing the buffers from 100 to 50 will save 26,600 bytes or approximately 26K of conventional memory. In CONFIG.SYS, set the "Buffers=XX,X" line to a smaller number. Some guidelines are:

  - If using DoubleSpace and DOS 6.2, set "Buffers=10,0"
  - If using SMARTDrive and Windows, set "Buffers=10,0"
  - If using an 80286 with 1MB or more, set "Buffers=43,0" (unless either of the above conditions applies)

- Reduce the space reserved for environment variables. The environment space is defined in the "SHELL=" line of CONFIG.SYS. A typical line might read:

```
SHELL=C:\DOS\COMMAND.COM C:\DOS\ /E:512 /P
```

  The environment size is specified by the "/e:512" portion where the environment is set to 512 bytes in this example. The default is set at 256 bytes. Unless you have seen the error message "Out of environment space," you do not have a problem and may not need to set it higher than the default.

- Reduce the number of stacks DOS reserves for handling hardware interrupts. If you're not running Windows, you most likely don't need to have the "Stacks=" line set to anything greater than the default (9,128). Windows needs stacks to be set to 9,256. The stacks line specifies stacks in the following manner: Stacks=number of stacks,bytes in each stack. Therefore, "stacks=9,256" sets up 9 stacks at 256 bytes per stack for a total of 2304 bytes or 2.25K.

I am unable to load SHARE at all. Is something wrong with the SHARE command?

The probable cause for this condition is the other programs loaded into the UMA. This condition happens frequently with network shells/redirectors which must intercept

DOS commands to check for network-specific commands. Due to the nature of the drivers and how they process all commands before passing functions to DOS, they need to function correctly before SHARE can function correctly. SHARE may fail to load, or it may load properly but fail to function (sharing violation errors, hangups, damaged data files) if the "interceptor" programs are not passing commands back to DOS properly.

This condition is not limited to network drivers, but could happen with any driver that tries to process a command first before letting DOS have access to the command.

Try loading all drivers into conventional memory. If SHARE works, start placing drivers and TSRs back into upper memory one at a time, until SHARE fails again. The last item moved into upper memory is the culprit.

I was running a terminal emulator for an IBM 3270 to connect my computer to a mainframe, and I was downloading a big file when my computer hung. Is this a memory problem?

Assuming everything else works fine, and you have no TSRs running or any hardware problems, you may want to adjust the DMA buffer size. You can change the DMA buffer size by changing the "DEVICE=C:\DOS\EMM386.EXE" line in the CONFIG.SYS. DOS 6 changed the default size from 16K to 32K. A recommended size when you run into this problem is 48K. Change your EMM386.EXE line to read: DEVICE=C:\DOS\EMM386.EXE D=48. This creates a 48K buffer for direct memory access (DMA) in extended memory. Reboot and then retry the operation. Most 3270 emulator software has been updated to correct DMA problems. Ideally, you should contact the software's vendor for an upgrade.

Since I upgraded to DOS 6.2, my computer hangs with a DoubleGuard message. What is going wrong?

The DoubleGuard feature of DoubleSpace in DOS 6.2 has detected that some other program is trying to overwrite the memory area that the DoubleSpace compression engine occupies in memory. You'll need to try to duplicate the problem, so that you can determine which program is damaging the DoubleSpace program in memory. If the problem happens while running more than one program, look for drivers and TSRs loading in the CONFIG.SYS and AUTOEXEC.BAT as the source.

You can disable the DoubleGuard feature, although this is dangerous—data loss could result if the DoubleSpace program is damaged and tries to write data to the hard drive. Type **DBLSPACE /DOUBLEGUARD=0** and press ENTER to disable DoubleGuard. You'll need to reboot for this change to take effect. If you are using the QEMM memory manager, you should also look at the question "I just ran the Stepup upgrade for DOS 6.2. When I boot the computer, I get a DoubleGuard Alarm error and the computer hangs up. I am using QEMM386 for my memory management functions. What's wrong?" in Chapter 11 for more information about the DoubleGuard message you might receive while using this memory manager.

I received a "WARNING: EMM386 installed without a LIM 3.2 compatible page frame" message when I booted my computer, and my programs don't recognize the expanded memory that EMM386 created. What is wrong?

Nothing is wrong. The warning you saw is designed to alert you that the expanded memory that EMM386.EXE created does not meet LIM 3.2 specifications. The expanded memory that EMM386.EXE created instead meets LIM 4.0 specifications. Programs that are designed to use expanded memory following LIM 3.2 specifications cannot use expanded memory that follows LIM 4.0 specifications if the page frames this expanded memory uses are partial or noncontiguous page frames. EMM386.EXE can create a partial or a noncontiguous page frame in 16K blocks using the Pn parameter. For example, this command in CONFIG.SYS will create a noncontiguous page frame:

```
DEVICE=C:\DOS\EMM386.EXE P0=C800 P1=CC00 P2=D800 P3=DC00 RAM
```

This command in CONFIG.SYS will create a partial page frame:

```
DEVICE=C:\DOS\EMM386.EXE P1=D800 RAM
```

Both of these options creates page frames following the LIM 4.0 specification. Therefore, any application written to conform to LIM 3.2 will not recognize any expanded memory. With either option in your CONFIG.SYS file, you will receive the message during bootup so you are aware that programs that use the expanded memory must accept the LIM 4.0 specifications for expanded memory.

Configuration Issues

Although you can use DOS as it is installed, many users want to tailor its features to their own needs. Making better use of memory, utilizing device drivers, defining work areas, and customizing their use of hardware are just a few of the changes desired. Because these changes are made once and stored in AUTOEXEC.BAT or CONFIG.SYS, it is easy to forget how to make a specific type of change. Even experienced users tend to forget what command to use, which file to store the instruction in, and what to do when things go wrong.

Because each person's environment and needs are different, software manufacturers cannot supply one set of configuration options to meet everyone's needs. If you want to utilize your computer effectively, you should customize your configuration. The entries in the following Frustration Busters box offer some guidelines that can help you prevent problems before they start.

FRUSTRATION BUSTERS!

The first step in avoiding bootup problems is understanding what happens when your computer boots up. Your computer performs several steps between startup and the appearance of the final DOS prompt. In the boot process, your computer:

- Performs the Power-On-Self-Test (POST). POST tests that your computer's memory is functioning correctly, that all expected equipment is present, and that the disk drives are working.

- Determines on which drive to load the operating system as described in the system's BIOS settings. Most systems are configured to check drive A first, then drive C, in the following steps:

  1. If you have a boot disk in drive A, your computer boots from drive A.

  2. If you have a disk in drive A that is not a boot disk, you see the message "Non-System disk or disk error; Replace and press any key when ready."

  3. If you do not have a disk in drive A, your computer looks at the beginning of your first hard disk. The first sector of the drive tells the computer where to find the information it needs to boot. This information is included in two hidden files, called IO.SYS and MSDOS.SYS. If you have a compressed disk, your computer also uses DBLSPACE.BIN. Additionally, you usually have a CONFIG.SYS and an AUTOEXEC.BAT file. These files are not required but make parts of your computer work or work better. You also have DBLSPACE.INI if you have a compressed drive.

- Loads the information in the hidden system files.

- Processes the information in CONFIG.SYS if this file is available. CONFIG.SYS is where you put certain types of commands. Some of the DOS features such as HIMEM.SYS and EMM386.EXE require that they be loaded in CONFIG.SYS. "FILES=" and "BUFFERS=" in CONFIG.SYS set up file handles and buffers in your computer's memory that other programs use as they open and work with the contents of your files. CONFIG.SYS often loads the software that runs your mouse. It can put information into UMB that is a special part of memory beyond conventional and before extended memory. HIMEM.SYS, if loaded, will also perform memory testing that is more extensive than the initial memory test (DOS 6.2 only).

■ Loads the COMMAND.COM in the root directory, or the command interpreter specified in the "SHELL=" line in CONFIG.SYS.

■ Processes the information in AUTOEXEC.BAT if this file is available. AUTOEXEC.BAT is a batch file that contains DOS commands that you want performed every time you start your computer. Some DOS programs such as SMARTDrive and SHARE are loaded at this point. AUTOEXEC.BAT frequently has the PATH command to set where DOS looks for files you are using when the files are not in the current directory. AUTOEXEC.BAT also frequently contains the PROMPT command to change the DOS prompt.

I have an application whose Setup program requires installation from floppy drive A, but my disks fit in my floppy drive B. Is there any way to install the program?

Most likely you can either reverse the letters or make drive B function as drive A with the DOS SUBST command. Usually, the DOS SUBST command will work with setup routines that specify drive A. To make drive B function as drive A, make your DOS directory the current directory and type **SUBST A: B:** and press ENTER. To see if it worked, put a disk in drive B and type **DIR A:** and press ENTER. You should get a directory listing of the disk you just placed in the drive you normally refer to as drive B. To revert back to the original configuration, type **SUBST A: /d** and press ENTER.

Older versions of DOS included the ASSIGN command, which could be used for the same purpose. For DOS 6.*x*, this command is available only with the supplemental disk. Contact

Tech Tip: Some programs cannot be "fooled" by SUBST or ASSIGN. For example, this technique cannot be used on the MS-DOS 6.*x* Setup program.

Microsoft Consumer Sales at (800) 426-9400 for more information on obtaining the supplemental disk for your 6.*x* version of DOS.

To use ASSIGN to make the switch, you must first make sure ASSIGN is installed in your DOS directory. Then, simply make your DOS directory the current directory and type **ASSIGN B=A** and press ENTER. This should have the same effect as the SUBST command outlined above. If you want to *reverse* the drives temporarily, type **ASSIGN B=A A=B** and press ENTER. Then, when you type commands for drive A, you'll be accessing drive B. When you type commands for drive B, you'll be accessing drive A. To cancel the effects of the ASSIGN command, simply retype **ASSIGN** without any parameters and press ENTER, or reboot the computer.

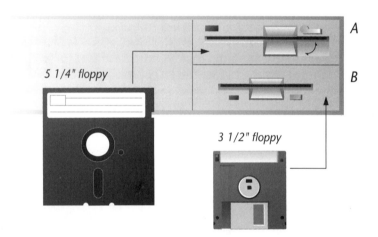

5 1/4" floppy

3 1/2" floppy

A

B

Every time I boot my computer since installing MS-DOS 6.2, HIMEM.SYS says there are problems with my RAM. If I boot without HIMEM.SYS, it runs fine. How do I turn off this warning?

This error message occurs when memory chips fail the more extensive memory test that HIMEM.SYS performs. The regular memory test that occurs at the beginning of the boot process is

Chapter 10 *Configuration Issues*

191

not finding a problem and that is why you do not see the message without HIMEM.SYS. Most of the time, it means that there is a problem with hardware. As long as your application had not accessed the bad memory, you would not have encountered a problem if this is the cause. In addition to problems with the RAM chips, problems could exist in the on-board cache. To disable the test until you can get the memory checked, add the "/TESTMEM:OFF" switch on the HIMEM.SYS line in CONFIG.SYS. For example, you might change the line to look like this: C:\DOS\HIMEM.SYS /TESTMEM:OFF. However, this is only a temporary solution until you get your computer tested.

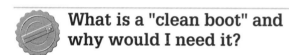

What is a "clean boot" and why would I need it?

A "clean boot" is booting, or starting, the computer without invoking either the CONFIG.SYS or AUTOEXEC.BAT file. These files are automatically processed if they are present in the root directory of the boot drive. Some reasons you may want to "clean boot" your computer are:

- To troubleshoot a problem: For example, you are having trouble with an application's performance, such as frequent locking up or other unexplained behavior. Clean booting and retrying the application lets you attempt to use the program without other programs loaded in memory. If this takes care of your problem, you know that the other applications loaded in CONFIG.SYS and AUTOEXEC.BAT are conflicting with the new program.

- To install a new product: Sometimes, installation procedures will instruct you to disable certain types of software when installing a new product. Clean booting is an easy way to accomplish this.

To "clean boot" DOS 6.x, reboot the computer, and the instant you see the phrase "Starting MS-DOS," press F5. DOS will display the following message:

```
Starting MS-DOS...

MS-DOS is bypassing your CONFIG.SYS and AUTOEXEC.BAT files.


Microsoft(R) MS-DOS(R) Version 6.20
          (C)Copyright Microsoft Corp 1981-1993.

C:\>
```

If you are using Microsoft Windows, you will need to execute a few of the commands in CONFIG.SYS. Reboot the computer, and the instant you see the phrase "Starting MS-DOS," press the function key F8. DOS will then display the first message shown in Figure 10-1 and then for every command in CONFIG.SYS, MS-DOS will prompt you to type **y** or **n** to select whether you want each command in this file performed.

Type **y** to the four lines that contain HIMEM.SYS; FILES; BUFFERS; and SHELL. Type **n** to any other line. If you want to process AUTOEXEC.BAT, type **n** when prompted to skip processing the commands in this file. Since skipping the AUTOEXEC.BAT file also skips your Path statement, you'll need to change to the WINDOWS directory, then type **WIN** and press ENTER to start Windows.

```
Starting MS-DOS...

MS-DOS will prompt you to confirm each CONFIG.SYS command.
DEVICE=C:\DOS\HIMEM.SYS [Y,N]?Y

HIMEM is testing extended memory...done.
DEVICE=C:\DOS\SMARTDRV.EXE /DOUBLE_BUFFER [Y,N]?N
DEVICE=C:\DOS\EMM386.EXE NOEMS [Y,N]?N
BUFFERS=10,0 [Y,N]?Y
FILES=50 [Y,N]?Y
DOS=UMB,HIGH [Y,N]?N
LASTDRIVE=E [Y,N]?N
STACKS=9,256 [Y,N]?N
SHELL=C:\DOS\COMMAND.COM C:\DOS\  /p [Y,N]?Y
```

FIGURE 10-1   Stepping through your CONFIG.SYS file

Tech Tip: If you have a version of DOS prior to 6.*x*, you can clean boot a computer by starting your computer from a bootable floppy disk. To do this, format a bootable system disk for your A drive with the /S switch. Simply type **FORMAT A: /S** and press ENTER. This command formats the disk and includes the minimum files needed to start your computer. Then, to "clean boot," just start the computer from that disk.

I created a "clean boot" system disk and rebooted my machine with it in drive A, but my system ignored it and just booted from drive C. Did I do something wrong?

If your system does not look at drive A for a disk to boot from, your machine's hardware settings may be configured *not* to look for a boot disk in drive A. Some machines have an option to only boot from drive C. Consult your hardware documentation for information on how to change this.

Tech Tip: If you are using a workstation on a network, this option may have been set up by your network administrator as a security measure.

I just installed MS-DOS 6.2 on my computer, and now it hangs every time I try to access my A or B drive. Why?

This can be caused by the presence of a third-party disk caching utility such as Norton's NCACHE. Disable the third-party cache and use SMARTDrive instead. See the question "What is SMARTDrive and how will it benefit my system?" later in this chapter for more information about the SMARTDrive utility.

Tech Terror: Although it is illegal to install multiple copies of utilities and other programs on multiple computers, some users do it anyway. This leaves them without documentation for how to remove the software if they need to.

I have heard coworkers use the term "cash" when referring to their computer. What is it?

What a *cache* (pronounced "cash") actually does is to "buffer" or store disk information that has been read or is about to be written. It is a temporary holding area for information that the computer is not ready to process yet.

For example, suppose you just opened a database and looked at the first three records. The disk cache stores the records as they are read from the hard disk. When you switch back to the second or first record, the data is already in memory so your computer does not have to look at the disk again. When saving data, the information first goes into the cache. When the computer's processor is finished with other computing tasks, it uses some otherwise idle time to actually write the data to the hard disk. This caching or buffering acts as a fast intermediate step that speeds up the computer's response time. Caching makes your computer faster because accessing data in memory does not require as much time as accessing data from a disk.

A cache is actually a process or an operation and not a physical entity. A cache can be implemented with either hardware or software. A hardware cache is a special type of memory chip(s) that has a much faster access time and can read and write from and to memory very quickly. The memory is dedicated to this task and cannot be used for any other purpose. A software cache is a software program that uses some of the general purpose RAM for cache purposes. This software borrows nondedicated RAM and configures it to be used as cache. A software cache provides time savings but does not offer as big of an advantage as the dedicated hardware cache. A software cache is much less expensive compared to the high cost of the very fast RAM used for a dedicated cache. The cache that MS-DOS provides is called SMARTDRV, pronounced "smart drive." See the question "What is SMARTDrive and how will it benefit my system?" later in this chapter for more information about the SMARTDrive utility.

What does it mean when DOS displays "Bad command or file name"?

When you see the "Bad command or file name" message, it is usually caused by one of three things:

1. The command you entered may be misspelled. Correctly spelling the command fixes this problem.

2. The filename you specified was not in the current directory and the Path statement does not contain the directory that the file/command you are typing is in.

3. The file does not exist on the disk/drive that the current prompt indicates. Switching to the directory containing the executable file fixes the last two problems.

If you see this message when you start your computer, it means that one of the commands in your AUTOEXEC.BAT file did not execute due to one of the three reasons listed above. Commands in CONFIG.SYS must specify the entire path and filename in order for the program or device driver to be found. Commands in AUTOEXEC.BAT will work with just the program/filename only if the command is located after the PATH line and the proper directory is included in the PATH.

What is the BUFFERS command used for in the CONFIG.SYS file?

The BUFFERS command sets up a built-in disk cache. This disk cache can cache all drives and loads into the high memory area with DOS, provided that there is enough room to fit all the buffers specified. Each buffer uses approximately 532 bytes and there will always be at least one buffer loaded low. The maximum number of buffers that can be is 48. The buffers cache is only good for small amounts of data while SMARTDrive is good for much larger data transfers.

What is SMARTDrive and how will it benefit my system?

SMARTDrive is a read/write cache that improves performance by writing the most recently used information to RAM temporarily. This allows the actual disk write operation to be performed when the system has a fraction of a second of idle time. SMARTDrive is run with the SMARTDRV DOS command. All data read from the hard drive is also stored in RAM temporarily—if the same data is needed again, SMARTDrive reads from RAM rather than from the disk. Accessing data from RAM is much faster than even the fastest hard disks. The system can retrieve data from RAM in nanoseconds (one-billionth of a second) while retrieving from hard disks takes milliseconds (one-thousandth of a second).

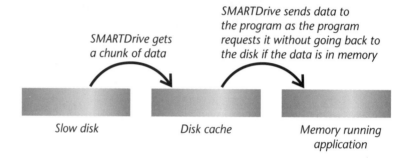

SMARTDrive gets a chunk of data

SMARTDrive sends data to the program as the program requests it without going back to the disk if the data is in memory

Slow disk   *Disk cache*   *Memory running application*

What does the FCBS command in the CONFIG.SYS mean?

FCBS stands for "file control blocks," which contain information about open files—the name, physical location, etc. The number specified by "FCBS=" indicates how many files can be open at one time using file control blocks. File control blocks are only important to programs that use them to keep track of the open files. Programs can use file handles rather than file control blocks to keep track of the open files. Since newer programs use file handles set with the FILES command, the number after "FILES=" is usually more important than the number after the "FCBS=".

I always see the line "@ECHO OFF" in AUTOEXEC.BAT files. If I don't add that line, what will happen?

"@ECHO OFF" simply prevents all subsequent lines from being displayed on the screen. An "@" at the beginning of any line suppresses the display of that line only. If "@ECHO OFF" is the first line of AUTOEXEC.BAT, you will not see any of the lines of AUTOEXEC.BAT displayed (although you will see information displayed by any programs that run as AUTOEXEC.BAT commands are processed). "@ECHO OFF" reduces the messages you see when you start your system. If you want to see the messages from when you start your system, type **REM** at the front of this line to have this line ignored.

When I booted my computer, I got the message "Unrecognized command in CONFIG.SYS line" and a line number. How do I fix this problem?

The line DOS threw a fit over probably has a spelling mistake or describes a file that is in a different location. First, reboot your system and press F8 when you see "Starting DOS...." Next, type **y** for each command *except* the one that caused the problem before (type **n** for that one). Then edit the CONFIG.SYS file and fix the error.

I'm getting the "Bad or Missing Command Interpreter" message, but then I get a DOS prompt. Still, nothing seems to work. I've seen the error message in MS-DOS 5 before, but I was never able to get a DOS prompt. What's going on?

This is a new feature in MS-DOS 6.*x*. Instead of simply halting the system, you have the opportunity to tell MS-DOS where to look for the COMMAND.COM. COMMAND.COM is a command interpreter that takes your entries at the DOS prompt and processes them. You can type **C:\COMMAND.COM** or **C:\DOS\COMMAND.COM** and then press ENTER. Or you can put a boot disk into a floppy drive and tell the system to look there by typing **A:\COMMAND.COM**, for example, and pressing ENTER. If a command interpreter is successfully found, you'll get a "real" prompt that functions normally. To keep the "Bad or Missing Command Interpreter" message from coming back, copy the COMMAND.COM from the location you specified in the last step into the root directory of your boot drive. For example, if you have to put a boot disk in drive A and use the COMMAND.COM there, type **COPY A:\COMMAND.COM C:** and press ENTER.

Sometimes, when exiting programs like Windows, I get the message "Invalid COMMAND.COM." What's causing this?

The program is trying to start a new copy of COMMAND.COM and can't find the file. Try adding or verifying the line in the CONFIG.SYS file, ensuring that the /P is present, as shown here:

```
SHELL=C:\DOS\COMMAND.COM C:\DOS /P
```

And verify that the following line references a correct path in the AUTOEXEC.BAT if present:

```
SET COMSPEC=C:\DOS\COMMAND.COM
```

Also check to see that there is a copy of COMMAND.COM in the root directory of the C drive.

I get the error message "Out of environment space." What's environment space and how can I get more?

Environment space is a section of conventional memory where MS-DOS stores small pieces of information it needs to use frequently. The most common example is your PATH statement. DOS is constantly checking this information, so it stays in memory all the time. DOS defaults to setting up 256 bytes of environment space, but you can create more using the "SHELL=" line in CONFIG.SYS. For example, in the following line:

```
SHELL=C:\DOS\COMMAND.COM C:\DOS\ /E:1024 /P
```

the number after the /E: sets up the amount of environment space (in bytes).

Can I change the drive letter of my RAM drive?

No, but you can control which drive letter the RAM drive uses to a certain extent. The RAM drive is assigned the next available drive letter when the RAMDRIVE.SYS device driver is loaded in memory to create the RAM drive. For example, if you have a C hard drive and another device such as an external floppy drive which you want assigned the letter D, put the command that loads RAMDRIVE.SYS after the command that loads the other item's device driver in the CONFIG.SYS file. You will then have your hard drive as C, the external floppy drive assigned as D, and RAMDRIVE.SYS will take the next available drive letter for the ram drive, in this case E.

After performing an MS-DOS upgrade, I receive the "Incorrect DOS version" error message whenever I try to execute some DOS commands. Why?

The MS-DOS upgrade will update the DOS files in the DOS directory, but DOS files on the root directory (other than COMMAND.COM) are not updated. As a result, the error message will appear when an old DOS command is encountered in the root directory. The easiest way to correct this situation is to delete the outdated DOS files from the root directory.

I heard someone mention something called CMOS. What is it and do I have one?

In technical terms, CMOS stands for complementary metal-oxide semiconductor. It's a type of RAM that consumes very low amounts of power. In lay terms, it's the place where the computer stores its basic hardware configuration. It is a chip on the motherboard that has backup power provided by a small battery so that when the computer is turned off it will retain the information. In response to the question "do I have one?": yes, if you have an 80286 or higher processor. With few exceptions, all 80286s and above have a CMOS. If the settings contained in your CMOS are lost (as can happen if the battery runs low), your system will be unable to communicate with hardware such as RAM, floppy drives, and hard drives. The battery which powers the CMOS typically lasts 3-5 years or more.

I hate the comma separators when I do a DIR in DOS 6.2. How can I get the output to look like 5.0?

The comma separators are a permanent addition to MS-DOS 6.2 and cannot be changed.

After I make a change to my AUTOEXEC.BAT file, do I have to reboot my machine to get those changes to show up?

It depends on the type of change you made. You can reinitialize some of your computer's settings by typing **AUTOEXEC** at the DOS prompt and pressing ENTER. Things like the PATH line, the PROMPT statement, and any SET statements will be updated, but programs like SMARTDRV are already loaded and will not take any new parameters. If you removed such an item from the AUTOEXEC.BAT, it will still be loaded into memory. If you're unsure whether the change you made will take effect, go ahead and reboot. When you reboot, your system is starting with a "clean slate."

I just changed my AUTOEXEC.BAT or CONFIG.SYS file. When I boot my computer, either file displays strange characters and no longer works. What happened?

You probably edited AUTOEXEC.BAT or CONFIG.SYS with a word processor rather than with EDIT. Word processors add special characters that describe how you want the data to appear. These special characters don't appear when you look at the file in the word processor. When you use the file from DOS, however, DOS doesn't know how to process these commands. This doesn't mean you can't use a word processor to change AUTOEXEC.BAT or CONFIG.SYS; it just means that when you save the file using the word processor, you need to tell the word processor to save it in a text format. Most word processors can do this and the steps vary with each word processor. After editing, you may need to reboot your computer and press F5 to skip over CONFIG.SYS and AUTOEXEC.BAT or F8 to selectively perform commands in these files. The EDIT command in DOS *only* saves files in a plain text format, so use it if you're unsure how to make your word processor save in plain text.

I upgraded from MS-DOS 3.1 to 6.2 and now my floppy drives don't format properly. Why?

There are two likely causes for this.

1. The old DOS was tailored specifically to support the hardware (the floppy drives). Microsoft's MS-DOS 5.0, 6.0, and 6.2 are not going to provide that specific hardware support. This is particularly likely if the old version of DOS was supplied with the machine—known in the industry as an OEM (original equipment manufacturer) version of DOS.

2. If the machine is older, it may need a BIOS upgrade. (BIOS chips are ROM chips with specific subroutines built into them. DOS handles many I/O operations by calling those subroutines. As hardware has become more complex, the set of those subroutines has grown.)

Depending on your hardware, you might be able to use the DRIVPARM command in CONFIG.SYS to get things working. This is the solution when you receive the error message "Invalid media type _ track 0 bad" when trying to read a disk, or "Parameters not supported by drive" when trying to format a disk. For example, if your drive B is a 3.5" 720K drive, try this line in CONFIG.SYS:

```
DRIVPARM=/D:1 /F:2
```

These settings indicate that floppy drive number 1 (drive A is number 0) is a 720K drive (the 2 after /F: indicates a 720K drive). The other numbers you can include after the /F: are:

Drive size	Disk capacity	Number after /F:
5.25"	160K, 180K, 320K, or 360K	0
5.25"	1.2MB	1
3.5"	720K	2 (and /I)
3.5"	1.44MB	7 (and /I)
3.5"	2.88MB	9

There are a number of other parameters that can be added which may apply to your hardware. Consult the online help by typing **HELP DRIVPARM** and pressing ENTER at the DOS prompt for more information. This is not guaranteed, though it does work in a majority of cases.

If you are having trouble reading or formatting disks in a floppy drive and the DRIVPARM command doesn't help, try using DRIVER.SYS instead. For example, for a high-density disk (1.2MB or 1.44MB) in a 5.25" drive, use the following statement:

```
DEVICE=\DOS\DRIVER.SYS /D:0 /F:1
```

The number after /D: is the number for the disk drive and the number after /F: corresponds to the drive size as shown in the table above.

Ideally, you should contact the hardware manufacturer to check for possible hardware incompatibility and to see if a BIOS upgrade is available.

I just installed 6.2 on my machine and when I reboot, I see "HIMEM is testing extended memory ..." and my machine stops. It does not go any further. What has happened?

The main new feature of MS-DOS 6.2's HIMEM.SYS is its extended memory test function. If the memory test is encountering a serious problem, it may not be able to report it. It's also possible that your machine requires a special switch for HIMEM.SYS to effectively use your computer's extended memory. Pressing F5 when you see "Starting MS-DOS..." will bypass CONFIG.SYS and take you directly to a DOS prompt. Edit CONFIG.SYS and add /TESTMEM:OFF to the HIMEM.SYS line. This switch disables the extended memory test that HIMEM.SYS performs. Save the file and reboot. If HIMEM.SYS installs without displaying error messages, then it's very likely that there is a problem with some of your system RAM. If HIMEM.SYS still hangs in the same place, make sure you are using the proper machine switch for HIMEM.SYS. HIMEM.SYS defaults to using the /MACHINE:1 switch. Your machine may require a different number for this switch. Type **HELP HIMEM.SYS** and press ENTER at the DOS prompt for a list of known machine types. If your machine is not listed, you may have to try each setting until you find the proper one.

I'm running MS-DOS 6.2 and I'm having problems accessing my floppy drives. I don't understand it. Everything was fine under 6.0. Now what?

There have been two major changes from 6.0 to 6.2 that might affect the floppies: Automount and DoubleGuard. For troubleshooting purposes, you can disable both from the DOS prompt. To do this, type **DBLSPACE /DOUBLEGUARD=0**, press ENTER, type **DBLSPACE /AUTOMOUNT=0**, and press ENTER again. Because each command will change the DBLSPACE.INI file, you will have to reboot to make these changes take effect. Although this is a good way to uncover the source of your trouble, it should not be the final fix. Other things to think about include memory conflicts and hardware incompatibilities.

What is a RAM drive and how do I get one?

A RAM drive is an imaginary drive where part of your extended memory behaves as if it is a disk drive instead of being used as RAM memory. A RAM disk has a drive letter just like other disk drives. A RAM disk is faster than hard disks, floppy disks, and CD-ROM disks. However, like all of your computer's RAM memory, when you

estart your computer, the RAM disk's contents are erased. A
AM disk is a wonderful place to store temporary files.

To create a RAM drive, you need to add a Device line
ontaining RAMDRIVE.SYS to your CONFIG.SYS file. It is
commended that you create the RAM drive in extended
memory (or expanded memory if extended is not available). To
do this, the line containing RAMDRIVE.SYS needs to appear after
the Device lines for your memory management device drivers
(HIMEM.SYS and EMM386.EXE), if any. Use the DOS Editor to
add the needed line. For example:

```
DEVICE=C:\DOS\RAMDRIVE.SYS 256 /E
```

creates a 256K RAM drive in *extended* memory. DOS assigns the
next available drive letter to the RAM drive. RAMDRIVE.SYS can
be loaded high into the UMBs with the DEVICEHIGH command.
For example, the following commands in CONFIG.SYS create a
256K RAM drive in the UMB:

```
DEVICE=C:\DOS\HIMEM.SYS
DEVICE=C:\DOS\EMM386.EXE
DEVICEHIGH=C:\DOS\RAMDRIVE.SYS 256
```

Tech Tip: You may be better off using your extended memory as
extended memory rather than as a RAM drive. Programs that are
designed to use extended memory may be faster by having more
extended memory than by accessing their temporary files faster.

I heard that I can speed up my applications by placing my temp files on a RAM drive. How do I do this?

Many applications create temporary files while they are running,
and if these files can be accessed with greater speed, then the
applications will run faster too. Once you create a RAM drive,
you can direct programs to place their temporary files there. To
do this (assuming your RAM drive has been assigned drive letter
D), add the following lines to your AUTOEXEC.BAT file:

```
MD D:\TEMP
SET TEMP=D:\TEMP
```

You need to create the directory each time because the contents of the RAM drive disappear each time you restart your computer.

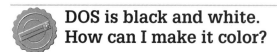

DOS is black and white. How can I make it color?

You can use the ANSI.SYS driver to change color settings at the DOS prompt. ANSI.SYS provides functions for graphics such as screen colors, cursor movement, and key assignments. Changing the DOS screen colors with ANSI.SYS will not affect the colors on most DOS programs, as they set up their own colors and video modes. To change the screen colors:

1. Make sure you have a line similar to this one in CONFIG.SYS:

```
DEVICE=C:\DOS\ANSI.SYS
```

2. Type a PROMPT command to set the screen colors and press ENTER. Put this command in your AUTOEXEC.BAT file when you want the screen color changed every time. You can also enter it at the DOS prompt when you want to change the color only until you restart your computer. This example:

```
PROMPT $e[1;34;43m
```

yields a yellow screen with bold blue characters. This PROMPT command sends an escape sequence (the $e equals the ESC key code) that sets the screen colors. The text attribute, foreground color, and background color are replaced by one of the following numbers.

Text attributes		Foreground colors		Background colors	
0	All attributes off	30	Black	40	Black
1	Bold on	31	Red	41	Red
4	Underscore	32	Green	42	Green
5	Blink on	33	Yellow	43	Yellow
7	Reverse video on	34	Blue	44	Blue
8	Concealed on	35	Magenta	45	Magenta
		36	Cyan	46	Cyan
		37	White	47	White

When I boot my machine up I get the error message "Cannot run SMARTDrive 4.0 with DoubleSpace." I have a SMARTDRV.EXE file in my Windows and DOS directories. Which one should I use?

A good rule is to always use the driver that has the most recent date on it. Most of the time this will be the most recent version of the driver. In this case, using the version of SMARTDRV.EXE that ships with MS-DOS 6.*x* will fix this problem. The version of SMARTDRV.EXE that ships with Windows 3.1 does not recognize a DoubleSpace compressed drive and therefore cannot operate when you are using the DoubleSpace compression.

The computer executes the CONFIG.SYS, but then freezes without giving me a DOS prompt. Why?

The COMMAND.COM file, which displays the DOS prompt on your screen, may be damaged. There must be one copy of this file on your hard drive, normally on the root directory and optionally in the C:\DOS directory. Start the computer up from a boot disk containing the same operating system that is running on your C drive, and copy over new copies of COMMAND.COM by typing either **SYS C:** or **COPY A:COMMAND.COM C:** and pressing ENTER.

I have just upgraded to DOS 6 and the Num Lock light is on! It never used to be on. How can I make it go away?

The default is to set Num Lock on. To change the default, add a line that says:

```
NUMLOCK=OFF
```

to the CONFIG.SYS file.

At bootup, I get the error message "Missing operating system." Why?

There are three reasons why you would receive this error. Check them in this order:

1. The CMOS settings for the hard drive could be incorrect. The computer stores information about your hard drive with battery-backed memory called CMOS. These settings can change spontaneously as a result of a static charge, poor battery contact, or a weak battery. If the CMOS settings are wrong, you may not have access to the hard drive at all, even after booting up with a system disk. You will need to start the setup procedure for your computer (not DOS) and provide the correct settings.

2. The system files on your hard drive could be missing or damaged. Boot with a system disk, then use the SYS.COM utility to recopy the system files. From the C:\DOS directory, type **SYS A: C:** and press ENTER.

3. Your DOS partition on the hard drive may have been set to inactive. To correct this, you'll need to boot up with a system disk from drive A, then run FDISK from the C:\DOS directory. Choose FDISK menu item #4, "Display partition information." If your C partition does *not* show status as Active, go back to the main FDISK menu and choose item #2, "Set active partition," then select the C partition as active. When you press ESC to leave FDISK,

you will reboot your system with the selected active partition.

How do I use SMARTDrive from DOS 6.2 to cache my CD-ROM drive?

The CD-ROM drive must be supported by MSCDEX.EXE (the Microsoft CD-ROM Extensions), which is included with MS-DOS 6.2, and MSCDEX.EXE must be loaded prior to SMARTDRV.EXE. Check your AUTOEXEC.BAT file for the lines containing MSCDEX.EXE and SMARTDRV.EXE. The line containing MSCDEX.EXE *must* appear before the line containing SMARTDRV.EXE. If you do not load MSCDEX.EXE in your AUTOEXEC.BAT file, then you cannot load SMARTDRV.EXE there either.

Another reason SMARTDrive might not be caching the CD-ROM drive is that the line containing SMARTDRV also contains /U. The /U is a command line option which instructs SMARTDRV to unload the CD-ROM support code even if MSCDEX.EXE is already loaded.

You can save a little memory if you don't want your CD-ROM to be cached by adding /U to the SMARTDRV line. However, if MSCDEX is not resident in memory when SMARTDRV is loaded, SMARTDRV will automatically unload the CD-ROM support so /U isn't necessary.

After I turn it on, my computer freezes during the list of programs loading into memory. Why?

Your computer may be locking up because CONFIG.SYS or AUTOEXEC.BAT cannot load one of the programs. Restart the computer and press F8 when "Starting MS-DOS..." appears. It will go through each line in the CONFIG.SYS and AUTOEXEC.BAT files, and ask you whether or not you wish to process each one. Type **y** for each line and watch for the line which causes the computer to freeze. Now restart the computer and, using the same F8 procedure, type **y** to every line *except* the line which previously caused the computer to freeze. Type **n** to that one. Does the computer still freeze?

If it doesn't freeze, then the line that you typed **n** to probably needs to be changed to work properly on your machine. If it does freeze, then the problem is elsewhere. Try typing **n** to other lines on bootup. Problems like this are often caused by the way the EMM386.EXE program allocates memory. Typing **n** to this line may stop the computer from freezing. Once you know which line in CONFIG.SYS or AUTOEXEC.BAT causes the problem, here are some suggestions as to what to do next:

1. If the problematic program is loading into upper memory, try loading it into conventional memory. Some programs are unstable when loaded in upper memory.

2. The problematic program may require different settings to function properly under your current configuration. Check the software's documentation for additional ideas.

3. If the problematic program still hangs the system, the file itself could be damaged, or the program may be incompatible with your new version of DOS.

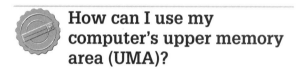

How can I use my computer's upper memory area (UMA)?

UMA is memory in a computer that DOS 5.0 and later started making available for device drivers and memory-resident programs. Initially, the UMA was used for video display adapter information and BIOS extensions and you couldn't use what was left. You load programs into this memory in your CONFIG.SYS file with the DEVICEHIGH command and from AUTOEXEC.BAT, a batch file, or a DOS prompt with the LOADHIGH command. For example, to put ANSI.SYS into the UMA, your CONFIG.SYS file will contain this line:

```
DEVICEHIGH=C:\DOS\ANSI.SYS
```

To make the UMA available, you need the following commands in your CONFIG.SYS file:

```
DEVICE=C:\DOS\HIMEM.SYS
DEVICE=C:\DOS\EMM386.EXE NOEMS
DOS=UMB
```

The second command can include other switches used by EMM386.EXE as well as using RAM in place of NOEMS. If you use both the RAM and NOEMS parameters, the RAM parameter is ignored and NOEMS takes precedence. The third command can also include HIGH and a comma separating HIGH from UMB when you want to put DOS into the high memory area (HMA).

On most personal computers running MS-DOS 5.0 or later and EMM386.EXE with the NOEMS switch set, you have only about 92K of upper memory blocks available.

```
DEVICE=C:\DOS\EMM386.EXE NOEMS /I=B000-B7FF
```

The amount of upper memory you actually get varies greatly depending on hardware installed, CMOS cache and shadow RAM options, and display adapter type.

Tech Tip: Some memory-resident programs and device drivers cannot be loaded into a UMB. You will discover which ones cannot by trial and error, or, in some cases, by reading the program's documentation. If a memory-resident program does not work when loaded into a UMB, reboot your system using another system disk or by using F8 so you can selectively run lines in CONFIG.SYS and AUTOEXEC.BAT to skip over the one loading the memory-resident program into a UMB. Then, edit the CONFIG.SYS or AUTOEXEC.BAT file to load the memory-resident program into conventional memory.

I am running out of memory. Can DOS use less so my other programs have more?

You can reduce how much conventional memory DOS uses by putting part of DOS into your computer's high memory area. To load part of the DOS kernel into the high memory area (the first 64K of extended memory above 1MB), your system must have an Intel 80286 or higher processor and more than 384K of extended memory. The CONFIG.SYS must have a DEVICE command for HIMEM.SYS, for example, DEVICE=C:\HIMEM.SYS. The command DOS=HIGH should also be in the CONFIG.SYS. This works for most systems. The question "How can I use my computer's upper memory area (UMA)?", earlier in this chapter, has more information on using the upper memory area and conserving conventional memory by using upper memory blocks.

Tech Tip: Do not use this command on a machine that runs DESQview because it will show a loss of conventional memory inside DESQview. This command also does not work with Quarterdeck's QEXT.SYS file dated earlier than June 1991.

Why does booting take longer with DOS 6?

As the Frustration Busters box at the beginning of the chapter described, your computer is doing a lot before you see the DOS prompt. However, you can shorten the booting process by two seconds by adding "SWITCHES = /F" to your CONFIG.SYS file. DOS has this two-second delay to give you more time to press F5 or F8 before continuing with the boot process. It's important to realize that adding "SWITCHES=/F" will make the F5/F8 boot options more difficult to use, so unless the extra two seconds are critical to you, it's recommended that you leave "SWITCHES=/F" out.

I heard that I can set DOS to extend my laptop's battery usage. How?

DOS includes a Power program that conserves battery power for laptop computers. The power savings range from 5 to 25 percent depending on whether your computer conforms to the Advanced Power Management specification. To install this program, add the following line to your CONFIG.SYS file:

```
DEVICE=C:\DOS\POWER.EXE
```

After you save CONFIG.SYS, you will need to reboot your computer. Once Power is installed, you can see a report of power usage by typing **POWER** and pressing ENTER. The following shows a sample of its report.

```
C:\>POWER

Power Management Status
----------------------
Setting =  ADV: REG
CPU: idle 43% of time

C:\>
```

In my multiple configuration, how can I have a choice in my submenu to return me to the previous menu?

It is easy to add a menu choice to return to a previous menu. All you have to do is make a submenu entry in your configuration block that references the previous menu item. The example on the next page shows what this would look like.

The choices to return you to the previous screen are set up in the sample Charlene and Tomb menu blocks. (Usually, your menu blocks will have more meaningful names.) Note that although you are returning to the previous screen, there is nothing stopping you from going back two or three levels. (For simplicity's sake, this example is set up to go back just to the previous screen.) Also note that the description states that this choice will take you back to the previous screen.

When you boot your system, you will initially see the menu defined by the [menu] block. If you select Additional Menus from the primary menu, you will see the menu defined by the [Tomb] block. In this second menu, you can select Previous Screen to return to the primary menu. You can also select Charlene and select one of the items from the menu defined by the [Charlene] block. This third menu includes a menu item called Previous Screen. Selecting this menu item returns you to the menu defined by the [Tomb] block.

All you have to do to be able to choose the previous menu is set the submenu to point to the desired menu name. In the example, the previous menu names are Menu and Tomb. Therefore, when you choose the submenu, DOS will bring up the previous menu.

```
[menu]
Menuitem=Network,Load Network
Menuitem=Local,Run Local Without Network
Menuitem=Class,Used For Different Classes
Submenu=Tomb,Additional Menus
Menucolor=3,1
Menudefault=Network,10


[Network]
DEVICE=C:\DOS\HIMEM.SYS /v
DEVICE=C:\DOS\EMM386.EXE 512 RAM HIGHSCAN X=c800-cfff
I=e000-efff I=b000-b7ff D=48
FILES=50
BUFFERS=50
SHELL=C:\DOS\COMMAND.COM C:\DOS\ /E:512 /P
LASTDRIVE=Z
DEVICEHIGH=C:\LANMAN.DOS\DRIVERS\PROTMAN\PROTMAN.DOS
/i:C:\LANMAN.DOS
DEVICEHIGH=C:\LANMAN.DOS\DRIVERS\ETHERNET\3COM\ELNKII.DOS
INSTALL=C:\WINDOWS\LMOUSE.COM


[Local]
DEVICE=C:\DOS\HIMEM.SYS /v
DEVICE=C:\DOS\EMM386.EXE RAM HIGHSCAN X=c800-cfff I=e000-efff
I=b000-b7ff D=48
DEVICEHIGH=C:\DOS\RAMDRIVE.SYS 2048 /E
DEVICEHIGH=C:\DOS\ANSI.SYS
FILES=50
BUFFERS=50
SHELL=C:\DOS\COMMAND.COM C:\DOS\ /P
LASTDRIVE=Z


[Class]
DEVICE=C:\DOS\HIMEM.SYS > TEST.TXT
DEVICE=C:\DOS\EMM386.EXE RAM > TEST.TXT


[Tomb]
Menuitem=Windows,Loads Windows With Optimal Memory
Menuitem=Word,Loads Word For DOS With Optimal Memory
Menudefault=Windows,20
```

```
Menucolor=4,1
Submenu=Charlene
Submenu=Menu,Previous Screen

[Windows]
DEVICE=C:\DOS\HIMEM.SYS
DEVICE=C:\DOS\EMM386.EXE NOEMS WIN=d000-efff I=b000-b7ff
DEVICEHIGH=C:\DOS\RAMDRIVE.SYS 1024 /e

[Word]
DEVICE=C:\DOS\HIMEM.SYS
DEVICE=C:\DOS\EMM386.EXE RAM I=e000-efff I=b000-b7ff
DEVICEHIGH=C:\DOS\RAMDRIVE.SYS 1024 /a

[Charlene]
Menuitem=Gail,Diagnose Disk
Menudefault=Gail,2
Menucolor=2,0
Submenu=Tomb,Previous Screen

[Gail]
DEVICE=C:\DOS\HIMEM.SYS

[common]
DOS=HIGH,UMB
BUFFERS=10,0
DEVICEHIGH=C:\DOS\DBLSPACE.SYS /MOVE
DEVICEHIGH=C:\DOS\SETVER.EXE
```

Why does my multiple configuration menu flash on and off when I use the MENUCOLOR command to set the color of the multiple configuration menu?

You are getting a flashing effect because you are using colors that are not supported by your display adapter. The most common colors that may flash are numbers 8-15. Change the colors to numbers below 8.

I just got the message "Inconsistency between startup and MemMaker STS file." What is this problem and how do I solve it?

This error message appears because MemMaker never completed the optimization process. If you ran MemMaker only once, type **MEMMAKER /UNDO** at the DOS prompt and press ENTER to restore your original configuration. Reboot the system and watch carefully. If the system does *not* boot up to a DOS prompt, such as when a menu program comes up, then you must edit your AUTOEXEC.BAT and type **REM** before any lines associated with the menu program. Once your system boots straight to a DOS prompt, you're ready to run MemMaker. Once MemMaker is finished, go back and remove those REMs.

Another possible solution is to edit the CONFIG.SYS file and remove the first line, which reads "DEVICE=CHKSTATE.SYS." Next, remove the command "C:\DOS\SIZER.EXE" from any line in the CONFIG.SYS or AUTOEXEC.BAT file. SIZER.EXE is a utility used by MemMaker to determine how much memory each program needs, and is never seen in a completed CONFIG.SYS or AUTOEXEC.BAT file. Finally, remove the last line in the AUTOEXEC.BAT file, which reads "C:\DOS\MEMMAKER /SESSION." This allows you to boot without receiving the error.

How do I set up a path with more than 127 characters?

DOS 6.*x* no longer has a limit on the length of the Path statement. Use the PATH command in CONFIG.SYS instead of in AUTOEXEC.BAT. If issued in CONFIG.SYS, the path can be any length, up to the amount of available environment space. If you need more environment space, see the question "I get the error message 'Out of environment space.' What's environment space and how can I get more?", earlier in this chapter. Once the path is set in CONFIG.SYS, any changes made to the path in AUTOEXEC.BAT or at the DOS prompt will result in a path truncated to 127 characters. For example, if a long path is specified in CONFIG.SYS, this command in AUTOEXEC.BAT:

```
PATH C:\DIR1;C:\DIR2;%PATH%
```

will result in a path that has been truncated, with the new directories at the beginning.

I want to run Interlnk but when I try to use it, it tells me I must install it. I thought Interlnk was installed when I installed DOS. What's wrong?

Installing DOS makes the files needed to run Interlnk available but it does not install it for you. Install Interlnk by adding the following line to your CONFIG.SYS file:

```
C:\DOS\INTERLNK.EXE
```

You will need to reboot your computer to install Interlnk.

What is the top transfer rate if I am using Interlnk with a serial cable?

The maximum transfer rate of Interlnk through a serial cable is 115.2K per second. The transfer rate can be changed with the INTERSVR command. The switch would be /BAUD:*rate*, where *rate* is a valid value for Interlnk. Valid values are 9600, 19200, 38400, 57600, and 115200. The default is 115200. For example, to set the rate at 9600 baud, start Intersvr by typing **INTERSVR /BAUD:9600** at a DOS prompt and pressing ENTER. For more information, see the DOS 6.*x* online help for Intersvr, Interlnk, and INTERLNK.EXE.

I am trying to install Interlnk and I continue to get the "Connection not established" message. Why?

Interlnk is a device driver that lets you connect two computers with a cable to exchange data. For example, you may be using it to transfer information from your laptop computer to the computer on your desk at work after a trip away from the office.

This error message usually indicates a hardware problem. First, make sure you are using the correct cable. Next, test the ports themselves. If they are serial ports, connect a modem to each computer's serial port and test it using any standard terminal emulation software. If both serial ports work, the problem is most likely with your null modem cable. For parallel port connections, connect a printer to the port for testing. Make sure the pin-to-pin connections internal to the cable are as shown in Tables 10-1 and 10-2. (This information can also be found in the Notes section of the Interlnk help screen.)

Is Interlnk faster with a serial or parallel cable?

Interlnk is faster with a parallel cable because the parallel method of transfer sends data streams side by side, while the serial method sends data one stream at a time. If you are going to use a parallel cable, make sure you have a cable which conforms to the Interlnk requirements. See the answer to the previous question for information about the cable requirements.

9 pin	25 pin		25 pin	9 pin	
pin 5	pin 7	⇔	pin 7	pin 5	(Ground-Ground)
pin 3	pin 2	⇔	pin 3	pin 2	(Transmit-Receive)
pin 7	pin 4	⇔	pin 5	pin 8	(RTS - CTS)
pin 6	pin 6	⇔	pin 20	pin 4	(DSR - DTR)
pin 2	pin 3	⇔	pin 2	pin 3	(Receive-Transmit)
pin 8	pin 5	⇔	pin 4	pin 7	(CTS - RTS)
pin 4	pin 20	⇔	pin 6	pin 6	(DTR - DSR)

TABLE 10-1   Serial cable connections

I recently upgraded to a 400MB hard drive. After I restored all of my data, something's changed! Why does CHKDSK report that the data that used to fit on my 200MB drive now uses 230MB?

Your 200MB drive was using a 4K cluster size and your 400MB drive is using a 8K cluster size. DOS writes data in clusters, and can address a maximum of 65,536 clusters. To accommodate larger hard drives, clusters get larger as drives get larger. If a given file is smaller than 1 cluster, the remainder of its cluster is empty and wasted. Since the cluster size is larger on your larger

25 pin		25 pin	
pin 2	⇔	pin 15	
pin 3	⇔	pin 13	
pin 4	⇔	pin 12	
pin 5	⇔	pin 10	
pin 6	⇔	pin 11	
pin 15	⇔	pin 2	
pin 13	⇔	pin 3	
pin 12	⇔	pin 4	
pin 10	⇔	pin 5	
pin 11	⇔	pin 6	
pin 25	⇔	pin 25	(Ground-Ground)

TABLE 10-2   Parallel cable connections

drive you are wasting more space than you were with your 200MB drive. To get around this, you could partition your 400MB drive into two or more smaller partitions using DOS's FDisk program.

My computer says that "SMARTDrive cannot cache a compressed drive." I want to cache my C drive, so what can I do?

If you are running DoubleSpace, SMARTDrive must operate on the DoubleSpace host drive (the uncompressed disk), not on the compressed drive itself. For example, if drive H is host for compressed drive C, then change the SMARTDrive line in your AUTOEXEC.BAT file from "C:\DOS\SMARTDRV C+" to "C:\DOS\SMARTDRV H+". Another solution is to omit the drive letter altogether. SMARTDrive will automatically detect a DoubleSpaced drive and cache its host drive.

What is a Master Boot Record?

The Master Boot Record (MBR) is the first place your system looks to find out about a physical hard drive. Your hard drive may have more than one partition, but it has only one MBR. The MBR contains the partition table and a description of how many and what type of partitions are on the drive. The MBR is located on the first physical sector of the drive. If the drive is your boot drive, the MBR also contains code to start the operating system.

I set up CONFIG.SYS and AUTOEXEC.BAT perfectly. How do I prevent someone else from skipping over their contents by pressing F5 or F8?

To prevent a user from skipping over CONFIG.SYS or AUTOEXEC.BAT with F5 or F8, include "SWITCHES = /N" in your CONFIG.SYS file. Then, pressing F5 or F8 during the bootup process has no effect.

I just got an "EMM386 exception error #12" message. What does that mean and what can I do?

Error #12 for EMM386 is a stack exception error. This error is usually caused when the "STACKS=" line is "STACKS=0,0", which disables the registers that DOS sets up to handle hardware interrupts. You can usually solve this problem by increasing the "STACKS=x,xxx" line in the CONFIG.SYS file. Set the line to "STACKS=9,256", which creates 9 stacks at 256 bytes per stack. If that is not enough, try "STACKS=18,256" or "STACKS=18,512."

Tech Tip: An exception error #12 can also occur as the result of a memory conflict.

I just got an "EMM386 exception error #13," what can I do?

Exception error #13 for EMM386 indicates a general protection violation—memory assigned to one program is being over-written by another. As for the solution, the most common fix is to use a different machine switch on the HIMEM.SYS line in the CONFIG.SYS. The line reads as follows:

```
DEVICE=C:\DOS\HIMEM.SYS /MACHINE:X
```

X is the machine number (that is simply read from a table that is included in the DOS online help file). A good starting place is setting the machine number to 1, with numbers 3, 7, 11, 12, 13, and 17 as alternates.

I have installed MS-DOS 6.x and compressed both drives C and D using DoubleSpace. Now my computer tells me there are "Too many block devices." What is a block device? Why do I now have too many?

A block device is any device that uses a drive letter to access data, such as a RAM drive, floppy drive, hard drive, or CD-ROM drive. This message appears when there are too few drive letters set aside for DOS. It shows up after compressing drives because DoubleSpace needs one extra drive letter for every compressed drive on the system. As a default, DoubleSpace reserves five drive letters. You can lower the number of drives to leave more room for the drives that DoubleSpace uses. To do this, change the Lastdrive line in CONFIG.SYS to a lower value. Next, change the DoubleSpace host drive letter to a lower value. The question "Why, after installing MS-DOS 6.0 and DoubleSpace, do I get the error message 'Invalid drive specification' when I try to go to my login drive on my Novell network?" in Chapter 12 describes the steps for changing the DoubleSpace host drive letter.

Since installing DOS 6.*x*, my CD-ROM drive is not working properly. I also see the message "Incorrect DOS version" during bootup. Is there something that I need to do in DOS to make it function again?

There may be if the trouble is related to MSCDEX (the Microsoft CD-ROM Extensions). There is an updated version of MSCDEX.EXE with DOS 6.*x* that you may need to use in place of an older one. There should be a line in your AUTOEXEC.BAT file that looks similar to this:

```
C:\CDROM\MSCDEX.EXE /D:MSCD001 /L:D
```

(CDROM may be called something else, of course.) You can use the DOS Editor to change the path before MSCDEX to point to the MS-DOS 6.*x* directory, but leave everything else the same. For example:

```
C:\DOS\MSCDEX.EXE /D:MSCD001 /L:D
```

The new version of MSCDEX.EXE is required for compatibility reasons. Previous versions of MS-DOS did not include MSCDEX.EXE, so the file included with your kit is for use with previous DOS versions only.

DOS Answers: *Certified Tech Support*

I think I have a problem with DBLSPACE.BIN. Can I boot without loading it?

You can bypass DBLSPACE.BIN, although the steps are different for DOS 6.0 and DOS 6.2. In DOS 6.2:

- Bypass loading DBLSPACE.BIN and executing the CONFIG.SYS and AUTOEXEC.BAT files by pressing CTRL+F5 when you see the message "Starting DOS..."
- Bypass loading DBLSPACE.BIN and step through your CONFIG.SYS and AUTOEXEC.BAT by pressing CTRL+F8.

When you bypass loading DLBSPACE.BIN, however, you will not have access to any information on your compressed drive. These key combinations will not work if your DBLSPACE.INI file contains "SWITCHES /N", which disables using CTRL+F5 and CTRL+F8. To bypass DBLSPACE.BIN in DOS 6.0:

1. Make a system disk for drive A by typing **FORMAT A: /S** for an unformatted disk, or **SYS A:** for a formatted one. Press ENTER.
2. Copy over the CONFIG.SYS and AUTOEXEC.BAT files to the system disk (optional).
3. Change to the A drive by typing **A:** and pressing ENTER.
4. Type **DELTREE DBLSPACE.BIN** and press ENTER to remove DBLSPACE.BIN from the system disk.
5. Reboot with this disk in your A drive. DoubleSpace will not be in effect, so you cannot access any compressed drives.

I want to use different CONFIG.SYS and AUTOEXEC.BAT files. Do I need to create separate boot disks for each set of CONFIG.SYS and AUTOEXEC.BAT files?

You do not have to create different boot disks if you want to use different CONFIG.SYS and AUTOEXEC.BAT files as long as you have DOS 6.*x*, which handles multiple configurations. When you have multiple configurations, you are creating a menu that appears every time you boot your computer. When you select

one of the menu items, you are selecting which configuration
you will use. The CONFIG.SYS file will have a block for the menu
and a block for each set of configuration commands. You can
also create submenus in a CONFIG.SYS file, set the color of the
screen, and set which item and configuration setting is the
default. The menu block in a CONFIG.SYS file looks like this:

```
[Menu]
MenuItem=Windows,Configure for best Windows usage
MenuItem=Nowindows,Configure for best non-Windows usage
MenuDefault=Windows,10
```

The above block creates a menu with two menu items that
look like this when you start your system:

```
MS-DOS 6.2 Startup Menu

    1. Configure for best Windows usage
    2. Configure for best non-Windows usage

  Enter a choice: 1      Time remaining: 10

















F5=Bypass startup files F8=Confirm each line of CONFIG.SYS and AUTOEXEC.BAT [N]
```

When you select the first item, DOS uses the configuration
settings in the [Windows] block of the CONFIG.SYS file. When
you select the second item, DOS uses the configuration settings
in the [Nowindows] block. If no selection is made after 10
seconds, DOS uses the configuration settings in the [Windows]

block because of the MENUDEFAULT command. The [menu]
block can only include the MENUITEM, MENUDEFAULT,
MENUCOLOR, SUBMENU, and NUMLOCK commands.

After the commands in the [menu] block, add the blocks for
each choice of configurations. For the menu shown above, the
CONFIG.SYS file will have a block labeled [Windows] and
another that starts with [Nowindows]. A sample of one of these
is shown here:

```
[Windows]
DEVICE=C:\WINDOWS\SMARTDRV.EXE /DOUBLE_BUFFER
DEVICE=C:\DOS\CHKSTATE.SYS /S:FR1 /32415
DEVICE=C:\DOS\HIMEM.SYS
DEVICE=C:\DOS\EMM386.EXE NOEMS
BUFFERS=10,0
FILES=50
DOS=UMB
LASTDRIVE=E
FCBS=4,0
DEVICEHIGH /L:1,12048 =C:\DOS\SETVER.EXE
DOS=HIGH
STACKS=9,256
```

Another possible block to include in CONFIG.SYS is
[common]. The [common] block contains the configuration
commands performed for all configurations.

**I have multiple startup
configurations, and I have
problems running
MemMaker. Can this be
done?**

It takes a bit of extra effort. Essentially,
you must make each block of your
multiple configuration CONFIG.SYS
and AUTOEXEC.BAT into separate
startup files, run MemMaker on each
set, then re-combine the optimized
configurations. When you have
multiple configurations, it's important to avoid the use of
[common] blocks in CONFIG.SYS and AUTOEXEC.BAT. Since
each configuration is different, MemMaker will assign each
program item to different memory locations for each
configuration.

To run MemMaker with different configurations, follow these
steps:

1. Create a backup copy of your CONFIG.SYS and AUTOEXEC.BAT files. You may want to copy them to the filenames of CONFIG.OLD and AUTOEXEC.OLD.

2. Copy your CONFIG.SYS and AUTOEXEC.BAT files for as many times as you have different configurations. Use names like CONFIG.1 and AUTOEXEC.1 for the first configuration.

3. Edit each of the copied CONFIG.SYS and AUTOEXEC.BAT files so they can be used for a single different configuration. This means removing the [menu] block that defines the menu in CONFIG.SYS, removing the "GOTO %CONFIG%" line in AUTOEXEC.BAT, and removing the configuration and startup commands for the remaining blocks, as well as removing all block headers. Remember to include the [common] block, if any, in each unique CONFIG.SYS, and duplicate any lines found above "GOTO %CONFIG%" inside each unique AUTOEXEC.BAT.

4. Rename the first set of configuration files to CONFIG.SYS and AUTOEXEC.BAT.

5. Restart the computer by pressing CTRL+ALT+DEL.

6. Run MemMaker.

7. Rename the CONFIG.SYS and AUTOEXEC.BAT files to their prior names (CONFIG.1 and AUTOEXEC.1, for example).

8. Repeat steps 4 through 7 for the other configurations.

9. Edit your CONFIG.OLD file using the MS-DOS Editor and delete everything *after* your [Menu] section. In other words, delete all the individual sections which are now saved as CONFIG.1, CONFIG.2, etc. Delete the [common] section also; remember, you added the common items to each individual section in step 3. Choose Save As in the File menu and call this new file CONFIG.TOP.

10. Exit to the DOS prompt and use the COPY command to combine all the small files into one:

```
COPY CONFIG.TOP+CONFIG.1+CONFIG.2+...CONFIG.X CONFIG.SYS
```

11. Edit the new CONFIG.SYS and insert block headings to match each entry in your [menu] section.

12. Use the same procedure to combine the AUTOEXEC.BAT files:

```
COPY AUTOEXEC.1+AUTOEXEC.2+...AUTOEXEC.X AUTOEXEC.BAT
```

13. Edit AUTOEXEC.BAT and add "GOTO %CONFIG%" at the top of the file. Next, insert the block label with the colon at the beginning of the line (for example, :choice1) to match each item in your CONFIG.SYS menu section.

How do I set up my computer to use an alternate keyboard layout and character set for international use?

You can set your computer to use a different keyboard layout and character set so the characters in another language are easily accessible. Let's use Spanish (Latin American) as an example of how you do this. Edit the CONFIG.SYS file and add the following lines in the CONFIG.SYS file:

```
DEVICE=C:\DOS\DISPLAY.SYS CON=(EGA,437,1)
COUNTRY=003,,C:\DOS\COUNTRY.SYS
```

The DISPLAY.SYS driver tells the system which alternate character set you wish to use—in this case, 437 (Spanish). DISPLAY.SYS also needs to know what type of display adapter is in use; EGA is the setting to use for both EGA and VGA displays. The final "1" is the number of alternate character sets your display can support.

The COUNTRY= setting tells the system what country's conventions to follow for things like dates, times, and currency. Note that there's an extra comma there, since the middle parameter (the country character set) isn't needed in this example. The last entry tells the system where to find the alternate character set information.

Add these lines to the AUTOEXEC.BAT file:

```
NLSFUNC
MODE CON CP PREP=((850)C:\DOS\EGA.CPI)
KEYB LA,,C:\DOS\KEYBOARD.SYS
CHCP 850
```

NLSFUNC enables national language support. The MODE CON CP PREP command modifies your output to the screen to use the proper set of characters, also known as the code page. For our example, the proper code page is 850. The code page information file (xxx.CPI) contains code page information for different display types. Again, EGA.CPI works for both EGA and VGA displays. KEYB changes which keyboard layout is to be used with the system—again, note that the middle parameter is not used in this example. CHCP makes the specified code page active.

The language support installed using this procedure will only work for text-based DOS programs, which means a very small percentage of programs on the market today. Check with your software vendor for information on foreign language support.

One of my programs has problems recognizing which key I am pressing. Is something wrong with my keyboard?

Some programs do not properly recognize all keys from an enhanced keyboard. These programs require that you add "SWITCHES = /K" to your CONFIG.SYS file. "SWITCHES = /K" forces a 101- key keyboard to behave like an XT 84-key keyboard. If CONFIG.SYS also loads ANSI.SYS, you need to add the /K switch to the command that loads ANSI.SYS. Try the program again and see if this solves your problem.

I loaded something with DEVICEHIGH or LOADHIGH but it didn't work because the programs I loaded high are in conventional memory. What happened?

DEVICEHIGH and LOADHIGH load programs into conventional memory when your computer doesn't have enough upper memory. It's not that the commands didn't work, but rather, they tried to put the program in upper memory, it didn't fit, and so they put it in conventional memory instead.

Tech Tip: If you have not run MemMaker, try it. MemMaker evaluates the programs and devices you are loading to make the best possible use of the upper memory area.

Interoperability

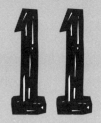

Most of the time, loading DOS is just the first of many steps in performing a task. Although you need to load DOS before you can start other programs, it is not the primary focus of your interest. Occasionally, the other programs that you load after DOS do not seem to work in tandem with it. It may be that the program has special features that do not seem to work with DOS or that the memory needed by the program is already used by DOS.

Hardware compatibility is also an issue if you want a system that runs smoothly with DOS. Often, device drivers are needed to control the operation of the hardware.

Although you may have the correct version of DOS, problems with either the software you want to run or the hardware you need to use will affect your ability to carry out the tasks you desire. These problems are all addressed in this chapter on interoperability since it is the combination of software or hardware that is the source of difficulty. The Frustration Busters box that follows outlines some tips to insure that you are doing everything possible to prevent these problems before they occur.

229

FRUSTRATION BUSTERS!

Trying to track down a problem caused by the interoperation of DOS and either hardware or software can be difficult. If you follow these suggestions you will have done everything you can to prevent problems before they occur.

■ **Terminate-and-stay-resident programs (TSRs):** These programs reside in memory until you need them. Most have a key combination that you press to activate an onscreen menu. After installing a new operating system, check that your old TSRs function without causing problems. Because new versions of DOS often use more memory or are loaded in a different area of memory than the earlier release, you should not be surprised if they are a source of difficulty. You can check with the manufacturer to see if an upgrade is available or if a new set of directions for loading the TSR in a different area of memory will fix any problems.

■ **Getting behind on upgrades:** If you continue to buy new application software but do not upgrade your operating system software, such as DOS, you may find that your new applications do not work as promised. Performance may be poor or you may experience other difficulties. Many newer software packages simply will not install unless a supported version of DOS is on the system.

■ **Shareware:** Although you can get some great software products at low cost with shareware, guaranteed compatibility and insured upgrades are not as likely as with software distributed by large software firms. Shareware authors usually can't test their products as extensively as commercial vendors do. If you experience problems with a shareware program after upgrading, you can contact the company you purchased it from, but there are no guarantees that they will still be in business.

■ **Older hardware:** It is difficult to pinpoint when a specific hardware system is outdated. As long as you are not trying to upgrade to new software,, the life of the machine is indefinite. Older machines are more likely to have incompatibilities between their BIOS and a newer operating system.

■ **Freeing memory:** Closing applications that you are no longer using frees their memory for other purposes and minimizes conflicts.

■ **File/disk utilities:** When you upgrade an operating system such as DOS,, major changes in disk and file input, output, and storage may be a part of the upgrade. Other file and disk utilities that you use may not yet be updated for these changes. This is especially true of the DOS 6.*x* DoubleSpace storage method.

■ **Device Drivers:** As you replace outdated peripheral equipment you might need to install new device drivers to enable your machine to communicate with this equipment. Check the documentation that comes with your hardware to see if a special installation procedure is recommended.

 I just installed DOS 6.*x* on my IBM PS/1 computer. A four-quadrant IBM screen used to appear when I started the computer, but now I only see the DOS prompt. Why?

You no longer see the four-quadrant screen because it is no longer accessed by DOS when you boot. The four-quadrant screen was preinstalled by IBM as part of the PS/1 boot process. Before you upgraded to DOS 6.*x*, the PS/1 probably booted using a copy of DOS that was stored in ROM. Now your computer is booting using the copy of DOS 6.*x* on the hard disk. Because you are booting from the hard drive instead of ROM, the command that displays the four-quadrant screen is no longer executed. If you would like to regain the four-quadrant screen, contact IBM PS/1 Support at (800) 765-4747 or (919) 543-9708.

I have 4MB of RAM. Since upgrading to MS-DOS 6.*x*, Windows tells me that there is not enough memory to start in Enhanced mode. Why?

You are getting the out-of-memory error message because some other program or utility is using memory that Windows needs to start in Enhanced mode. You can use the MEM command without Windows running to see what is loaded that is taking up memory.

At the DOS prompt, type **MEM /C /P** and press ENTER. The MEM command with the /C switch lists the programs that are in conventional and upper memory along with how much memory they use. The /P switch tells MEM to show you one screen of information, then wait for you to press a key before displaying any more information.

One possible cause of the out-of-memory message is that SMARTDrive uses too much memory. You can limit the memory SMARTDrive consumes. Edit your AUTOEXEC.BAT file and add **256 256** to the end of the SMARTDRV.EXE line. This tells SMARTDrive to use only 256K of memory for caching. The MEM command will show the upper memory being used, but won't attribute it to SMARTDrive.

After installing MS-DOS 6.x and DoubleSpace, Windows is much slower. What happened?

There are three things that can usually explain speed problems with Windows after installing MS-DOS 6.x:

1. If you've installed DoubleSpace, your Windows swap file may have been changed to a temporary swap file. To check this:

   a. Open the Control Panel application, usually found in the Main program group.

   b. Select the 386 Enhanced icon or 386 Enhanced from the Settings menu.

   c. Select the Virtual Memory button.

   d. If the Type listed is Temporary or None, choose Change and make a permanent swap file on your uncompressed host drive—usually drive H.

   e. Select OK, Yes, and Restart Windows to complete this change.

2. Check that SMARTDrive or another disk caching program is running. Look at your AUTOEXEC.BAT file for a line about SMARTDRV.EXE. It should look something like this: C:\DOS\SMARTDRV.EXE

3. If you only have about 2MB of RAM, the minimum for Windows, try adjusting the amount of RAM used by SMARTDrive. For example, change the line in your AUTOEXEC.BAT file which loads SMARTDrive to "C:\DOS\SMARTDRV.EXE 256 256". The "256 256" limits SMARTDrive's cache size to 256K.

Tech Tip: SMARTDrive makes a big difference in Windows performance, except when total system memory is so low that loading SMARTDrive forces Windows into standard mode.

Tech Tip: By default, the host drive will have only about 2MB of free space and it is usually best to have a larger swap file. You can change the amount of space available on the host using the DoubleSpace utility program. To resize the compressed disk, start DoubleSpace, select Change <u>S</u>ize from the <u>D</u>rive menu, and enter a smaller number for the remaining free space on the uncompressed drive.

My mouse stopped working in my DOS applications and the MS-DOS Editor. However, it still works in Windows. How can I fix this?

Your problem is that you are loading only one of two mouse drivers. DOS-based applications need to have a DOS-based mouse driver to use the mouse. Windows has its own internal mouse driver that Windows and its applications use to operate the mouse. You cannot use the Windows mouse driver to control the mouse in DOS applications. Only a DOS-based mouse driver lets you use the mouse with DOS-based applications. You may have accidentally removed the line that loads your DOS-based mouse driver from your AUTOEXEC.BAT file, or you may have deleted the mouse driver file.

DOS-based mouse drivers usually have a .COM or .SYS file extension such as MOUSE.COM or MOUSE.SYS, whereas MOUSE.DRV is the mouse driver that comes with Windows. To add mouse support to your DOS applications, add a line to your AUTOEXEC.BAT file that loads the DOS-based mouse driver. For example: you can add the line "C:\DOS\MOUSE.COM" if MOUSE.COM is your DOS-based mouse driver and it is stored in the \DOS directory. If you are unsure what file is the DOS-based mouse driver, check the documentation that came with your mouse. If the mouse driver file cannot be found on your hard disk, you need to reinstall it from the disk that came with your mouse.

Tech Tip: You must restart your computer in order for the changes to your startup files to take effect. This means that adding the mouse driver to the CONFIG.SYS or AUTOEXEC.BAT file won't actually load the mouse driver until you restart your computer.

I get a message saying "Permanent swap file is corrupt" when I start Windows. I create a new one in Windows, but when I restart Windows I get the same message again. Am I doing something wrong?

A corrupt swap file occurs most frequently in DOS 6 when your permanent swap file is on your compressed drive. Permanent swap files must be created on uncompressed drives. To avoid this error, create either a temporary swap file or a permanent swap file on an uncompressed drive. For example, if you compressed your hard drive using DoubleSpace, you should create your permanent swap file on the DoubleSpace host drive, which is usually drive H.

Tech Tip: When you create the permanent swap file, you will notice that Windows prompts you to create it on drive C, even though it is compressed. This is because Windows 3.1 was created before MS-DOS 6.*x* and its DoubleSpace feature. Windows does not realize that your C drive is compressed.

I can't use the DOS-based MS Backup when I'm in Windows. Why not?

DOS 6 has separate backup utilities for DOS and for Windows. Do not use the DOS-based MS Backup from within Windows. Instead, use DOS 6.x's Windows-based MS Backup. If you did not originally install the Windows version, you can install it by putting your first Setup disk in the disk drive, typing **SETUP /E** at the DOS prompt, and pressing ENTER.

What is a BIOS and how do I know what type and date I have?

BIOS stands for Basic Input/Output System. BIOS is what the central processing unit (CPU) of your computer uses to communicate with all other hardware inside the computer. Some of the things the BIOS communicates with, commonly called *peripherals*, are: a mouse, a floppy drive, a hard drive, a monitor, and a keyboard. This means that the BIOS is what allows your computer to talk with itself.

To find out about your computer's BIOS:

1. Type **MSD** at the DOS prompt and press ENTER, starting the Microsoft Diagnostics utility.

2. Select the Computer button by clicking it or pressing P. The BIOS information is displayed for you, as in the example shown in Figure 11-1.

3. Press ESC or ENTER to remove the BIOS information from the screen.

4. Select Exit from the File menu by pressing ALT+F, then X.

Tech Tip: Some BIOS versions do not report correct information when checked by MSD. Watch for BIOS messages during bootup, since BIOS versions are usually displayed there. If the information you see in MSD doesn't make sense (for example, if the date listed is several years older than your computer), contact your BIOS manufacturer to determine the correct date.

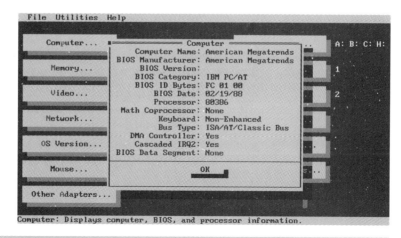

FIGURE 11-1　　Display of computer information with Microsoft Diagnostics

When I run Setup for any program, the Setup program won't accept the second Setup disk, but continually asks for it to be inserted. How can I install my program?

When a Setup or installation program keeps prompting for the second disk, even if it is in the drive, you probably have one of three possible problems. You can discover which is the true source of your problem and determine how to correct it by running simple tests. The three potential causes, and the tests to identify them are:

A Problem with the Hardware

1. Reboot your system.

2. Press F5 when you see the "Starting MS-DOS..." message to bypass your AUTOEXEC.BAT and CONFIG.SYS files. Booting without executing these files is called a *clean boot*.

3. Place any disk with files on it in the A drive.

4. Type **DIR A:** at the DOS prompt and press ENTER. Note the files in the directory.

5. Insert a different disk in the same drive and do another directory list, using the command given above.

   - If you see a different list of files, your system is correctly reading the disks. You now need to check if there is a conflict with another program, using the steps described in the next section.

   - If you see the same list of files for both disks, your computer is not recognizing that you have changed disks.

6. Follow steps 3 through 5, using your second floppy disk drive, if you have one.

   - If both of your disk drives have difficulty reading disks, the difficulty is either with your system's BIOS settings for the drives, or in the floppy disk drive controller.

   - If the second disk drive works correctly, the problem is either the BIOS settings for the one drive or a defect in the drive itself.

A Conflict with Another Program
If you test both of your disk drives as described above and they are both working

properly, your problem may be a conflict between the Setup program and another loaded program. To test if a program conflict is the source of your problem:

1. Reboot your system.
2. Press F5 when you see the "Starting MS-DOS..." message to bypass your CONFIG.SYS and AUTOEXEC.BAT files.
3. Restart the Setup program.

If you have no difficulty with the Setup program now, your problem was a conflict with another program. If you had unloaded all programs before attempting to run Setup the first time, then the conflict was with one of the programs loaded in CONFIG.SYS or AUTOEXEC.BAT.

For future reference, you will want to know which program caused the conflict. To find out, reboot your system and press F8 instead of F5 when you see the "Starting MS-DOS..." message. You can then choose which lines in the CONFIG.SYS file you want executed. Allow only one program or driver to load, then attempt Setup again. Continue this, until you isolate the one line that causes your problem.

A Problem with the Disks   Your problem may be with the Setup disks themselves. To test this, try the disk change test described under "A Problem with the Hardware," using the Setup disks themselves. If the other disks worked correctly but the Setup disks do not, the problem is most likely with your Setup disks. Confirm this by performing the disk change test with the Setup disks on another computer.

Tech Tip: If the problem is happening particularly with the DOS Setup program at the point where the Uninstall disk is inserted, a likely cause is a disk of the wrong density. Although this problem is rare, it would probably be a preformatted high-density disk inserted in a double-density drive.

I have a program with a built-in backup feature designed to back up its data files. Since upgrading to DOS 6.x, the backup feature doesn't work. Why?

The application probably used MS-DOS's BACKUP command to execute its backup feature. MS-DOS 6.x no longer includes the BACKUP command. Instead, it uses the new MS Backup utility, which works very differently.

To make the program's built-in backup feature work again, you need to make the old BACKUP command available. There are two possible ways to do this:

1. You can order the supplemental disk for DOS 6.x, which has the BACKUP command on it, and install the command on your computer. You can order the supplemental disk using the order form at the back of the DOS 6.x manual.

2. You can also use your old BACKUP command from a prior DOS version. To do this:

   ■ Copy the file BACKUP.EXE (or BACKUP.COM, depending on the DOS version) from your old DOS Setup disks or the OLD_DOS.x directory into your \DOS directory.

Use SETVER to add the BACKUP command to the SETVER version table, allowing it to run with MS-DOS 6.x. To do this, type a command like **SETVER BACKUP.EXE 5.00** at the DOS prompt and press ENTER. The 5.00 should be altered to the version number of the MS-DOS version the BACKUP command is from. You need to set the version with SETVER to the *actual* DOS version that the BACKUP command file came from when updating the SETVER table. See the online MS-DOS Help for more information on the use of SETVER.

I installed MS-DOS 6.2 and now I get "EMM386: Unable to start enhanced Windows mode due to invalid path specification for EMM386" when I try to start Windows. What's wrong?

This error message is rather deceiving because very often it has nothing to do with whether your Path statement is correct. Often, it is appearing because of your Anti-Virus software instead. The Microsoft Anti-Virus utility keeps track of the file conditions for each file in each directory using what are called Checksums to allow it to detect changes. After the MS-DOS 6.2 installation, many DOS files have been changed, including EMM386.EXE. Your Anti-Virus software now sees these changed files as being possibly infected by a virus. You must re-scan your hard drive with the Anti-Virus software and choose Update when it stops on your DOS files, or disable VSafe, the memory-resident portion of the Anti-Virus software. Since VSafe is typically started in your AUTOEXEC.BAT file, you can disable it by simply adding **REM** at the beginning of the line in your AUTOEXEC.BAT file that starts VSafe, then restarting your system.

If you are using the Windows version of the Anti-Virus utility, you use different steps to take care of this:

1. Start Windows in Standard mode, by typing WIN /S and pressing ENTER.
2. Start your Microsoft Anti-Virus utility.
3. Select Set Options from the Options menu and make sure the Create New Checksums check box is selected (it will be filled with an X).
4. Select OK.
5. Then choose Detect. Anti-Virus's virus detecting will pause on the modified DOS files with a warning.
6. Choose Update to update the Anti-Virus software with the new file conditions. You should then be able to run Windows in 386 Enhanced mode again.

Why do I get the error message "Incorrect DOS version" when I attempt to go to the DOS Prompt program item in Windows? This started after upgrading to DOS 6.x.

Your DOSPRMPT.PIF file, which Windows uses to find your COMMAND.COM file, may specify a previous version of COMMAND.COM. In order to prevent this, you need to find the previous versions of COMMAND.COM and delete them, then update the DOSPRMPT.PIF file so that it directs Windows to the updated version.

1. In the root directory of each hard disk, type **DIR /S COMMAND.COM** at the DOS prompt and press ENTER. This command will list each copy of COMMAND.COM on the disk.

2. Compare each copy of COMMAND.COM to the one found in the root directory of your boot drive. Delete any copy of COMMAND.COM whose file size and date do not match the COMMAND.COM for your version of DOS.

3. Within Windows, start the PIF Editor and edit the DOSPRMPT.PIF file so that it executes an up-to-date COMMAND.COM.

Windows and some other programs will not start since I upgraded to MS-DOS 6.x. Why?

Windows and the other programs will not start because you probably ran QEMM, 386MAX, Netroom, MemMaker, or another memory management program on your system while you were still using your previous version of DOS. All the memory optimization is specific to the files associated with that earlier version of DOS. Some of the drivers and programs loaded in CONFIG.SYS and AUTOEXEC.BAT have changed with the upgrade, and so has your memory configuration. Reoptimizing your memory to account for the changed size of some of the new MS-DOS files may help.

Tech Tip: This is only one of many possible causes, all related to changing memory configuration. Use the F5 and F8 keys to boot your system interactively, and temporarily disable anything not related to the program you're trying to run. If your problems are with Windows, try starting Windows in Standard mode by typing **WIN /S**. Standard mode does not use the upper memory area where most conflicts occur. If Standard mode works, use the F8 key interactive boot to troubleshoot the problem.

My printer isn't working. Is there a reliable way to test the printer to see if the problem is either hardware- or software-related?

When your printer isn't working, you can easily run a simple test to decide where the problem occurs. The easiest way to find the source of the problem is to print from DOS directly to the printer port. If you can print directly from DOS, then the source of your problem is probably the program you are using to print. If you cannot print from DOS, then your problem is probably the hardware.

To print to your printer port directly from DOS, do the following:

1. Make your root directory the current directory by typing **CD ** at the DOS prompt and pressing ENTER.

2. Type **COPY CONFIG.SYS LPT1** and press ENTER. The printer should start printing the contents of the file. Some printers (usually laser printers) require that you issue a form feed before they actually print. DOS doesn't issue form feeds automatically. To do that, take the printer offline, usually by pressing the On Line button on the front panel, press the Form Feed button once, then press the On Line button again.

Tech Tip: Many software-related printing problems occur when a program is sending the printing information to the incorrect port. Make sure your program is set up for the correct printer port.

If your printer is connected to a different port, simply substitute that port for LPT1 in step 2 above. If you are unsure which port the printer is connected to, try the test above using each of the port names: LPT1, LPT2, LPT3, COM1, COM2, COM3, and COM4. If the printer prints, you will then know which port it is connected to.

If the printer does not print when you copy a file to the printer port with the COPY command, your printing problem is probably hardware-related. Make sure your printer is turned on and is online. Check all cable connections between the printer and the computer. If you have a printer control box, bypass it and connect the printer cable directly to the printer and the computer. Now try the test again.

If your computer is connected to a network, the problem may relate to the network itself. In this case, you want to contact your network administrator and let that person resolve the difficulty.

Why did I lose my compressed Stacker drives after upgrading to MS-DOS 6.2?

Stacker compresses data on your hard disk, just as DoubleSpace does. Stacker 3.1*x* is also similar to DoubleSpace in that it loads as a system file, meaning that it loads before CONFIG.SYS is executed. (Older versions of Stacker load in the CONFIG.SYS; Stacker 3.1*x* also installs in CONFIG.SYS when it is first installed under DOS 5 or earlier.) Stacker accomplishes this by substituting its own DBLSPACE.BIN file. The Stacker 3.1*x* version of this file mounts Stacker's STACVOL file. When you upgraded to MS-DOS 6.2, the upgrade overwrote Stacker's DBLSPACE.BIN file with an updated Microsoft DBLSPACE.BIN file. The new DBLSPACE.BIN cannot read the STACVOL file, and as a result, the Stacker compressed volume files are not mounting.

The data saved in your Stacker drives is not lost. However, the steps needed to remodify the DBLSPACE.BIN file so that you can access these drives again are complicated and vary in each case. You should contact Stac, the manufacturer of Stacker, for instructions.

I have an older version of Norton Utilities/PC Tools. It worked fine with MS-DOS 5.0. Why do I need to upgrade, now that I have upgraded to MS-DOS 6.*x*?

You won't need to upgrade to a newer version of Norton Utilities or PC Tools, unless you install DoubleSpace. Older versions of Norton Utilities and PC Tools do not understand the DoubleSpace file structure. Therefore, some of the utilities will do more harm than good when used on a DoubleSpace compressed drive. You can continue to use these older utilities as long as you do not use DoubleSpace to compress the files on your hard disk.

Tech Tip: Norton Utilities 7.0 and PC Tools 8.0A are at this time the only third-party disk utilities that are compatible with the MS-DOS 6.*x* DoubleSpace compression utility. If you are using a different utility program, contact its manufacturer for an update that supports DOS 6's DoubleSpace compressed drives.

When I try to start a DOS program from Windows, I get the message "Insufficient File Handles." What can I do? I'm on a network.

If you get the error message "Insufficient File Handles" when trying to invoke a DOS application under Windows, first make sure that the proper network is selected under Windows Setup. Then change the following settings:

- Increase the Files statement in your CONFIG.SYS file.
- Insert **PerVMFILES=<# of files>** in the [386Enh] section of the SYSTEM.INI file.
- For Novell networks, add the statement **File Handles = 70** to the NET.CFG or SHELL.CFG file, which should be in your C:*NET* directory, where *net* indicates the directory that relates to your network.

Tech Tip:
Sometimes, just increasing the Files statement in the CONFIG.SYS file is sufficient to eliminate the error message.

The combination of all three of these settings cannot total more than 255.

Why can't Interlnk share my CD-ROM drive?

A CD-ROM drive is an actual device attached to your computer. As with many other attached devices, your CD-ROM drive requires a device driver to provide access to it. A device driver is a file that provides the information necessary for DOS to communicate with your device. In general, Interlnk can only access devices that do not require device drivers. This requirement also excludes access to network drives, some external hard drives and floppy disk drives, and other devices.

How do I configure Lotus 1-2-3 3.*x* to work in DOS Shell?

You need to create a program item in DOS Shell's Main program group for Lotus 1-2-3 3.*x*. You also need to set how much extended memory Lotus 1-2-3 3.*x* needs. To do this:

1. Move to the Program List area of the DOS Shell using TAB.
2. Go to the program group that you want to add the 1-2-3 program item to.
3. Select New from the File menu.
4. Select Program Item, then OK in the New Program Object dialog box.
5. Enter the information necessary for Lotus 1-2-3 3.x in the Add Program dialog box.
6. Select Advanced.
7. Type **384** in the XMS Memory KB Required text box.
8. Select OK twice to add the new program item to the Main program group. You can now select this program item to start Lotus 1-2-3 3.*x* from the DOS Shell.

When I start Windows 3.0, I see the message "You must have the file WINA20.386 in the root of your boot drive to run Windows in Enhanced Mode." How do I run Windows?

Add "SWITCHES = /W" to your CONFIG.SYS file. This switch tells Windows that the WINA20.386 file is not in your root directory. You also need to edit the SYSTEM.INI file in your Windows directory and add the following line in the section that has the header [386Enh]: DEVICE=*location of file*\WINA20.386. You can also solve this problem by copying the file WINA20.386 to your root directory. If you can't find this file, you can retrieve it from your DOS disks—be sure to use the WINA20.386 found on the original disks for your current version of DOS, since this file is version-specific.

Tech Tip: This message can show up erroneously if you're using an older version of the QEMM memory manager. Upgrade QEMM to version 6.0 or later to solve this problem.

I keep getting the error message "Memory parity error" when I open an application in Windows. How do I get rid of this message?

Memory parity errors frequently indicate a problem with your computer's hardware. To find out what is wrong, try starting Windows after doing a clean boot and only performing the minimum commands in CONFIG.SYS. To do this:

1. Restart your system by pressing CTRL+ALT+DEL or turning it off and then on again.

2. When you see the message "Starting MS-DOS...", press F8. DOS will now prompt you to confirm each line in the CONFIG.SYS file that you want to execute.

3. Type **Y** to only the five lines that load or set:

   - HIMEM.SYS
   - Files=
   - Buffers=
   - Shell=
   - Stacks=

Start Windows and the application that caused the parity error. If you no longer have this error message, the problem is caused by one of the lines in your CONFIG.SYS or AUTOEXEC.BAT file.

If you still get the same message after executing this boot process, one of your memory chips may be bad. You need to have your system's memory checked and repaired. Contact either the manufacturer of your computer or a computer repair service to have this done.

Tech Note: MS-DOS 6.2 checks your memory during the startup procedure if HIMEM.SYS is loaded in the CONFIG.SYS file. HIMEM.SYS has to be loaded for Windows to run. If you see errors listed here even occasionally, this is an additional indication of a hardware memory problem. In either case, have the system checked by a qualified technician. HIMEM.SYS may not detect parity errors, since they may only show up when certain values are stored in the affected memory location.

I want to delete a non-DOS partition on my hard drive. Can I do it with DOS?

You can delete a non-DOS partition, such as a partition created by another operating system, with MS-DOS 6.x, though not with previous versions of DOS. To delete the partition:

1. Create a boot disk with FDISK.EXE on it.

2. Insert your boot disk in the A drive and reboot your system.

3. Type **FDISK** at the DOS prompt and press ENTER.

4. Choose option 3, "Delete a partition or Logical DOS Drive."

5. Choose option 4, "Delete Non-DOS Partition."

6. Choose the number of the partition you want to delete.

7. When prompted, type **Y** to confirm you want to delete that partition.

8. Press ESC twice to exit FDISK.

Tech Tip: There are many flavors of UNIX and FDISK has been found to have trouble deleting a few types of UNIX partitions. Just about any other kind of partition can be deleted with FDISK.

You can now use FDISK to create a new partition, or create a new partition using some other software.

I'm having trouble with my Clipper database after installing MS-DOS 6.x. Any ideas about what to do?

The most likely cause of problems with a Clipper database after installing MS-DOS 6.x is memory errors. You may be receiving "Not enough memory" messages or your system may stop responding unexpectedly. If this is the problem, check the line in your CONFIG.SYS file that loads the EMM386 memory manager. If you're using the NOEMS switch to load EMM386, try adding the NOVCPI switch as well.

I'm using a virus detection program other than MSAV. It detects a virus infecting one of the MSAV files. Is my system in trouble?

In this case, your virus detection program is probably not detecting a potential problem. Most virus detection programs look for the "signature" of a viru—an identifying part of the virus, not the entire virus itself. The signature can consist of a banner screen, or actual code that the virus uses in its operation. In order for a virus detection program to recognize this signature, it must already have a copy of that signature. What is probably happening is that your other virus detection program is picking up the copy of the signature file that MSAV uses to recognize the virus, and is mistaking it for an actual virus. If the other program is detecting a virus in MSAV files, there is probably no virus infection at this point, just a case of mistaken identity.

I installed MS-DOS 6.x and no longer have the OS/2 Boot Manager. How do I get it back?

OS/2's Boot Manager functions on a 1MB partition at the beginning of your first physical hard drive. When the MS-DOS Setup program runs, it disables this partition, but does not delete it. The MS-DOS partition must be active during setup so that Setup can recover if there is a power failure or other interruption. To get your system back to normal:

1. Type **FDISK** at the DOS prompt and press ENTER.
2. Choose option 2, "Set active partition."
3. Select the 1MB partition.
4. Press ESC twice to exit FDISK.
5. Reboot your system. You should see OS/2's Boot Manager again.

Why can't I load DOS into high memory on my Zenith SuperSport?

The design of the Zenith SuperSport 80286 with 1MB of memory makes it impossible to load DOS high. Although these computers have memory that could be made available as extended memory with HIMEM.SYS, Zenith has set this memory as expanded memory. It cannot be reconfigured.

Each time I start my system it stops responding after loading Above DISC. What can I do to fix this?

A system using an older version of Above DISC may stop responding, beep repeatedly, or reboot itself if HIMEM.SYS is loaded and DOS is loaded into high memory. All three programs—DOS, HIMEM.SYS, and Above DISC—are using the high memory area, causing a conflict. According to Above Software, the latest version of Above DISC (1.4c) is fully compatible with DOS 6.*x*, so this error should not occur.

Networking

Every network that works with DOS installs as a program running on top of DOS. Therefore, network support for DOS comes from the network software, not from DOS. If you are attached to a network, you can use DOS commands to access both data on your hard disk and the network file server. Most network software also provides some type of file management program to handle basic file manipulation tasks. You can choose to use either approach unless your network manager specifies a preferred method.

If you choose to use DOS, many of your problems are likely to be the same ones that non-network users experience. In this chapter, you will find questions that are unique to network users. The questions related to a specific type of network are grouped together according to the network type. Some of the questions involving networks and DOS use terms that you do not encounter with other features of DOS. Several of these terms are described in the Frustration Busters box that follows.

FRUSTRATION BUSTERS!

Understanding a few of the most common terms relating to networks will help you reduce the frustration level of working in a new environment. The most common terms you see as a network user include:

- **Client:** A computer that requests information on a network.

- **Local:** The resources available to a user through his or her own computer rather than through a network. A network user may have a hard drive and printer available locally as well as the drives and printers available through the network.

- **Peer-to-peer:** A network which does not have a server that operates as the network's hub. Peer-to-peer networks can provide the basic network features when you do not have too many computers attached to the network. Each computer on the network can function as a client or server based on which computer prompts for information and which computer has the requested information.

- **Redirector**: The part of the network that locates the files and directories. A redirector monitors all commands and redirects those intended for the network to the appropriate network resource, while passing non-network commands to the local command interpreter. For example, if your network printer is identified as LPT2, any output destined for LPT2 is redirected to the correct network printer. This is also commonly referred to as a *network shell.*

- **Server:** The computer that sends files or other information to the computer user requesting it. Servers also may share available resources such as printers and modems with computers on the network. On a peer-to-peer network, any computer can be a server, even while operating simultaneously as a client. On a server-based network, the network server is always dedicated to its server function.

- **Server-based network:** A network which has one computer dedicated to the network server function. The network server coordinates the flow of information between the other computers,

called workstations, and usually has its own network operating system.

- **Workstation:** A computer connected to a network where users perform work. A workstation is not a server in a server-based network, but may operate as a server in a peer-to-peer network.

Will DOS 6 work with my network?

Tech Tip: If you are running Microsoft MS-Net or a 100-percent compatible network, and you run into an error message during DOS 6 setup, the solution is to get newer network files. You can get these newer network files by ordering the supplemental disks or by downloading the files from the Microsoft Product Support Download Service (MSDL).

Most popular networks are designed to work with DOS 6. However, some of them may require that you upgrade your network software before upgrading to DOS 6.

The following table shows the different network systems DOS 6 supports and the minimum version number needed to work with DOS 6. If you have an earlier version of the network software, contact your network vendor for an upgrade before upgrading to DOS 6. If your network software is too old to support DOS 6, you will see a message indicating that you need to check the NETWORKS.TXT file on the Setup disk. Usually, the solution is to get a newer version of the network software.

Network	Earliest Version Supported
Artisoft LANtastic	2.5
Banyan VINES	4.0
DCA 10Net	3.3 (41)
DCA 10Net Plus	4.20 (20)
DEC PATHWORKS for DOS	4.0
Farallon PhoneNET	2.02
IBM DOS LAN Requester	1.30.1
IBM PC LAN Program (PCLP)	1.34
Novell NetWare	2.1 (NETX Shell must be 3.32 or higher)
Sitka TOPS	3.0

Can I add a program item to DOS Shell for my network?

While DOS Shell will not stop you from creating a program item for logging into your network, it probably will not work. For example, if you run Novell's Login, Map, or Session commands from MS-DOS Shell or while MS-DOS Shell is running, these commands cannot add to the existing search path. You probably cannot use the network commands once you log in. Rather than trying to create a program item for the network from DOS Shell, log into your network, then start DOS Shell. You can add program items for the tasks you want to do on the network once you are inside DOS Shell.

Does MemMaker work if I am on a network?

MemMaker will work when your computer is part of a network. If you load network redirector programs, running MemMaker can help select how they are placed in upper memory blocks. However, if you are part of a token ring network, MemMaker may not work correctly. If this happens, run MemMaker by typing **MEMMAKER /T** at the DOS prompt and pressing ENTER. You should also check your network software documentation to see whether the network TSRs can run in upper memory. Some TSRs can load into upper memory but will misbehave after loading.

Tech Tip: You may want to skip over network drives when you run Microsoft Anti-Virus, depending on the anti-virus capabilities of your network and whether Microsoft Anti-Virus incorrectly reports viruses on your network server. To disable network drives, type **MSAV /L** and press ENTER to start the program. When you use MWAV, the anti-virus software that runs within Windows, you have the option to scan only the local drives.

Tech Terror: Banyan VINES may not work with MemMaker. For example, MemMaker does not work correctly if Banyan VINES puts some of the network software components into different upper memory block regions.

My programs do not run correctly when they use expanded memory and I am connected to a network. How do I get my programs to work?

If your network stores part of itself in upper memory, you need to tell EMM386.EXE in CONFIG.SYS to not to use the memory that the network adapter card uses for other purposes. Forgetting to exclude this memory may cause a problem with programs that use expanded memory. Edit CONFIG.SYS and add **X=** followed by the memory address your network adapter card uses. For example, if you are using the defaults for the LANtastic 2Mbps adapter, you will add **X=D800-DFFF** to the "DEVICE=" command for EMM386.EXE.

I'm on a LANtastic or 10Net network and can't run DoubleSpace on my local hard drive. How can I compress my local drive?

LANtastic and 10Net networks recognize all local drives as network drives. DoubleSpace cannot be installed on a network drive. When you try, you will see a message that DoubleSpace cannot be run on a network drive. The solution is to disable the network software, run DoubleSpace, then re-enable your network software.

To temporarily disable your network, reboot and press F8 immediately when you see the message "Starting MS-DOS." Pressing F8 allows you to process individual lines in your CONFIG.SYS and to skip the AUTOEXEC.BAT file. Type **N** for the lines that set up and process your network and type **Y** for all other lines. Once you are at the DOS prompt, run DoubleSpace on the local drive. After DoubleSpace finishes, simply reboot and you will return to normal, with the network software loaded again and your local hard drive compressed.

Besides using F8 as described above, you can use the DOS Editor to remark lines in your AUTOEXEC.BAT and CONFIG.SYS files containing your network software. To make a line a remark and prevent DOS from processing it, type **REM** and a space in front of the lines. Save the files with the changes and reboot. After rebooting, run DoubleSpace and compress your local hard drive. When DoubleSpace finishes, re-edit the files, remove the remarks, and reboot the computer.

Tech Tip: After you compress a local hard drive, some DoubleSpace features, such as the LIST, CHKDSK, MOUNT, and UNMOUNT features, do not work correctly unless you stop the server service for the LANtastic or 10Net network. Also, LANtastic's NET command does not display the drive configuration of your server correctly and does not display any drive that the DBLSPACE /INFO command labels as "Available for DoubleSpace." If you have problems accessing data from the compressed drive's host drive, you may need to change the host drive's drive letter. The steps for this are described in the question "Why, after installing MS-DOS 6.0 and DoubleSpace, do I get the error message 'Invalid drive specification' when I try to go to my login drive on my Novell network?", later in this chapter.

 ## I'm on a LANtastic network and I can't run ScanDisk to check my local hard drive. How do I run ScanDisk?

A LANtastic network recognizes all local drives as network drives. ScanDisk does not work on network drives. To run ScanDisk on your local drives, you must first disable the network software. The question "I'm on a LANtastic or 10Net network and can't run DoubleSpace on my local hard drive. How can I compress my local drive?", earlier in this chapter, describes how you can temporarily disable the network. With the network disabled, you can run DoubleSpace as well as ScanDisk.

Tech Tip: Just as with ScanDisk, you may also have problems with the Microsoft Defragmenter utility. Defragmenter will not work with your LANtastic or 10Net network if the server service is loaded. Defragmenter will work with your network only if the redirector is loaded.

 ## Why, after installing MS-DOS 6.0 and DoubleSpace, do I get the error message "Invalid drive specification" when I try to go to my login drive on my Novell network?

When DoubleSpace Express set up its host drive letter, DoubleSpace defined the host drive by assigning it the fifth available drive letter. If the network was not active at the time of setup, the host drive for drive C is then drive letter H. All drive letters in between are reserved for use by MS-DOS. If the first drive letter used by Novell is F, the host drive must be E or lower.

You can fix this problem by reassigning the drive letter for the host drive.

For MS-DOS 6.0:

1. Change to the host drive (usually H).

2. Type **ATTRIB -R -S -H DBLSPACE.INI** and press ENTER to clear all the attributes from the hidden file DBLSPACE.INI. This file stores the initial settings for DoubleSpace.

3. Type **EDIT DBLSPACE.INI** and press ENTER to modify this file. Your DBLSPACE.INI file will look something like:

```
MaxRemovableDrives=2
FirstDrive=D
LastDrive=H
MaxFileFragments=115
ActivateDrive=H,C0
```

4. Edit the LastDrive and ActivateDrive lines in DBLSPACE.INI to read:

```
LastDrive=E
ActivateDrive=E,C0
```

This will tell DoubleSpace to reassign the host drive letter and set the last drive equal to E.

5. Check your CONFIG.SYS, and, if needed, edit the "LASTDRIVE=" line to "LASTDRIVE=E."

6. Type **ATTRIB +R +S +H DBLSPACE.INI** and press ENTER to return all the attributes from the hidden file DBLSPACE.INI.

For MS-DOS 6.2:

■   Type **DBLSPACE /HOST=E** and press ENTER. This will automatically modify the DBLSPACE.INI. When you reboot, the system will use the new host drive letter.

How can I run MSD on my computer that is on an ArcNet network?

To run MSD on an ArcNet network, you need to type **MSD /I** at the DOS prompt and press ENTER. Once inside MSD, do not choose the <u>N</u>etwork option. /I tells MSD not to perform its regular suite of hardware detection at startup. The polling of hardware causes the workstation running MSD to disconnect from the net, and may cause other disconnects and disruptions on the net. As long as MSD does not try to talk to the network card, everything will be fine.

I cannot run my AT&T StarGroup network after running DOS 6 Setup. How do I get my network running?

If your AT&T StarGroup network will not run after running MS-DOS 6 Setup, you will need to follow these steps:

1. Type **SETVER SETUP.EXE 4.00** at the DOS prompt and press ENTER.

2. Type **SETVER ATTSTART.EXE 4.00** at the DOS prompt and press ENTER.

3. Restart your computer.

4. Remove the existing network software using your StarGroup installation disks.

5. Reinstall StarGroup. When the network installation prompts for the version of MS-DOS you are using, select MS-DOS version 4.0.

6. Once the network software installation is complete, type **SETVER SETUP.EXE /D** at the DOS prompt and press ENTER.

7. Restart your computer.

After upgrading to DOS 6.x, I frequently see the message "Incorrect DOS version" when I use DOS commands on a network. What causes this error message?

You are seeing this message because your computer found a different version of a DOS command before it found the DOS 6 version of the command. Your PATH setting probably includes a network drive with a directory containing old DOS files before your own DOS 6.x directory on your local hard drive. Your PATH setting typically changes when you log into the network. Type **SET** and press ENTER to see your current PATH settings. Look for the location of your current DOS directory in relation to the other directories in your path. The local DOS directory needs to appear before other directories that contain DOS files. See your network administrator about correcting problems with your network PATH modifications.

Novell typically maps search drives at the front of the PATH and many networks share a DOS directory. This is fine until a workstation upgrades its DOS version, logs in to the network, and the mapped search drive appears in their path before the location of the more up-to-date DOS files. When you use a DOS command from outside the DOS directory, DOS searches your PATH for the command. DOS finds the network DOS directory first and runs that version of the command. Since it is from a previous version of DOS, you get the error message. While this example uses a Novell network, it can happen on other networks where the operating system finds more than one copy of DOS files.

Another possible cause is that COMSPEC is set incorrectly in the system login script on a Novell network. COMSPEC is a DOS environment variable which DOS uses to keep track of where COMMAND.COM is stored. You want to check that it is pointing to the correct version of DOS, that the directory reference is correct, and that the file is not damaged.

When attempting to load my NETX.COM for my Novell network, why do I get an "Incorrect DOS version" or "Not running on DOS V3.0 through V5.0" message?

You will see this error message because your NETX.COM is a version developed before MS-DOS 6.*x* was released. Microsoft recommends you use NETX.COM version 3.32 or later with MS-DOS 6.*x*. As a temporary solution, you can "trick" NETX.COM into thinking it's running on a previous version of DOS by following these steps:

1. Check your CONFIG.SYS file and make sure it includes this line:

```
DEVICE=C:\DOS\SETVER.EXE
```

2. At the DOS prompt, type **SETVER NETX.COM x.xx** and press ENTER. *X.xx* equals the version number of MS-DOS that your NETX.COM file expects. For example, you can enter the following when NETX.COM expects DOS 5.0:

```
SETVER NETX.COM 5.00
```

This adds the program NETX.COM to the version table. When this program executes, MS-DOS notifies NETX.COM that it is operating on DOS 5.00.

If your network login script maps the COMSPEC DOS environment variable to the OS_VERSION environment variable, DOS may look to the network V5.00 directory. This information is only needed in certain Novell login script configurations. You can solve this problem by following these steps:

1. Create a net directory, such as V4.90, and give all MS-DOS 6.*x* users access to this directory. The name of the directory does not matter, as long as it's less than 5.00.

2. Copy the MS-DOS 6.*x* files into the directory.

3. Modify SETVER to match the directory. For example, if the directory is V4.90, you want to type **SETVER NETX.COM 4.90** and press ENTER.

Tech Tip: You can check the version of NETX.COM you are using by typing **NETX** at the DOS prompt and pressing ENTER. You can also use the NetWare VLM client version 1.*x*. To check the version number of the NetWare VLM, type **VLM** at the DOS prompt and press ENTER.

Can I back up my Novell network drive using DOS 6's Backup?

DOS 6's Backup program will not work on network drives although you can back up other drives to network drives. Your network administrator will handle backing up the network drives.

Tech Tip: The Complete field in the Backup Progress dialog box in Microsoft Backup shows you how far along the backup process is. It will initially move slowly when you back up files to a NetWare 286 network, due to the way NetWare 286 handles writing files to the network.

I'm running into several problems since I upgraded my Novell network. Did I do something wrong?

When a Novell network has a problem running DOS 6, the easiest solution is to get an updated version of the network shell software. Some of the problems that an updated network shell will fix include:

- The Task Swapper in MS-DOS Shell not working.

- The inability to load MS-DOS 6 on your remote-boot workstation. A new RPLFIX.COM file will fix this problem.

- The inability to reload COMMAND.COM after the Novell login program sets the COMSPEC variable. A new login program solves this problem. You can also solve it by removing any path information to the COMMAND.COM file since the file is in the root directory.

- The inability to use the UNDELETE command on a network.

I'm trying to load the hard disk driver for my Novell NetWare server but no matter what I do, it says that the file does not exist. I checked my DOS partition and it's there. What is happening?

The hard disk driver is one of the first things you need to load during a server installation. Since the driver is located in the DOS partition of your server, try typing **LOAD C:*filename*.DSK** at the DOS prompt and pressing ENTER. *Filename* is the name of the hard disk driver. If that does not work, exit the installation process and return to DOS. Check the attribute of this file by typing **ATTRIB *filename*.DSK** at the DOS prompt and pressing ENTER. (*Filename* is the same filename used earlier.) If this file has an *R* for read-only, then you found the source of your problem. NetWare does not see files in the DOS partition marked with this attribute. To correct the problem, remove the attribute by typing **ATTRIB -R *FILENAME*.DSK** and pressing ENTER. You can now continue with your server installation.

I am running Novell's NetWare Lite and now every time I try to use certain drives, I get the "Not ready" error message. What is wrong?

This error message occurs because Novell is using the same drives that DoubleSpace wants to use. You need to set the host drive letter to one that is lower than your lowest NetWare Lite network drive letter. The best way to do this depends on your DOS version. See the question "Why, after installing MS-DOS 6.0 and DoubleSpace, do I get the error message 'Invalid drive specification' when I try to go to my login drive on my Novell network?" earlier in this chapter for more information.

Error Messages

Error messages are a source of frustration to many DOS users. Often, they are not particularly descriptive and don't even provide a clue about how you might correct the error. The most common DOS error messages are listed in this chapter along with brief explanations of what the problem might be. In some cases, these messages are covered in more detail earlier in the book. In these cases, we've included a reference to the chapter that question is in, in case you need additional information.

Abort, Retry, Fail, Ignore?

This message can appear in three different forms: "Abort, Retry, Fail, Ignore?", "Abort, Retry, Fail?" or "Abort, Retry, Ignore?" Whichever version of the message you receive, the point is that DOS can't communicate with the hardware you are trying to access. This message most often appears when reading or writing to disks.

Tech Note: An error that occurs while trying to exchange data with another piece of hardware is called an I/O error. I/O stands for Input/Output. An I/O error is an error that prevents DOS from bringing information into memory (input), or sending information from memory to another device (output).

If you're using a floppy disk, first check that the disk is actually in the drive. If it is a 5 1/4" disk, make sure that the disk drive door is closed. After the disk is correctly inserted, type **R** for Retry. If the disk is correctly inserted, check to see if the disk is usable. To do this, type **A** for Abort, then use CHKDSK or ScanDisk to look at the disk. The disk may be unformatted, formatted incorrectly for your drive or computer, or may be damaged. If it is damaged, throw it out. Otherwise, reformat the disk to make it usable. This error message may also appear when there are problems with your hard drive, or when your computer tries to read or write data from a parallel or serial port, such as a modem or printer might use.

Access denied

One of the files you are attempting to work with has the read-only attribute set. To remove the read-only attribute, enter **ATTRIB -R MYFILE.TXT**, where **MYFILE.TXT** is the name of the file with the read-only attribute, and press ENTER. This message can also show up in a multi-user environment, such as a network. Another user may be accessing the file at the same time, or you may not have the necessary network rights to modify or delete the file.

Allocation error. Size adjusted.

If you see this message while running CHKDSK, it means CHKDSK found an error in the file allocation table indicating that a file was listed in the table as either longer or shorter than it actually was. CHKDSK corrected the entry in the file allocation table.

Bad command or file name

DOS can't find the command or filename you entered. Check your typing. Then check that you are in the directory where the file is located. If necessary, add a path to the filename so that DOS will look in the correct directory.

Bad or missing *C:\directory\filename.ext*
Error in CONFIG.SYS line *x*

One of the files loaded during startup is missing. Check the CONFIG.SYS line mentioned in the error message to make sure that the referenced file exists in the directory specified.

Bad or missing command interpreter

DOS can't find a command interpreter, usually the file named COMMAND.COM. Try rebooting your system with a system disk in drive A, then check the following:

1. Verify the "SHELL=" line in CONFIG.SYS. Make sure that it lists the correct path and filename for your COMMAND.COM. If you have no "SHELL=" line, DOS will look for a COMMAND.COM file in the root directory of your boot drive.

2. Verify that the COMMAND.COM (or the other command interpreter listed on the "SHELL=" line) actually exists on the disk you usually boot from. Restore or replace COMMAND.COM if necessary.

3. Make sure that the COMMAND.COM you locate is made to work with your version of DOS.

Cannot find file QBASIC.EXE

You attempted to start a program that uses the QBASIC.EXE file, such as the DOS Editor or the online MS-DOS Help. Check that the QBASIC.EXE file is still in the DOS directory. Ensure that your Path statement includes the DOS directory.

Tech Tip: To view your current path, type **SET** at the DOS prompt and press ENTER. The path, along with any other environment variables, will be displayed.

Cannot load COMMAND.COM, system halted

The command interpreter could not be loaded. This message appears after another program has been run. There are several possible causes:

- DOS could not find the proper COMMAND.COM file after the program finished executing. Verify that the "SHELL=" line in CONFIG.SYS points to a valid copy of COMMAND.COM. Verify that the COMSPEC environment variable (an optional variable set in AUTOEXEC.BAT) also points to a valid COMMAND.COM.

- There is an error or data corruption in your COMMAND.COM file. Reboot your system with a system disk and replace the COMMAND.COM file.

- Memory may not have been released back to DOS to allow COMMAND.COM to load, or memory may have been corrupted. This can happen as a result of a problem with the program you were running, or a memory conflict between the program and other memory-resident programs and device drivers.

Cannot make directory entry

You have either too many files in the directory or insufficient space on the disk to create the directory or volume label you just tried creating. The root directory of a hard drive can contain only 512 directory entries, including the volume label, directories, and files. High-density floppy disks have a limit of

224 directory entries, while low-density disks are limited to 112. If you do a directory listing with DIR and it lists fewer files than the limit, try running CHKDSK or ScanDisk to check for damaged directory entries.

Cannot move multiple files to a single file

You entered a MOVE command and specified multiple files to move. However, you also specified a single file to move these files to, instead of specifying a directory. For example, the command **MOVE MYFILES.* MYFILES.ALL** will generate this error unless MYFILES.ALL is a directory. If you are trying to combine small files into one larger file, use the COPY command instead.

Cannot run SMARTDrive 4.0 with DoubleSpace

You are running a copy of SMARTDrive that is too old to recognize DoubleSpace. The older copy is probably in your Windows directory. Edit your CONFIG.SYS or AUTOEXEC.BAT file to make sure that SMARTDrive is loading from the DOS directory. Delete the older SMARTDRV.EXE or SMARTDRV.SYS file on your system.

A CVF is damaged

This message appears when you are booting your computer and DoubleSpace detects problems with the compressed volume file (CVF), where all the data on your compressed drive is stored. Usually, when this message appears, the CVF can still be mounted. This means that the problems are minor, such as lost allocation units or crosslinked files. However, file structure damage to a compressed drive can very easily become more serious. You need to back up any important data from the compressed drive, then run a disk repair utility such as DOS 6.2's ScanDisk to locate and repair the damage.

Data error

DOS found a bad sector while attempting to read or write to a file. The "Abort, Retry, Fail?" message will appear with this one. Choose Abort. If you were saving, then discard the current disk and use another one. If you were opening a file, find your backup copy and use that.

Directory already exists

You cannot create two directories with the same name in the same parent directory. Give your new directory a different name, or use the MOVE command to rename the existing directory.

Disk unsuitable for system disk

You are trying to make a system disk out of a disk with some bad sectors. Try again with a different disk. You may continue to use this disk for data storage, or discard it.

Divide overflow

The program you were using tried and failed to perform a calculation, usually an attempt to divide a number by zero. Reboot your system and restart the program. If the error recurs, contact the manufacturer of the program you were using when you received this message.

DoubleGuard Alarm #nn

DoubleGuard, the error protection feature of DoubleSpace with MS-DOS 6.2, has detected that the DoubleSpace program's area of memory has been corrupted by another program. The system halts at this point to prevent corrupt data from being written to disk. See the question "I just got a DoubleGuard Alarm message. Is something wrong with my disk?" in Chapter 8 for some ideas on what to do next.

Drive not ready

The drive is not ready to be read. Check that the disk is completely inserted in the drive, and the drive door is closed. If you are using an external drive, be sure the drive power is on and all cables are properly connected. Verify that any necessary device drivers for the external device are properly loaded.

Drive or diskette types not compatible

This message appears if you attempt to use DISKCOMP or DISKCOPY to compare or copy disks of different size or density. These commands only work when the two disks involved are of the same type and density.

Duplicate file name or file not found

You tried copying or renaming a file and either specified the name of an existing file or directory for the copy filename, or did not specify the original filename correctly. Reenter the command with the correct filenames, and with a different original and copy name.

EMM386 DMA buffer is too small

The error appears when a program that uses direct memory access (DMA) needs a larger buffer than EMM386 is providing. To solve this problem, edit the CONFIG.SYS and add **D=#** to the EMM386.EXE line, where # equals a number between 46 and 256. The default buffer is 32K.

EMM386 Exception Error #6

Invalid operating code was sent to your central processing unit. This usually means that a program file is corrupted. Try reinstalling the program completely. If this does not correct the situation, it may be a TSR or memory-resident program causing the problem. Unload the TSRs until you have found the one whose absence resolves the situation. If the problem is not resolved by unloading the TSRs, you may have a bad RAM chip. In general, if the problem occurs in only one program, suspect a corrupt program file first. If the problem occurs in more than one program, suspect a memory conflict first.

EMM386 Exception Error #12

You need to set a larger Stack variable. To do this, edit your CONFIG.SYS file. Change the line starting with "STACKS=" to "STACKS=9,256", which creates 9 stacks at 256 bytes per stack. If that is not enough, try "STACKS=18,256" or "STACKS=18,512". A corrupt file or memory conflict may also cause this error.

EMM386 Exception Error #13

One program is accessing memory outside its normal memory boundaries. You'll find additional information on troubleshooting memory problems in Chapter 9. Again, if the problem only occurs in one program, damaged files could be the cause.

EMM386 Not Installed - Protected Mode Software Already Running

EMM386 cannot install if another protected mode program is already running. To prevent this problem, make sure that EMM386.EXE is loaded in CONFIG.SYS after HIMEM.SYS, but before any other protected mode device drivers or programs.

EMM386: Unable to start enhanced mode Windows due to invalid path specification for EMM386

Some files were changed when you installed DOS 6.2. MS VSafe is detecting the changed files and assuming this change was caused by a virus. The file changes are causing EMM386 to have problems since Windows accesses the upper memory area. See the question "I installed MS-DOS 6.2 and now I get 'EMM386:

Unable to start enhanced mode Windows due to invalid path specification for EMM386 when I try to start Windows. What's wrong?" in Chapter 1. This problem can also show up on a network using a diskless workstation if EMM386 cannot be found. For this situation, add the parameter "/Y=C:*DIR*\\EMM386.EXE", where *DIR* is the location of EMM386.EXE. Also add the line "SWITCHES=/W" to CONFIG.SYS.

Error creating image file. Diskcopy will revert to a multiple-pass copy

DOS tried creating an image file to store the contents of your source disk, but was unable to do so. Therefore it will finish the DISKCOPY process using several passes, instead of one pass. To avoid this error message and speed up the DISKCOPY process, clear space on your hard disk equal to the total capacity of the disk being copied for the image file and be sure the TEMP variable is included in AUTOEXEC.BAT. For example:

```
SET TEMP=C:\TEMP
```

Also, be certain the specified directory actually exists on drive C.

Error in EXE file

There is an error in an executable file that you are trying to load. Delete the file, and replace it from the program's original disks. If you continue to get this message, contact the manufacturer of the faulty program.

ERROR: missing parameter.

This message is provided by Setver. To avoid this error, do not specify the drive and path for the file you are entering in the SETVER table.

Expanded memory services unavailable

You need to edit your CONFIG.SYS file to change the settings for EMM386 to prevent this message and make expanded memory available. See the question "The message Expanded memory services unavailable displays when I start my computer. How can I use some of my upper memory?" in Chapter 9 for details on changing these settings.

An extended memory manager is already installed

Some other extended memory manager program is loaded in your CONFIG.SYS before HIMEM.SYS is loaded. Remove the line loading the other extended memory manager or HIMEM.SYS, depending on which one you plan to use.

File allocation table bad

Your file allocation table is corrupted. The file allocation table on a disk is used to tell DOS about the file and directory structure of the disk. DOS uses the information to locate files. Use the DOS CHKDSK or ScanDisk utility to try to repair the damage. Some errors cannot be corrected by CHKDSK or ScanDisk. The surest way to fix damage to your FAT is to back up any data that can be accessed, then reformat the drive.

File cannot be copied onto itself

You tried copying a file, but forgot to specify where you wanted it copied to. Reenter the command with the destination drive and directory, or a different filename to create a second copy of the file in the same directory.

File creation error

There are several possible causes for this error:

- You have reached the limit on root directory entries. Create the file inside a subdirectory, delete some files from the root directory and try again, or use a different disk.

- You specified an invalid path or filename. Check your spelling and be sure the name you entered does not contain illegal characters.

- There may be insufficient space on the disk. Delete some files and try again, or use a different disk.

- The disk has directory structure problems. Run CHKDSK or ScanDisk to clear the errors.

File not found

DOS cannot locate the file you specified. Check that you typed the path and filename correctly. Then check that the file actually exists where you think it does. Reenter the command with the file correctly identified. This message is common when you enter a filename but not a path.

Format terminated. Format another (Y/N)?

DOS cannot format the disk. The disk is either bad, write protected, or the wrong density for the drive. Format another disk.

From DoubleSpace: There is not enough free conventional memory

You do not have enough conventional memory to run DoubleSpace. Free up some additional conventional memory by rebooting and pressing F5 when you see "Starting MS-DOS...." If your machine has less than 640K total conventional memory, you may want to increase the amount of RAM installed before running DoubleSpace, since DoubleSpace will use at least 38K of conventional memory at all times after a drive is compressed.

General failure reading/writing to drive X:

There is an error relating to reading or writing to a disk. If drive *X* is a floppy disk drive, consider the following:

- Are the disk drives shut, with the disks correctly inserted?
- Are the disks of the correct density and format?
- Are any external cables attached firmly to the computer?

This message can also appear as the result of a defective disk or disk drive. If drive *X* is a hard drive, there may be a damaged file or a bad sector on the disk. Run ScanDisk or another program that tests for bad sectors. If the problem persists, have your system serviced, since there may be a failure in the hard drive or hard drive controller.

Incorrect DOS version

The DOS command or program you are trying to use was designed to work with a different version of DOS than the one you are using. Determine which DOS version you are using by typing **VER** and pressing ENTER. Also, there may be multiple copies of the problem program on the hard disk, and only some may be made for an older version of DOS. To check this, make the root directory the current directory and type **DIR *FILENAME*.* /S** and press ENTER. DOS will search the drive for any copy of the file. Delete or replace any copies that don't work with your current DOS version. If no newer version of the program is available, you can try adding an entry to the SETVER table. Entries in the SETVER table tell DOS to report a different DOS version number to the command when it tries to run. For example, type **SETVER BACKUP.EXE 5.00** and press ENTER to add DOS 5.00's BACKUP command to the SETVER table when you are running DOS 6.*x* and want to use the BACKUP command from DOS 5.00. This workaround does not work for every program because some can only work with a specific version of DOS. Check with the program's manufacturer if you aren't certain.

Insufficient disk space

There is insufficient space on the current disk for the file you are trying to write to it. You can get this message when saving, copying, or moving files. Replace your destination disk with a disk with sufficient space on it, or delete some files and try the operation again.

Insufficient memory

You are trying to load a program that requires more memory than you currently have available. You need to unload some other programs, such as drivers for peripherals, which are not essential to the task you are trying to carry out.

Tech Tip: This message usually refers to conventional memory. If you have DOS 6.*x*, try using MemMaker to free up some additional conventional memory.

Internal stack overflow. System halted

Requests from software to access hardware such as serial and parallel ports, disks, and other hardware go into buffers, to be handled as soon as the requested hardware is available. Your system has received more requests to access the hardware (called *hardware interrupt calls*) than its buffer can hold. Increase the number of buffers by changing the "STACKS=" entry in CONFIG.SYS. The format of the line is: STACKS= *# of buffers, size of each buffer in bytes.* Try increasing one or both numbers. If you don't already have the line in CONFIG.SYS, try "STACKS=9,256".

Invalid COMMAND.COM

DOS is trying to load a new COMMAND.COM and cannot find the file. Make sure that COMMAND.COM appears in both the DOS and root directory and that the Path statement includes the DOS directory. Verify that the "SHELL=" line in CONFIG.SYS is pointing to a valid copy of COMMAND.COM. If your AUTOEXEC.BAT file contains a "SET COMSPEC=" line, make sure this is also pointing to a valid COMMAND.COM, ideally, the same copy the "SHELL=" line mentions. If COMSPEC is set, you can check it by typing **SET** at a DOS prompt and pressing ENTER.

Invalid date

The date you entered in response to DOS's request for a new date was in an unacceptable format. Make sure that you enter the date using the format shown in the prompt for the date.

Invalid directory

You specified a directory that DOS can't find. Check the path name you entered for spelling. Use DIR and CD to make sure that the directory actually exists where you think it does. Make sure that you are in the appropriate directory when you issue this command.

Invalid drive specification

You specified a drive that DOS cannot find. Make sure that you used a valid drive letter, and that you used a colon after it.

Invalid media type or track 0 bad - Disk unusable

You are trying to format a disk using the wrong density, or there may be a defect near the beginning of the disk that prevents it from being used.

Tech Tip: Some older systems may not recognize high-density disk drives, resulting in this error. See the question "I upgraded from MS-DOS 3.1 to 6.2 and now my floppy drives don't format properly. Why?" in Chapter 10 for further information.

Invalid number of parameters

You entered your command with too many or too few parameters for DOS to understand what you wanted to do. Review the command you just entered and correct it. See also the sections on the "Required parameter missing" and "Too many parameters" messages.

Invalid parameter

You included a parameter that the command does not use. Therefore, DOS does not know what to do with the extra text. Edit the command to make sure it matches DOS's required syntax.

Invalid path, not directory, or directory not empty

You tried removing a directory and could not. Make sure you typed the name of the directory correctly and that the directory actually exists. Make sure that all of the files in the directory are deleted. Then retry the command. This message often appears if there are subdirectories beneath the one you are trying to delete, or if there are hidden files within the directory. Remove subdirectories first, then type **DIR /A:H** and press ENTER in the problem directory to check for hidden files. Use the ATTRIB command to remove attributes from the hidden files, then delete them. You should then be able to remove the directory.

Tech Tip: If you have DOS 6.*x*, use the DELTREE command instead. DELTREE removes a directory and any files and subdirectories it may contain in one step. DELTREE will also delete hidden and read-only files.

Missing operating system

Your computer cannot find its operating system during setup. There are several possible reasons for this error message, including errors in your CMOS, damaged system files, or inactive main DOS partitions. See the question "At bootup, I get the error message 'Missing operating system.' Why?" in Chapter 10 for some possible solutions.

No room for system on destination disk

DOS cannot copy the system files on the destination disk, either because there is insufficient space, or because the sectors it wants to use for the system files are already in use. Either delete all unnecessary files from the disk, or use a different disk for the system disk. If you don't need any of the files on the disk, use **FORMAT A: /S** instead.

Non-system disk or disk error

The disk you are trying to boot from is not a system disk. Remove it or replace it with a system disk. This message can also appear if the system files on the disk are missing or damaged. If you get this message when booting from the hard drive, boot with a system disk in drive A, then recopy the system files onto the hard drive using the SYS command.

Not ready reading/writing drive *X*:

Drive *X* is not ready to be read. Make sure that the disk is inserted, and the disk door is closed, then retry accessing the disk. If the message refers to a hard disk, there may be a hardware defect.

Out of environment space

You are out of space in memory to save environment variables. To correct, you need to assign more space to environment variables. For example, the line "SHELL=COMMAND.COM /E:1024 /P" in your CONFIG.SYS file will supply 1024 bytes of environment space. The default setting is 256 bytes, but you can set a value between 160 and 32768.

Parameters not supported by drive

You have tried to format a disk using settings that the drive cannot use, such as formatting high density on a low-density drive. Correct your command to match the capabilities of the drive.

Path not found

You typed a non-existent path name in the command you just entered. Check your typing for errors. Then check that the path you have specified actually exists.

Probable Non-DOS disk. Continue (Y/N)?

CHKDSK will display this message if it does not recognize the specified disk or drive as a standard DOS disk.

Choose to continue only if you know that the selected disk is a DOS disk. CHKDSK cannot function on disks created by other operating systems.

Required parameter missing

The command you issued cannot be completed with the information you supplied. For example, if you use the RENAME command to rename a file without specifying both the old name and the new name, you will see this message. For more information, type **HELP** *command* at the DOS prompt and press ENTER to see exactly which parameters are required.

Syntax error

There is an error in the command that you typed. First check the spelling, then check that you have spaces where required. Then type **HELP** followed by the command and press ENTER to see what syntax to use with the command.

Target disk bad or incompatible

The disk you are attempting to write to using the DISKCOPY command cannot be formatted to match the size or density of the source disk. The disk may be formatted at the wrong density, or formatted for another operating system, such as Macintosh or UNIX. Replace the disk.

Too many parameters

You have too many spaces, parameters, or other entries in the command you just entered. You need to check the syntax of the command before reentering it.

Unable to create directory

The directory name you specified is already assigned to a file in the current directory. A directory cannot have the same name as a file in the parent directory. Delete, move, or rename the file first, or choose a different directory name.

Unable to load COMMAND.COM or DOSSWAP.EXE

You attempted to switch a program from within DOS Shell, but the DOSSHELL.INI file is corrupt. You need to re-create the DOSSHELL.INI file. See the question "When I try to switch between programs, DOS Shell just stops functioning, and I need to reboot my computer. Why?" in Chapter 7 to discover how to re-create this file. You may also have run out of memory. Exit DOS Shell, then type **EXIT** at the DOS Prompt and press ENTER. If you return to DOS Shell, you have multiple copies of DOS Shell running.

Unable to write BOOT

Throw the disk out and use another one for the command. The disk is defective and cannot be used. If the disk is a hard disk, contact your hardware vendor.

Unrecognized command in CONFIG.SYS
Error in CONFIG.SYS line *X*

Line *X* in your CONFIG.SYS file is incorrect. Reboot your system, press F8 when you see the "Starting MS-DOS..." message, and type **y** only to those lines you want executed. Then edit your CONFIG.SYS file to correct the incorrect line.

Unrecoverable read/write error on drive A, side 1, track 29

DOS tried writing a file to a bad sector on the disk. Copy any files you want to use later to another disk, then throw this one out. If the problem is a read error, you may not be able to recover the data from this disk. Try using DOS 6.2's ScanDisk utility to recover the data.

WARNING: EMM386 installed without a LIM 3.2 compatible page frame. Press any key to continue

Emm386 has created expanded memory that fits the LIM 4.0 standards instead of the LIM 3.2 standards. Programs that require the LIM 3.2 standards may not be able to access this memory, unless the page frames are contiguous. See the question "I received a 'WARNING: EMM386 installed without a LIM 3.2 compatible page frame' message when I booted my computer and my programs don't recognize the expanded memory that EMM386 created. What is wrong?" in Chapter 9 for an explanation of how to resolve this memory issue.

Write failure, diskette unusable

DOS cannot write to the disk. Copy any files you want to use in the future to another disk and throw this one out.

Write Fault error reading/writing to device XXX:

DOS cannot exchange data with the device mentioned. Check the connections to the device and be sure that it is ready to communicate. For example, if the device is a printer, make sure the printer is online.

Write Protect Error

You attempted to write to or format a disk with write protection enabled. To remove write protection, remove the sticky tab from your 5 1/4" disk or close the notch on the right side of your 3 1/2" disk.

You must specify the host drive for a DoubleSpace drive

In your AUTOEXEC.BAT file, you have specified that SMARTDrive cache a DoubleSpace compressed drive. You need to edit this line so that SMARTDrive caches on the DoubleSpace host drive, which is uncompressed. You can also remove the drive letter entirely since SMARTDrive automatically caches using the host of any DoubleSpace compressed drive.

Glossary

Few things are as frustrating as hearing terms that you don't know or understand. To help you avoid this frustration, we've provided many of the most common computer terms in this glossary. Although some of the terms do not relate to DOS directly, they are used frequently, and you're likely to encounter them.

Access method   A set of rules used by network software and hardware that directs traffic over the network.

ACR (actual compression ratio)   Used with DoubleSpace. A ratio which represents the amount of compression being applied to all data on the compressed volume. An ACR of 1.5 to 1 indicates that files are compressed by 33% on average. *See also* ECR (estimated compression ratio).

Address   A unique set of numbers that identifies a location in computer memory, a workstation in a LAN, or a packet of data traveling through a network.

ANSI (American National Standards Institute) An organization that sets standards for languages, database management systems, etc.

Anti-virus   A program that checks your system for evidence of viruses.

Application module   Any single unit of an integrated package, i.e., database, spreadsheet, word processor.

Application servers   PC LAN workstations that perform a specific network task separate from the central file server. These are usually machines that are dedicated to specific tasks, such as database servers, electronic mail servers, asynchronous servers, gateway servers, and print servers.

Architecture   Describes how a system is constructed and how its components are put together. Open architecture refers to a non-proprietary system design that allows other manufacturers to design products that work with the system.

Archive   A copy of files stored on a separate disk as protection from data loss.

ARCnet (Attached Resource Computer Network)   A popular 2.5Mbps local area network developed by Datapoint. Novell sells ARCnet products under the name RX-Net.

ASCII (American Standard Code for Information Interchange)   A set of definitions for the bit composition of characters and symbols. ASCII defines 128 symbols using seven binary bits and one parity bit. It is used by many microcomputers and minicomputers.

ASCII text files   Text stored using this coding structure is stored in the same order as it appears on a printed page; no characters are added or deleted. ASCII text files are often called "print" files.

Asynchronous   A communications mode in which data is sent character by character, controlled by adding start and stop bits to each character. No timing information or clocking information is exchanged between parties. Asynchronous communication is also called "start/stop" or "TTY."

Auto-answer   A modem that can answer an incoming call without operator intervention by a modem-generating carrier tone which signals the originating modem that its call has been received.

Autodial   A modem that can simulate a telephone dialer modem using either pulse or touch tone dialing signals. It can be programmed to operate unattended.

AUTOEXEC.BAT   A batch file that automatically executes when the computer is turned on. It can run any DOS command,

and is used to load information such as the PATH command. (*See* CONFIG.SYS.)

AUX   The default DOS communications port.

Background task   A secondary job performed while the user is performing a primary task. For example, an emulation session performing a file transfer between PC and mainframe can be running in background while the user is running a word processing application program in the foreground.

Back up   To copy files in order to protect against data loss.

Backup   An MS-DOS utility to make a copy of important files.

Backup set catalog   File used by MSBACKUP and MWBACKUP to keep track of files that were backed up. A copy of this file should be on the hard drive that the backup was run from and also on the last disk in the backup itself.

.BAK   An extension assigned by many programs to the previous version of a file.

Baseband   A technique for transmitting data on a single cable in which the entire bandwidth is used for the data. Only one signal can be transmitted at a time.

Baseband LAN   A LAN category in which the entire bandwidth of the LAN cable is used to transmit a single digital signal at a time. The signals from the sending device are put directly into the cable without modulation. Baseband LAN is less expensive and less sophisticated than broadband LAN.

BASIC (Beginners All-Purpose Symbolic Instruction Code)   A programming language designed to solve mathematical and business applications.

Batch File   An ASCII file that combines several DOS commands into a single file.

Baud   A measure of the signaling speed of a data-transmission device. The speed in baud is equal to the number of times the line condition (frequency, amplitude, voltage, or phase) changes per second.

Bernoulli   Removable, high-capacity disk storage that uses fluid dynamic principles to prevent damage to the disk during power failure.

.BIN   A binary file such as the one used by DoubleSpace.

Binary   A numbering system that uses only two digits, 0 and 1.

BIOS (basic input/output system)   Software built into a PC that controls how your computer communicates with hardware and DOS.

Bit (binary digit)   The elemental unit of digital information, written as one (1) or zero (0).

Bitmapped graphics   The image that results when an illustration is drawn into the graphic (bitmapped) memory of the computer. When an image is stored in bitmap form, it is stored as a set of single pixels or dots. For contrast, see Object-oriented graphics.

Block   A collection of information sent together on a communication line, normally associated with synchronous protocols. Also called a "frame."

Boot   To start a computer.

Boot sector   The first sector on a logical drive. This area is used to contain the program that is responsible for booting the machine.

bps (bits per second)   The instantaneous bit speed with which a device or channel transmits a character during serial transmission.

Bridge   Equipment that connects several LANs and allows communications between devices across the bridge.

Broadband LAN   A method for conveying information across LANs. More complex, expensive, and sophisticated than baseband LAN, broadband LAN carries several signals simultaneously. The channels are kept separate with frequency division multiplexing, with each channel occupying a different frequency slot on the cable. At the receiving end, it is demodulated to its original frequency. This technique is used by cable TV to fit 50 channels into a single coaxial cable.

Buffer   A temporary storage place for data. For example, a printer buffer holds data in storage until the printer is ready to print the data. Also called a "capture buffer."

Bus   A communication channel that connects the processor, memory, and peripherals of a computer, or connects workstations and servers in a network.

Bus Network   A LAN in which all workstations are connected to a single cable. All stations hear all transmissions on the cable and each station selects those transmissions addressed to it based on address information contained in the transmission. Ethernet is the best known bus topology. Also called "linear bus topology."

Byte   A unit of eight bits. A byte is approximately equivalent to a single character.

C   A high-level programming language, known for its portability, developed at Bell Laboratories.

Cache memory   Part of a computer's or a network server's RAM that operates as a buffer between the system memory and the microprocessor. The most recently used data and instructions are stored in the cache memory. Because of the speed at which RAM is accessed, data called for again is more quickly available, therefore improving system response time.

Carrier   A steady signal whose tone can be changed or modulated to transmit data.

CD-ROM (compact disc read-only memory)   An optical form of disk storage that uses a laser rather than a magnetic head to read information from the disk. The laser scans the disk and detects the appearance of minute pits on the disk which represent binary data.

CGA (Color Graphics Adapter)   CGA offers two palettes of four colors in a low-resolution 320 x 200 pixel mode. It has a higher resolution of 640 x 200 pixels, but only in monochrome.

CGM (Computer Graphics Metafiles)   A graphic file in a standard format defined by ANSI which can be imported and exported by most business graphics packages.

Checksum   A method of totaling bits for the purpose of checking errors in data transmission or detecting viruses.

Chip   An integrated circuit containing thousands of transistors.

Circuit   Two-way communication between two points, comprising associated go and return channels.

Clean boot   To start the machine without processing the CONFIG.SYS or AUTOEXEC.BAT. This is done by pressing either SHIFT or F5 when the machine displays "Starting MS-DOS."

Clipboard   A storage place used for cutting and pasting information on the Macintosh and in Microsoft Windows. It holds whatever was last cut or copied.

Clock   An oscillator-generated signal that provides a timing reference for a transmission link.

Clock/calendar   Built-in computer hardware which keeps track of the date and time. A battery powers the clock when the computer is turned off.

CMOS (complementary metal oxide semiconductor)   A type of computer chip that requires little power to operate and generates little heat, thereby making it advantageous to use in computer components.

CMYK (Cyan, Magenta, Yellow, blacK)   A file format used for four-color separations.

Coaxial cable (coax)   A cable that supports high data rates with high immunity to electrical interference and low incidence of errors. It is a popular medium in local area networks and with cable television.

COBOL (COmmon Business-Oriented Language)   A compiler developed primarily for business.

COM1   A communications port, usually the first serial port.

Command   An instruction that starts a program or alters its execution.

Communication Protocol   The means used to control the orderly communication of information between stations on a data link.

Compiler   A very fast high-level programming translator that translates source code (programming language text) to object (machine-readable) code.

Compressed drive   A DOS drive that contains DoubleSpace compressed data. The data exists in a CVF on the hard drive.

Compression   Reducing the space required for a file on disk by storing the file in a special coded format.

CompuServe   A bulletin board information service that can be accessed from a computer using a modem.

CON   The name DOS uses for the keyboard and the display screen.

CONFIG.SYS   A file that holds configuration information, such as device drivers, and automatically loads when the computer is turned on. *See* AUTOEXEC.BAT.

Contiguous   Files that are not fragmented or on separate sectors on a hard disk. Contiguous files can be accessed more quickly and efficiently than files that are non-contiguous or fragmented.

Control characters   ASCII characters that do not print out but are used to control communications. Control characters can, for example, signal a sender to stop transmitting information when the receiver is busy.

Controller   A device that relays information and administers the communication between two devices, such as a hard drive and the main processor.

Conventional memory   The first 640K of RAM memory.

Coprocessor   An additional processor that takes care of specific tasks such as I/O or disk access to reduce the load on the CPU.

CP/M (Control Program for Microcomputers) A once-popular but outdated microcomputer operating system which preceded the IBM Personal Computer and MS-DOS.

cps (characters per second) A measure of printer speed.

CPU (central processing unit) The primary functioning unit of a computer system. Its basic architecture consists of storage elements called registers, computational circuits designated as the Arithmetic Logic Unit (ALU), the Control Block, and Input/Output (I/O) ports.

CRT (cathode-ray tube) Television-like picture tube used in visual-display terminals.

CTRL+BREAK A key sequence that cancels a command.

CTRL+PRTSC Tells DOS to print everything it displays until you press this key sequence again.

Current directory The directory where DOS checks for files and writes files unless you specify otherwise.

Current drive The drive where DOS writes files or reads them unless you specify otherwise.

CVF (compressed volume file) A dblspace.### file that is on a host drive. This file contains all the data in compressed format for one compressed drive.

Daisy wheel A type of printer with letters arranged on a wheel that spins around to bring the letters into place to strike the ribbon.

DASD (direct access storage device) A storage medium that is permanently mounted and therefore always available, for example, a hard drive.

Database A structured system for storing data using records and fields, with capabilities for searching, analyzing, and reporting on the data.

Data-Link Control The set of rules used by two nodes or stations on a network to perform an orderly exchange of information over the network.

Data validation   A method that checks input from the keyboard to determine if that data falls within specified criteria. For instance, an inventory number entered on an invoice could be checked against the actual inventory file to determine if that item number was valid.

DBMS (database management system)   A way of managing data that allows you to structure, query, and change the data; change the structure; and generate reports.

DCE (Data Communications Equipment)   The equipment or modem that sits between Data Terminal Equipment (DTE) and a network.

DDE (Dynamic Data Exchange)   A method used by Microsoft Windows and IBM OS/2 Presentation Manager to allow the exchange of information between applications. The linked information is updated in one application whenever it is changed in another.

DDP (distributed data processing)   A technique in which some processing is done by connected devices such as PCs rather than by the processor at the heart of a network. Using a PC for local editing and validation of input data to a mainframe system is an example of DDP.

Debugger   A program used for locating, identifying, and editing mistakes that impede the operation of another program.

Defrag   MS-DOS utility included with DOS 6.*x* used to eliminate file fragmentation. During its operation, files are reorganized so that each file is placed in one contiguous cluster chain.

DELTREE   MS-DOS command included with version 6.*x*. Its function is to delete a directory, all of its subdirectories, and all files contained within them. Can also be used to delete individual files (even if they are hidden or read-only files).

DES (Data Encryption Standard)   Developed by IBM, this is the most widely used method of encryption for PCs.

Desktop publishing   A program that reads in information from many formats, such as word processing, graphics, spreadsheets, or databases, and provides tools to create a final format for typesetting.

Dialog   The conversation between the user and the program.

DIP (dual inline package) switch   Small on-off switches, usually mounted on a printed circuit board, used to configure options on the device.

Directory   A logical representation for disk space, it is used to organize files on a disk.

Disk cache   Memory set aside for data read from disk to speed up operations.

Display   The computer screen.

Distributed architecture   A networking capability that lets programs access data residing on PCs, minicomputers, or mainframes.

DLL (dynamic link library)   A self-contained object of code that allows a link between Microsoft Windows and another application.

DMA (direct memory access)   A fast method of moving data from a storage device directly to RAM which speeds processing.

DOS (disk operating system)   A program or set of programs that instructs a disk-based computing system to schedule/supervise work, manage computer resources, and operate/control peripherals.

DOS Extender   Software that uses the capabilities of 80286 or 80386 processors to allow programs running under DOS to use more than 640K of RAM (the limit under DOS).

DOSKEY   A program that allows you to store DOS keystrokes and reuse them.

DOS Shell   A mode that allows the user to jump to DOS for formatting disks, copying files, and performing other functions without leaving the application software. Also refers to a user-friendly interface for performing DOS tasks and executing programs.

Dot matrix   A type of printer that forms letters from a collection of dots; the resolution is measured in dots per inch.

DoubleSpace   Disk compression utility included with MS-DOS 6.*x*. This utility provides on-the-fly compression and decompression of files and will virtually double the capacity of your hard disk drive.

Download   To bring data to a microcomputer from another computer, usually over a modem or network connection.

DPI (dots per inch)   A measure of the resolution of a monitor, a dot matrix printer, or a laser printer.

DPMI (DOS Protected Mode Interface)   A memory management specification that allows programs to access extended memory.

DSR (Data Set Ready)   A modem-interface signal defined in RS-232 which indicates to the attached data terminal equipment that the modem is connected to the telephone circuit.

DSS (decision support system)   A system that integrates information from different sources and provides management with useful reporting for making decisions.

Dumb terminal   A workstation, often just a keyboard and screen, without a computer in it, which is limited in its ability to process data.

Duplex   Refers to the two-way nature of modem communications. In full-duplex communications, both terminals can send and receive information simultaneously. In half-duplex communications, both terminals can send and receive information, but not at the same time.

ECR (estimated compression ratio)   The ratio used to calculate projected free disk space in a DoubleSpace compressed drive.

Editor   A program used to perform line and block edits and copy between files.

EGA (Enhanced Graphics Adapter)   EGA provides higher resolution graphic and color capabilities while maintaining compatibility with CGA programs and monitors. The EGA card's 640 x 350 resolution in 16 simultaneous colors generates sharper graphics than the CGA and uses an 8 x 14 pixel matrix for text characters.

E-mail (electronic mail)   Electronic mail programs allow users or groups of users to send messages and files to one another electronically across a LAN.

Embedded formula   In a spreadsheet, a built-in formula for which the user defines values rather than operators or functions.

EMM386.EXE   Expanded memory manager included with MS-DOS version 5.0 and higher. Used on 80386 and higher computers to convert extended memory into expanded memory, and also to gain access to the upper memory area where programs and device drivers are placed when they are loaded high.

Emulation   The imitation of one device by another, usually referring to the ability of a PC or microcomputer to act like one of several dumb terminals.

Encryption   A fail-safe measure that prevents files from being read even if they are accessed. The file is coded in a way that is not readable. Decryption decodes the files into a readable format.

EPROM (erasable programmable read-only memory)   A non-volatile semiconductor memory that can be erased, usually by exposure to ultra-violet light, to permit reprogramming.

EPS (Encapsulated PostScript File)   A graphics format developed by Adobe Systems.

Ethernet   A CSMA/CD network system that uses coaxial cable, developed by Xerox and popularized by 3Com and DEC. One of the most popular LAN topologies in use today.

Expanded memory   Additional memory added to older model computers that required an expanded memory manager to utilize it. The LIM (Lotus-Intel-Microsoft) specification standardizes its use.

Extended memory   Memory above 1MB added to IBM/PS2, IBM/AT, or clone computers. An extended memory manager is used with this memory.

File   A collection of related information, stored as one unit on a disk or tape.

File allocation table (FAT)   A table used by DOS that indicates which clusters and sectors on disk are available, which have been used by files, and which are defective.

File attributes   The DOS identifier that denotes special characteristics of a file, such as copy-protected system files, read-only files, and archival files.

File encryption   *See* Encryption.

File locking   A scheme that allows only one station to have access to a DOS file at a given time.

Files area   Also known as the data area. This is the area on the disk where the user's data is stored.

File server   A computer providing shared resources to LAN users, usually including centralized file storage, access to printers, and PC-to-PC communications such as electronic mail.

Font   A complete set of type (letters, numbers, and other characters) with a consistent style and type size.

Fragmentation   The state of a hard disk when files are stored in many small pieces, rather than in one sequential location.

Front end   The user interface seen on screen.

Full duplex (FDX)   Communication that allows data to be sent and received simultaneously.

Full-length   An expansion board that installs in a long slot in an IBM PC, XT, or AT.

Gateway   A computer system and its software that permit two networks using different protocols to communicate with each other, often a PC LAN to an IBM SNA network.

Gigabyte (Gb)   A billion bytes.

Groupware   Software that increases group productivity by providing common utilities over a network where multiple users can work together to reach common goals.

GUI (graphical user interface)   A program—such as the Macintosh System, Microsoft Windows, or OS/2 Presentation Manager—that provides a consistent look to all the applications that run under it. GUI applications make use of graphical features, such as windows and pull-down menus, and support the use of a pointing device such as a mouse.

Half duplex (HDX)   Communication that allows data to be sent in one direction at a time.

Half-length   A board that fits into a short slot in an IBM PC, XT, or AT.

Hard copy   Contents of a computer data file which are in printed form on paper.

Hexadecimal   A base 16 numbering system, used in printer codes, for example. Hexadecimal numbers are represented by the digits 0–9, along with the letters A–F.

Hidden file   A file that is not listed in the directory listing.

High memory area (HMA)   The area of memory from 1,024K to 1,088K that is sometimes used by DOS.

High Sierra Group Format   A standard physical format for CD-ROM disks.

HIMEM.SYS   Extended memory manager included with MS-DOS version 5.0 and higher. Also responsible for managing the use of the high memory area (HMA), the area where DOS is placed when it is loaded high.

Host   A large, central computer whose resources can be accessed and shared by terminals, workstations, or microcomputers.

Host Drive   A drive that contains one or more DoubleSpace compressed drives stored in dblspace.### files.

Hotkey   Some combination of the ALT, CTRL, or SHIFT key and another keyboard choice used to activate a TSR program or other special function.

Hotlink   A link between files or applications such that if one is changed, the other is automatically updated; both files or applications must be loaded in RAM.

Hub   The center of a star topology network or cabling system. May be a file server acting as a hub or a dedicated box with a number of connectors on it.

Hypertext   A method of linking text so that a reader can jump easily between related ideas, rather than reading in a specified sequence.

Incremental backup   Backing up only files that have changed since the last backup.

Index   A file separate from a database that determines the order in which the data will be viewed. An index contains two fields. The record number field points to the record in the main database with the corresponding key-value field.

.INI   Initial settings file used by DOS utilities and Windows programs.

Integrators   Programs that integrate other stand-alone programs so you can toggle between applications without exiting and reloading each one.

Interactive   Programs that allow you to type commands while the program is running and often let you correct your mistakes.

Interactive start   To start the machine processing the CONFIG.SYS and AUTOEXEC.BAT one line at a time. This is done by pressing F8 when the machine displays "Starting MS-DOS."

Interface   A hardware or software connection that allows components to be connected and information to be transferred.

Interpreter   A high-level programming environment that works interactively to translate code. It is slower than a compiler.

I/O (Input/Output)   Communication between the CPU and peripheral devices.

ISO and OSI   The International Standards Organization (ISO) is a major standards committee which defined Open System Interconnection (OSI), a model for communications networks that would be independent of manufacturer.

K   Abbreviation for kilobyte.

Kbps   Abbreviation for kilobytes per second.

Kermit   An asynchronous communications protocol for microcomputers.

Keyword   Word used in searches by a text-retrieval program.

Kilobyte (K)   1,024 bytes.

LAN (local area network)   A data communications network spanning a limited geographical area to provide communications between computers and peripherals.

Laptop   A very small, lightweight, portable computer.

Laser printer   A printer that uses a laser beam to transfer images onto a print drum, which is then dusted with toner ink. Heat and pressure transfer the images from the drum onto paper to produce high-quality letters and graphics.

Layout   The arrangement of images and text on a page.

LIM/EMS (Lotus/Intel/Microsoft Expanded Memory Specification)   A standard used by some memory boards which frees the user from the 640K memory limitation of DOS 2.*x* and 3.*x* when used with programs compatible with EMS. LIM/EMS 4.0 allows up to 32MB of expanded memory.

Linking   The ability to combine or share data from separate files. The linked information may be relational with information from one file depending upon another file.

Locking   Preventing more than one person from accessing the same data simultaneously.

Login   The process of identifying and authenticating oneself to a computer system or network, used to control access to a system.

LPT1   A logical name assigned by DOS to the first parallel printer port in an IBM-compatible computer system. The second parallel printer port is called LPT2 and the third parallel printer port is called LPT3.

Machine code   An executable version of a program that has been converted from a high-level source code. Machine code is in binary format, which can be run directly from the DOS prompt.

Macro   A sequence of commands and/or data-entry keystrokes that is stored and invoked using a single keystroke.

Master boot record (MBR)   The first physical sector on a hard drive. The MBR is responsible for determining which partition the hard drive is going to boot from, and then passing control to the boot sector of that partition.

Math coprocessor   An additional processor that handles arithmetic calculations for the CPU to speed up operations. Math coprocessors can be helpful in certain applications such as CAD or graphics.

Mbps   Abbreviation for megabytes per second.

MCGA (Multicolor Graphics Array)   A standard for color monitors, used in the IBM PS/2 models 25 and 30, providing a 640 x 480 graphics mode.

Megabyte (MB)   A million bytes (actually 1,048,576 bytes).

Megahertz (MHz)   One million cycles per second. A measure of the operating speed of a processor which determines how fast a processor can execute instructions; also referred to as clock speed.

Menu A user interface that allows the user to pick from a selection of commands, rather than typing in the commands.

Metafile An interchangeable format for transferring files between graphics programs; uses the .CGM extension. Microsoft Windows uses a .WMF format, which is also called a metafile, but has a different format.

Micro Channel Architecture (MCA) Bus design used by IBM in the PS/2 Model 50, 60, 70, and 80 computers.

Modem (MOdulator/DEModulator) A device that links a computer to other computers through telephone lines.

Motherboard The main card in a PC that holds the CPU.

Mouse An input device for a graphical interface, which points to areas on the screen and can be used in addition to a keyboard.

MTBF Abbreviation for "mean time between failure," a measure of the reliability of hardware.

Multi-config A way of starting your computer with different configurations by using a startup menu.

Multisynchronous Display A type of high-resolution color monitor that automatically synchronizes itself to whatever video signal it receives.

Multitasking Running two or more applications products simultaneously.

Multithreading Running two or more copies of one application simultaneously. For example, running a database query and printing a report on the same database.

Multi-user version A network-compatible version of a product that often includes file-, record-, or cell-locking.

Native 80386 Mode   Processor operating mode that provides up to 4Gb of RAM and can address an additional 64Tb of virtual memory.

NetBIOS   A LAN transport protocol used by IBM's PC Network and Microsoft's LAN Manager and MS-Net.

Network   A communication channel among computers that allows them to exchange information and share files, applications, printers, and other peripherals.

Network architecture   The physical structure and protocols used by a computer network.

Network interface card   Electronic circuitry on a card that fits into a slot inside a PC that connects a workstation to a network cable. Works with the network software and the computer's operating system to transmit and receive messages on the network.

Network-ready   A product that can run either on an individual PC or on a network.

Network shell   Network software loaded into a workstation's memory forms a shell around DOS to let the workstation communicate with the network. The shell intercepts workstation requests before they reach DOS and reroutes network requests to the file server.

Network topology   The physical layout or geography of a network such as Star, Bus, or Ring.

Node   A PC connected to a LAN at which an operator can execute programs and access shared network disk storage and resources such as printers.

Noise   Random disturbances that degrade or disrupt data communications, present to some degree in all transmission links.

Null-modem cable   A serial cable in which pins two and three are crossed. A null-modem cable is used to establish a connection between two PCs using a program such as Interlink.

Object linking and embedding (OLE)   A method of data exchange that is more advanced than DDE. OLE allows the creation of compound documents where one application (the client) creates the main document, but another application (the server) provides the special functions needed to create and maintain an object within the main document

Object-oriented graphics   Graphic designs that are manipulated and edited as objects or elements rather than as single pixels. As objects are resized or scaled, they maintain their integrity. For contrast, *see* "Bitmapped graphics."

Object-oriented programming (OOP)   A programming technique in which data and the code that acts on that data are combined into self-contained modules or objects. Objects can be created from scratch or derived from a parent object to inherit its characteristics.

OCR (optical character recognition)   Process by which a scanner recognizes text and images from hard copy and converts them into an electronic form, such as word processing or spreadsheet.

One-finger mode   Allows you to execute with one finger command sequences that otherwise require two or more simultaneous keystrokes, such as CTRL-ALT-DEL to reboot. Particularly useful for handicapped users.

Online help   Information about how to use a program that is available from within that program.

Operating system   The interface between the hardware and the application software running on your PC.

OS (Operating System)   IBM's original mainframe operating system.

OS/2   IBM's operating system that provides multitasking and uses a graphical interface. It uses applications developed under Systems Application Architecture (SAA).

Parallel port   A physical connection on a computer used to connect output devices through which data is transmitted as multiple bits simultaneously over separate wires. Used to send a byte of data at a time to a printer. Picture eight people walking out of a room shoulder to shoulder, rather than in single file.

Parameter   An option for a DOS command to provide additional specifications for the command's use.

Parity   A means of checking for errors by adding an extra bit to each character transmitted. The extra bit is the result of a calculation performed at each end of the transmission. If the bit does not match after being transmitted, the data may be corrupt and is re-sent.

Password protection   A method of limiting login access to a network by requiring users to enter a password.

Path   A full description of the location of a file, including the drive letter and all directories above and including the file's parent directory.

.PCX   A pixel-based format generally used by painting programs for the IBM PC to export files.

.PIF (program information file)   Allows Microsoft Windows to run a non-Windows application.

PIM (personal information manager)   A type of software used for organizing personal information. Types vary from those designed to manage structured information, such as phone numbers or appointments, to those designed for unstructured information, such as free-form ideas, goals, or objectives.

Pipe   Sending the output of one DOS command to be used as the input for a second DOS command. The pipe symbol (|) is used to represent this action.

Pixel (contraction of picture element)   A single dot on a computer display.

Point and shoot   A method of executing commands by positioning the cursor on the desired command and pressing ENTER.

Polling   Interrogation by a central site of a number of remote sites simultaneously and the response of the remote sites in a particular sequence.

Port   A connector and its associated circuitry that enable data to be input to or retrieved from a communications network.

PostScript   A page description language (PDL) built into an output device. It lets you develop a page consisting of text and graphics and can manipulate elements on a page without losing their integrity. Most desktop publishing programs support PostScript printers.

Print server   A computer attached to a network to provide access to centralized printer resources, a function usually provided by the file server.

Printer driver   The instructions a program uses to communicate with a printer. A printer driver keeps track of the attributes of the printer and what codes the program must send to access those attributes.

Prompt   An indication displayed on the screen that DOS is waiting for your next request.

Protected mode   Allows the 80386 to emulate the 80286, which makes the 80386 compatible with all software written for the 80286. In protected mode, the 80386 can address 16MB of memory.

Protocol   A set of rules for communicating between computers that govern format, sequencing, and error control.

Protocol Converter   A device that translates from one communication protocol to another.

Queue   A series of tasks, such as computer print jobs or messages, lined up waiting for processing.

Radio button   A type of menu choice with at least two options, all of which are mutually exclusive. Used in Microsoft Windows, IBM OS/2, and on the Macintosh; the button consists of a circle, the center of which turns dark when an option is selected.

RAM (random access memory)   Memory that provides immediate access to any storage location point.

RAM disk   Allows you to use portions of memory as if they were a disk, allowing the CPU to access programs and data files faster than if they remained on the hard or floppy disk.

RAM-resident   A program that resides in memory and provides some utility in your use of an application program. *See also* TSR.

Raster graphics   Graphic designs that are interpreted and manipulated as a group of many dots or pixels; also called "bitmapped graphics."

Read-only   An attribute indicating that you can display a file's contents but not alter them.

Redirection   Sending the output from a command to a device other than the default device.

Remote digital loop-back   The ability of a modem to test another device's ability to process digital signals (remote loop-back), or to test its own ability to process signals (local loop-back).

RFT (revisable format text)   A word processing file format used by IBM.

RGB (red, green, blue)   A type of color monitor. Also a color specification based on the red, green, and blue components of a color.

Ring   A LAN topology in which each workstation is attached to two other workstations forming a loop or ring. Each PC receives a message, checks the address on the message, and forwards it to the next PC on the ring.

ROM (read-only memory)   A chip or chips that contain the central core logic that provides instructions that tell the computer or a device how to function.

Root directory   The uppermost level in the directory structure. To get to the root directory, you would type **CD** and press ENTER.

RS-232C   A standard for transmitting serial data that covers hardware configurations and transmission parameters. Different manufacturers implement some or all of the RS-232 standard in their communications products.

RTF (rich text format)   A word processing file format used by Microsoft that retains text and graphics formatting.

Runtime version   An execute-only version of a program that allows a user to run an application written by a programmer without letting the user access the source code to modify the application.

ScanDisk   Utility included with MS-DOS 6.2 which is used to detect and correct problems with standard drives and DoubleSpace drives. This utility virtually replaces DOS's CHKDSK as it is much more powerful and corrects many more disk errors.

Scanner   A device that converts an image on a printed page into an electronic format.

Screen saver   A software program that causes the screen to go blank after a specified length of inactivity until the keyboard is touched again, to protect the screen from phosphor burn-in.

Script files   A set of commands that lets you specify a list of directories and/or files to be backed up or restored. Often used in backup utilities.

SCSI (small computer system interface)   The interface for a hard drive controller used in both Macintoshes and IBM compatible computers.

.SDF (standard data format)   A text file with fields separated by spaces so that they line up in columns.

Selective backup   Backing up only those files selected by the user.

Separation   A technique for dividing a picture into its component colors for color printing. Full-color images can be separated into cyan, magenta, yellow, and black using the CMYK color model.

Serial data   Data sent one bit at a time, as opposed to parallel data sent several bits at a time. Modems operate on serial data.

Serial port   A communications adapter used to connect a serial printer or plotter, a serial input device such as a mouse or graphics tablet, or an external modem that uses an RS-232 plug (also known as COM1 or COM2).

Server   *See* File server or Application servers.

Shell   An interface between a user and a program. The DOS shell offers a simplified way to use DOS, shielding the user from DOS's complex commands.

Shielding   The process of protecting a cable with a grounded metal surround so that electrical signals are not transmitted by the cable and signals from outside the cable cannot interfere with transmissions inside the cable.

SIMM (single in-line memory module)   Memory units used on most modern PCs. SIMM modules are pre-assembled with memory chips soldered onto a carrier board that snaps into a socket on the memory board or motherboard.

SMARTDrive   Disk caching utility provided with MS-DOS. Used to speed up a computer's performance by storing information in memory or RAM which has previously been read from a disk drive. The computer can then retrieve the information from memory instead of re-reading the disk.

Source code   High-level language that can be read by programmers. For a program to execute source code, it must be converted to machine-readable code through an interpreter or a compiler.

Spreadsheet   A software program for storing and analyzing numbers, especially financial data. A spreadsheet contains cells organized in rows and columns, like a financial worksheet. Formulas provide powerful automatic calculations on the data, which are recomputed whenever the data changes.

SQL (structured query language)   A database query language that allows PCs to access data on mainframes and minis.

Stand-alone program   A product with a specific single application, not a unit of an integrated package.

Star   A LAN topology in which all workstations are wired directly to a central server or hub.

SYLK (SYmbolic LinK)   A Microsoft file format used for data transfer for spreadsheets and databases.

Synchronous   A communications mode in which data has a constant time interval between successive bits or characters. Implies that all equipment in the system is in step.

Terabyte (Tb)   A trillion bytes.

Terminal   A keyboard-display terminal connected to a controlling computer.

TIFF (tag image file format)   A file format for transporting computerized versions of scanned images into graphic or desktop publishing applications.

Token   A unique combination of bits. When a LAN workstation receives a token, it has been given permission to transmit.

Token passing   A network access method in which a token is passed among workstations carrying message and address information. When a workstation receives the token, it looks at the address and sends it on or receives it as appropriate. This method is used by ARCnet and IBM Token-Ring.

Token-ring   A LAN with ring topology that uses token passing as its access method.

Topology   The physical layout or geography of a network, such as Bus, Ring, or Star.

TSR (terminate and stay resident)   A program that resides in memory and can be invoked from within another application.

TTY (teletypewriter)   A low-speed asynchronous communications protocol.

TWAIN   An interface standard for capturing images.

Twisted pair   Two insulated wires wrapped or twisted around each other. May be shielded with a jacket of insulation or other pairs of wires. Usually used for telephones or dumb computer terminals.

UMA (upper memory area)   The memory area between 640K and 1MB reserved for hardware use.

UMB (upper memory block)   A contiguous free area in the UMA. These areas are where device drivers and TSR programs are loaded by memory managers. The result is more free conventional memory.

UNIX   A multi-user, multitasking operating system from AT&T that runs on many types of computers, including microcomputers and mainframes.

Upload   To send data from a microcomputer to a mainframe or minicomputer.

UPS (uninterruptible power supply)   A mechanism used to provide short-term backup power to a PC so that data can be saved after a power failure.

Utility software   Software that lets a board perform functions such as setting and reading the clock, spooling data to be printed, and using extra memory as a RAM disk.

VCPI (virtual control program interface)   A standard for addressing extended memory on 80386-based computers. It was developed by PharLap Software, Inc. Programs using DOS extenders that conform to the VCPI standard (such as Lotus 1-2-3 Release 3.0) can be run simultaneously.

VDISK   A RAM disk, introduced in DOS 3.0, that allows the use of extended memory as if it were a small hard disk.

Vector graphics   Graphic designs that are interpreted and manipulated as objects or elements; also called object-oriented graphics.

VGA (Video Graphics Adapter)   VGA offers two display modes—640 x 480 in 16 colors or 320 x 200 in 256 colors. Third-party vendors offer cards that have various compatibility levels with IBM's VGA display and provide additional features such as 800 x 600 in 16 colors and 640 x 400 in 256 colors. VGA cards are generally compatible with the previous display modes.

Virtual 8086 mode   Employs hardware unique to the 80386 to provide a safe, fast multitasking environment. Creates separate, secure, 1MB regions of memory that simulate an 8086 environment, with each region acting as if it were an independent PC. Programs compatible with DOS 3.*x* will run in virtual 8086 regions.

Virtual memory   The ability of software to use the computer's hard disk as additional working storage. Virtual memory is slower than but not as limited as RAM memory.

Virus   A program designed to enter a system without the user's consent or knowledge in order to alter normal operations.

Volume label   An optional name of as many as 11 characters that you can assign to a disk.

Wildcard   A special character (such as an asterisk) used as a variable in searches.

.WK1   The extension of Lotus 1-2-3 Release 2.*x* files.

.WK3   The extension of Lotus 1-2-3 Release 3.*x* files.

.WKS   The extension of Lotus 1-2-3 Release 1A files.

Word processor   An application for creating, editing, printing, and saving text documents. Many word processors also offer more sophisticated page layout features.

Workstation   *See* Node.

.WPG   A WordPerfect graphics extension.

.WR1   The extension of Lotus Symphony 1.0 and 1.01 files.

Write-protect   Fixes a disk to prevent the data it contains from being overwritten. You can uncover the hole on a 3.5-inch disk by sliding a small piece of plastic, or apply a small tab to a 5.25-inch disk to do this.

.WRK   The extension of Lotus Symphony 1.1, 1.2, and 2.*x* files.

WYSIWYG (what you see is what you get)   Viewing the format, layout, and fonts of a document on the screen as it will appear when it is printed.

.XLC   The extension of Microsoft Excel chart files.

.XLM   The extension of Microsoft Excel macro files.

.XLS   The extension of Microsoft Excel files.

.XLW   The extension of Microsoft Excel workspace files (groups of Excel files that can be opened at the same time in the same order by opening the workspace).

Xmodem   A simple asynchronous communications protocol that detects most transmission errors.

XMS (Extended Memory Specification)   A standard for using extended memory on computers with 80286 or higher processors.

XON/XOFF   A simple asynchronous communications protocol based on the use of transmit-on and transmit-off signals.

Ymodem   An advanced version of the Xmodem asynchronous communications protocol that uses cyclic redundancy check (CRC) and batch file transfers.

Zoom   Magnifying an area of a screen or drawing.

Index

A

"A CVF is damaged", 265
"Abort Retry Fail Ignore?", 262
Above DISC, 248
"Access Denied", 67, 262
Access method, 281
ACR (actual compression ratio), 281
Add Program dialog box (DOS Shell), 126
Address, 281
"Allocation error. Size adjusted.", 262-263
Allocation units, lost, 66
"An extended memory manager is already installed", 270
ANSI (American National Standards Institute), 281
ANSI escape sequences, using, 94-95
ANSI.SYS, 205
Anti-virus software, 4-5, 17, 103-104, 108, 239, 246-247, 281

Application module, 281
Application servers, 281
Applications (*See also* Programs)
    with a backup feature, 238
    installation from drive A, 189-190
    key recognition in, 227
    mouse drivers for, 233-234
    not working with DoubleSpace, 153-156
Architecture, 282
Archive, 282
ARCnet, 256, 282
ASCII, 282
ASCII text files, 107, 282
Assembly language programming, 112
ASSIGN, 190
Asynchronous, 282
AT&T StarGroup network, 256
ATTRIB, 56-57, 67
Auto-answer, 282
Autodial, 282
AUTOEXEC.BAT, 282

after making changes,
200-201
bypassing, 7, 12
choosing from a menu,
222-224
CLS command in, 85
deleting accidentally, 118
DOS Shell in, 122
@ECHO OFF in, 196-197
hiding display of, 89-90
Path statement in, 82-84
at startup, 189
AUTOEXEC.UMB, 161
AUX, 283

B

Back up, 283
Background task, 283
Backing up data, 13-14
BACKUP command, 5-6, 102,
283
vs. MS Backup, 99
and RESTORE, 110
Backup disks
formatting, 99
installing from, 34
Backup feature of an
application, 238
Backup set catalog, 283
Backup utility, 109 (*See also*
MS Backup utility)
and DoubleSpace, 133
and networked drives, 259
"Bad command or file name",
107, 122, 194-195, 263
"Bad or Missing Command
Interpreter", 197, 263
"Bad or missing file name",
178-179, 263
.BAK file, 283

Baseband, 283
Baseband LAN, 283
BASIC, 283
Batch files, 85-86, 283
DOS Shell, 117-118
getting user input, 93-94
including explanations in,
91
a line at a time, 93
screen saver, 91-92
using CHKDSK in, 93
Battery usage (laptop),
211-212
Baud, 283
Bernoulli, 284
.BIN file, 284
Binary, 284
BIOS (basic input/output
system), 235, 284
checking the date, 20-21
and DoubleSpace, 132
Bit (binary digit), 284
Bitmapped graphics, 284
Black-and-white display, 205
Block, 284
Block devices, 220-221
Boot, 284
Boot Manager (OS/2), 247
Boot process, 188-189. *See
also* Booting
Boot sector, 284
Bootable disk, making, 90-91
Booting (bootup), 7-8
clean boot, 191-192, 286
with CTRL+ALT+DEL, 172
and DoubleSpace,
139-140, 147
freezes while loading
programs, 208-209
and HIMEM.SYS, 190-191
and MemMaker, 3-4, 169
memory information
displayed, 174

and no files displayed, 44
role of AUTOEXEC.BAT, 189
role of CONFIG.SYS, 188
takes longer, 211
Bps (bits per second), 284
Bridge, 284
Broadband LAN, 284
Broken computer, 49
Buffer, 285
Bus, 285
Bus network, 285
Byte, 285

C

C language, 285
Cable connections, tables of, 218
Cache memory, 173, 285
Caches, 194
Caching a CD-ROM drive, 208
"Cannot find file QBASIC.EXE", 91, 264
"Cannot find a hard disk on your computer", 16-17
"Cannot load COMMAND.COM. System halted", 264
"Cannot make directory entry", 264-265
"Cannot move multiple files to a single file", 265
"Cannot run SMARTDrive 4.0 with DoubleSpace", 8, 206-265
Carrier, 285
Catalog files (MS Backup), storing, 112-113
CD command, vs. CHDIR command, 81-82

CD-ROM (compact disc read-only memory), 285
CD-ROM drives
caching, 208
and Interlnk, 243
CGA (color graphic adapter), 285
CGM (Computer Graphic Metafiles), 286
Changed files, copying, 104-105
Character set, accessing international, 226-227
CHDIR command, vs. CD command, 81-82
Checksum, 286
Chip, 286
.CHK files, erasing, 69
CHKDSK command, 7-8, 69, 218
vs. DIR command, 66-67
DoubleSpace/CHKDSK routine, 146
CHKDSK /F, 58, 60
using in a batch file, 93
CHOICE command, 93-94
Circuit, 286
Clean boot, 191-192, 286
Clean boot system disk, 193
Client computer, 250
Clipboard, 286
Clipper database, 246
Clock, 286
Clock/calendar, 286
CLS command, 85
Clusters (disk), 66-67
CMOS (complementary metal oxide semiconductor), 199-200, 286
CMYK (Cyan Magenta Yellow Black), 286
Coaxial cable (coax), 286

COBOL (COmmon Business-Oriented Language), 286
Color display, setting, 205-206
.COM files, creating, 112
COMMAND command, 93, 287
Command history, accessing, 76
COMMAND.COM, 28, 197-198, 206
Commands
  displaying the last command, 86-88
  external and internal, 81
  onscreen help with, 81
  slowing down the display from, 90
  stopping, 78
COM1 port, 286
Communications protocol, 287
Comp utility, 107
Compaq computers, 28
Compiler, 287
Compressed disks/drives, 287
  Defrag on, 145
  identifying, 145
  resizing, 143-144
"Compressed drive C is currently too fragmented to mount", 150-151
Compressed files, changing the drive letter for, 158-159
Compressing data, 141, 287. *See also* DoubleSpace
CompuServe, 287
CON, 287
CONFIG.SYS, 287
  after making changes, 200-201
  and boot process, 188

BUFFERS statement, 33, 195
bypassing, 7
choosing from a menu, 222-224
DEVICE statement, 95
disabling, 12
editing, 47
FCBS statement, 196
PATH command in, 215-216
SHELL= statement, 198
stepping through, 192
unrecognized command in, 197
CONFIG.UMB, 161
Configuration issues, 187-228
Contiguous, 287
Control characters, 287
Controller, 287
Conventional memory, 162, 287
  displaying, 176
  limits of, 168-169
"Convert to file?", 60
Coprocessor, 287
COPY command, 70-71, 75
Copying files
  by date, 111
  large files, 65
  multiple files, 67-68
  only changed files, 104-105
Corrupted files, 24-25, 701
CP/M (control program for microcomputers), 55, 288
Cps (characters per second), 288
CPU (central processing unit), 288
Cross-linked clusters, 66
CRT, 288
CTRL+ALT+DEL, 172
CTRL+BREAK, 288

CTRL+PRTSC, 288
Current directory, 288
Current drive, 288
CVFs (compressed volume
    files), 131, 139, 288
    limit, 147
    preventing from using
        drive, 151
"CVF is damaged", 7-8

D

Daisy wheel, 288
DASD, 288
Data compression. *See*
    DoubleSpace
Data compression (MS
    Backup), 141
"Data error", 266
Data validation, 289
Database, 288
Data-link control, 288
Date, copying files by, 111
DBLSPACE.BIN, 222
DBMS, 289
DCE, 289
DDE, 289
DDP, 289
Debugger, 289
Defrag utility, 101-102, 289
    on compressed drives, 145
    with many files, 113-114
    when to run, 113
DEL command, 55
Delete Sentry, 101
Delete Tracker, 100-101
Deleted files, 23, 41-42
Deletion protection levels,
    99-101
DELTREE command, 51, 57,
    60, 65, 71, 289

Densities, disk drive, 13, 59
DES, 289
Desktop publishing, 289
Device drivers, 231
Dialog, 290
DIP switch, 290
DIR command
    vs. CHKDSK, 66-67
    setting display of, 68-69
    slowing down the display
        from, 90
    DIR /S, 42-43
Direct memory access (DMA),
    179, 290
Directories, 290
    deleting, 65
    removing, 71
    renaming, 59
    root, 21, 61, 303
"Directory already exists", 266
Disk cache, 290
Disk drive densities, 13, 59
Disk space, run out, 46
Disk space to run Setup, 30
"Disk unsuitable for system
    disk", 266
Disk utilities, 231
Disk volume labels, 61, 80, 308
DISKCOPY command, 63-65
Disks (*See also* Drives)
    accessing, 45
    formatting backup, 99
    making bootable, 90-91
    uncompressing, 140, 142
    using DoubleSpace on,
        136-137, 147
Display
    enlarging, 92
    printing out, 84
    setting, 205, 206
Display dialog box (DOS
    Editor), 106
Distributed architecture, 290

"Divide overflow", 266

DLL, 290

Direct memory access (DMA),
  179, 290

DOS, 290

DOS Editor
  Display dialog box, 106
  large files in, 106
  margin settings, 107
  scroll bars, 105-106

DOS extender, 290

DOS files. *See* Files

DOS prompt, 78-80, 94-95,
  205, 302

DOS Shell, 115-129, 290
  adding to the Program
    List, 126-127
  adding a program for a
    network, 252
  associating files in, 124-126
  in AUTOEXEC.BAT, 122
  batch files, 117-118
  Command Prompt option,
    122
  and deleted
    AUTOEXEC.BAT, 118
  deleting files from, 62
  disappearing program
    items, 123
  dual file lists in, 119
  file lists in, 120
  Lotus 1-2-3 in, 244
  opening Windows from,
    116
  program list in, 120
  switching between
    programs, 122-123,
    128-129
  switching mouse buttons,
    129
  using the mouse in,
    116-117
  view options, 119-120

DOSKEY, 86-88, 290

DOSSHELL.COM, 127

DOSSHELL.EXE, 127

DOSSHELL.INI, 121, 128

Dot matrix, 291

DoubleGuard Alarm, 27, 149,
  184-185

"DoubleGuard Alarm #nn",
  266

DoubleSpace, 131-159, 291
  activating, 40
  application does not work
    with, 153-156
  and BIOS, 132
  and boot up, 139-140, 147
  changing the drive for
    compressed files,
    158-159
  CHKDSK routine, 146
  to compress a Hardcard,
    157-158
  converting Stacker to, 134
  on drive D, 148
  FORMAT and, 146-147
  free space reported, 141
  and hard drives, 133
  host drive backup, 135
  how it works, 131-132
  identifying compressed
    disks, 145
  and insufficient memory,
    170-171
  insufficient memory for
    games, 164-165
  level of compression, 152
  memory for, 6-7
  memory to install, 152
  memory use in 6.0 vs. 6.2,
    152-153
  and MS Backup, 141
  need for backups, 133
  preventing from using
    drive, 151

programs known to have problems with, 155

removing, 2-3, 21-22

resizing a compressed drive, 143-144

running, 135

setting MaxFileFragments, 150-151

in 6.0 vs. 6.2, 132

with SMARTDrive 4.0, 8

and system slow down, 149

uncompressing with, 140, 142-143

using on floppy disks, 136-137, 147

volume files limit, 147

"DoubleSpace could not mount drive C due to problems with the drive", 151

Download, 291

Downloading from IBM 3270, 184

DPI, 291

DPMI, 291

Drive D

DoubleSpace on, 148

running Setup from, 25

Drive densities, 13, 59

"Drive or diskette types not compatible", 267

Drive letter

changing, 158-159

RAM drive, 199

"Drive not ready", 267

Drives (*See also* Disks)

accessing floppy, 203

formatting floppy, 201-202

uncompressing, 143

Drives A and B

accessing, 193

application installation, 189-190

DRIVPARM, 201-202

DR-DOS, 22

DSR, 291

DSS, 291

Dual file lists in DOS Shell, 119

Dumb terminal, 291

Duplex, 291

"Duplicate file name or file not found", 267

E

ECHO command, 90

ECR, 291

EDIT command, 91

Editor, 291

Editor, DOS, 105-107

EGA, 292

EISA computers, 178

E-mail, 292

Embedded formula, 292

"EMM386 DMA buffer is too small", 179, 267

"EMM386 Exception Error #6", 170, 267-268

"EMM386 exception error #13", 220, 268

"EMM386 Exception Error #12", 268

"EMM386 Not Installed-Protected Mode Software Already Running", 268

"EMM386: Unable to start enhanced Windows mode due to invalid path specification for EMM386", 4, 239, 268-269

EMM386.EXE, 36, 168-169, 171, 292

HIGHSCAN parameter, 174

and page frames, 180-181
Emulation, 292
Encryption, file, 292
Environment space, 198
Environmental variables, 64
EPROM, 292
EPS, 292
ERASE command, 55
"Error in CONFIG.SYS line x",
    263, 278
"Error creating image file.
    DISKCOPY will revert to a
    multiple-pass copy", 63-64,
    269
"Error in EXE file", 269
Error messages, 261-280
"ERROR: missing parameter",
    269
Escape character, creating,
    94-95
Ethernet, 292
EXE2BIN.EXE, 112
EXIT, 118
EXPAND, 25, 107
Expanded memory (EMS),
    163, 292
    with MemMaker, 167-168
    and networking, 253
    services unavailable,
        166-167
"Expanded memory services
    unavailable", 166-167, 270
Extended memory, 163, 293
Extended memory manager,
    169-170
External commands, 81

F

FAT, 63, 100, 293
FDISK, 34, 71, 73

and hard disk formatting,
    70
partitioning with, 66
"File allocation table bad", 270
File allocation table (FAT), 63,
    100, 293
File attributes, 293
"File cannot be copied onto
    itself", 270
"File creation error", 270-271
File lists in DOS Shell, 119-120
File locking, 293
"File name is invalid", 60
"File not found", 271
File server, 293
File utilities, 231
Files, 293
    apparently lost at reboot,
        40
    copying after a certain
        date, 111
    copying large, 65
    copying multiple, 67-68
    copying only changed,
        104-105
    currupted, 24-25
    creating .COM, 112
    deleted, 23
    deleting from DOS Shell,
        62
    deleting hard disk, 60
    displaying contents of,
        88-89
    displaying hidden, 55
    finding, 42-43
    finding corrupted, 70
    with odd characters in
        names, 51
    overwriting, 56-57
    printing, 89
    recovering deleted, 41-42
    restoring, 6
    in root directory, 21, 61

temporary, 57-58, 118
updating, 9
verifying integrity of, 107
viewing hidden, 144
Files area, 293
Finding corrupted files, 70
Finding a file, 42-43
Floppy disks/drives
accessing, 203
accessing data on, 45
formatting, 201-202
using DoubleSpace on,
136-137, 147
Font, 293
FORMAT command
and DoubleSpace, 146-147
FORMAT /F, 59
FORMAT /S, 37, 90
"Format terminated. Format
another?", 271
Formatted disk, recovering
data from, 49-50
Formatting
backup disks, 99
floppy drives, 201-202
a hard disk, 70
Fragmented disks, using
Defrag on, 101-102,
113-114, 293
Free space
to install DOS, 17-18
reported by DoubleSpace,
141
Front end, 293
Frozen screen
rebooting, 46-47
while loading programs,
208-209
Full duplex, 293
Full-length, 293
Function key, using to start a
program, 95

G

Games, memory for, 164-165
Gateway, 294
"General failure
reading/writing drive X",
271-272
Gigabyte (Gb), 294
Groupware, 294
GUI, 294

H

Half duplex, 294
Half-length, 294
Hard copy, 294
Hard disks/drives, 58-59
compatibility, 31-32, 36-37
and DoubleSpace, 133
formatting, 70
head parking, 63
setting up, 27
Hardcard, 157-158
Hardware (*See also*
Interoperability)
compatibility, 15-16
outdated, 230
Hardware cache, 194
HELP command, 54
Help
accessing, 91
with DOS commands, 81
Hexadecimal, 294
Hidden files, 294
deleting, 57
displaying, 55
viewing, 144
High memory
displaying, 172
loading TSR programs into,
172-173
using, 166-170, 209-210

High memory area (HMA), 162-163

High Sierra group format, 294

"HIMEM is testing extended memory", 202-203

HIMEM.SYS, 168-169, 190-191, 202-203, 294

HMA, 294

Host, 295

Host drive, 131, 295

Host drive backup, 135

Hotkey, 295

Hotlink, 295

Hub, 295

Hypertext, 295

Hyundai computers, 29

I

IBM 3270, downloading from, 184

"Incompatible hard disk or device driver", 31-32

"Inconsistency between startup and MemMaker STS file", 215

"Incorrect DOS version", 5, 6, 8, 102, 199, 221, 240, 257-259, 272

Incremental backup, 295

Index, 295

.INI files, 295

Installing, 4-7 (*See also* Setup)
    applications from drive A, 189-190
    from backup disks, 34
    disk space required for, 30-31
    manually, 18-19
    PS/1, 8

utilities for DOS and Windows, 19

"Insufficient disk space", 272

"Insufficient file handles", 243

"Insufficient memory", 113-114, 164-165, 273

Insufficient memory for and DoubleSpace, 6-7, 170-171

Integrators, 295

Interactive, 295

Interactive start, 295

Interface, 296

InterInk, 216-217, 243

Internal commands, 81

"Internal stack overflow. System halted.", 273

International character sets, accessing, 226-227

Interoperability, 229-248

Interpreter, 296

"Invalid COMMAND.COM", 8, 198, 273

"Invalid date", 273

"Invalid directory", 274

"Invalid drive specification", 254-255, 274

"Invalid media type or track 0 bad - Disk unusable", 274

"Invalid number of parameters", 274

"Invalid parameter", 274

"Invalid path or file name", 59

"Invalid path not directory or directory not empty", 275

I/O, 296

IO.SYS, 36

ISO, 296

K

Kbps, 296

Kermit, 296
Key recognition in
    applications, 227
Keyboard, setting up
    alternate, 226-227
Keyword, 296
Kilobyte (K), 296

L

LABEL command, 34, 61, 80
Labels, disk volume, 61, 80
LAN, 296
LANtastic, 253-254
Laptop, 296
Laptop battery usage, 211-212
Large files
    copying, 65
    in DOS Editor, 106
Laser printer, 296
Last command, displaying,
    86-88
Layout, 296
LIM/EMS, 296
Linking, 297
LOADHIGH, 228
Local drive, compressing,
    253-254
Local resources, 250
Locking, 297
Login, 297
Lost allocation units, 66
Lotus 1-2-3, in DOS Shell, 244
LPT1, 297

M

Machine code, 297
Macro, 297
Manual installation, 18-19

Master Boot Record (MBR),
    219, 297
Math coprocessor, 297
Mbps, 297
MBR, 297
MCA, 298
MCGA, 297
Megabyte (MB), 297
Megahertz (MHz), 297
MEM command, 165, 172
    and cache and video RAM,
        173
    MEM /C /P, 176
MemMaker utility, 161
    and booting, 3-4, 169
    and DOS=HIGH, 177-178
    and DOS=UMB, 177-178,
        180
    with expanded memory,
        167-168
    and multiple startups,
        224-226
    on a network, 252
    and parity error, 175
    and RAM, 171
    STS file, 215
Memory, 161-186 (*See also*
    Conventional memory;
    Expanded memory)
    displaying loaded, 172
    DoubleSpace use of,
        152-153, 170-171
    extended, 163, 169-170,
        293
    for games, 164-165
    getting information about,
        165-166
    information displayed at
        boot up, 174
    to install DoubleSpace, 152
    optimizing, 182-183
    RAM vs. hard disk, 58
    RAM vs. ROM, 164

reserved, 162
types of, 162-164
"Memory parity error", 245
Memory switches, 171
Menu, 298
Menu choices, adding,
212-214
MENUCOLOR, 214
Metafile, 298
Microsoft Diagnostics (MSD),
72-75, 181-182, 235, 256
"Missing operating system",
207, 275
MODE command, 88, 92
Modem, 298
MORE command filter (|), 90
Motherboard, 298
Mouse, 298
Mouse buttons, in DOS Shell,
129
Mouse drivers for DOS
applications, 233-234
MOVE command, 55-56, 59
MS Backup utility, 6, 65
vs. BACKUP and RESTORE,
99
compatibility test, 99-110
data compression, 141
restoring files, 111
storing catalog files,
112-113
using in Windows, 234
MSAV, vs. Vsafe, 108
MSD (Microsoft Diagnostics
utility), 72-75, 181-182,
235, 256
MS-DOS, upgrading PC-DOS
to, 23
MS-DOS utilities. *See* Utilities
MTBF, 298
Multi-config, 298
Multiple files, copying, 67-68
Multisynchronous display, 298

Multitasking, 298
Multithreading, 298
Multi-user version, 298

N

Native 80386 mode, 299
NetBIOS, 299
NetWare, 254-255, 258-260
NetWare Lite, 260
Network, 299
Network architecture, 299
Network interface card, 299
Network shell, 250, 299
Network topology, 299
Networking, 249-260
from DOS Shell, 252
terms, 250-251
and using expanded
memory, 253
and using MemMaker, 252
Network-ready, 299
Networks supported, table of,
251
NETX.COM, 258-259
New features, 29-30
"No room for system on
destination disk", 275
Node, 299
NOEMS, 171, 210
Noise, 299
Non-DOS partition, deleting,
246
"Non-system disk or disk
error", 50, 275-276
Norton utilities, 242-243
"Not ready reading drive A",
24
"Not ready reading/writing
drive X", 260, 276

"Not running on DOS V3.0
through V5.0", 258-259
Novell NetWare, 258-260
Novell NetWare Lite, 260
Novell network, 254-255
Null-modem cable, 299
Num Lock light, 207

O

Object-oriented graphics, 300
OCR, 300
Old computers, upgrading,
20-21
Old versions, using new
utilities with, 112
OLD_DOS.1 subdirectory, 11,
32
OLE, 300
One-finger mode, 300
Online help, 81, 91, 300
OOP, 300
Operating system, 300
OS, 300
OSI, 296
OS/2, 300
OS/2 Boot Manager, 247
"Out of environment space",
198, 276
"Out of memory", 106
Overwriting files, 56-57

P

Packard Bell computers, 177
Page frames, 180-181
Parallel cable connections,
table of, 218
Parallel port, 300
Parameter, 301

"Parameters not supported by
drive", 276
Parity, 301
Parity errors, 175, 245
Parking the hard disk head, 63
Partitions (disk), 33-34, 37-38
combining, 72-75
deleting, 246
with FDISK, 66
with two hard drives, 71-72
Password protection, 301
Path, 301
PATH command in
CONFIG.SYS, 215-216
"Path not found", 276
PC Tools, 242-243
PC-DOS, upgrading with
MS-DOS, 23
.PCX files, 301
Peer-to-peer, 250
Peripherals, 235
"Permanent swap file is
corrupt", 234
.PIF files, 301
PIM, 301
Pipe, 301
Pixel, 301
Point and shoot, 301
Polling, 301
Port, 302
"Possible virus!", 17
PostScript, 302
Power-On-Self-Test (POST),
188
PRINT command, 89
Print server, 302
Printer driver, 302
Printer ports, setting up, 88
Printer test, 241-242
Printing
hung up, 43-44
files, 89
the screen, 84

"Probable Non-DOS disk.
  Continue?", 276-277
Program list in DOS Shell,
  120, 126-127
Programs (*See also*
  Applications)
  assembly language, 112
  function key to start, 95
  known to have problems
    with DoubleSpace, 155
  loading into high memory,
    172-173
  in root directory, 61
  switching between in DOS
    Shell, 122-123, 128-129
PROMPT command, 78-80,
  94-95, 205, 302
Protected mode, 302
Protection levels for deletions,
  99-101
Protocol, 302
Protocol converter, 302
PS/1 computers
  four-quadrant screen, 231
  installation, 8
  wrong DOS or
    COMMAND.COM, 28

Q

QEMM386, and Setup, 27-28
Quantum Hardcard, setting
  up, 27
Queue, 302

R

Radio button, 302
RAM, 171, 302
  vs. hard disk memory, 58

and MemMaker, 171
  vs. ROM, 164
RAM disk, 303
RAM drive
  accessing, 203-204
  temp files on, 204-205
RAM drive letter, 199
RAMDRIVE.SYS, 203-204
RAM-resident, 303
Random access memory. *See*
  RAM
Raster graphics, 303
Read-only, 303
Read-only files, deleting, 57
Read-only memory (ROM),
  162
Rebooting, 46-47
  with CTRL+ALT+DEL, 172
  and finding no files, 40
Recovering data from a
  formatted disk, 49-50
Recovering deleted files, 41-42
Redirection, 303
Redirector, 250
REM, 91
Remote digital loop-back, 303
Renaming directories, 59
REPLACE command, 104-105
"Required parameter
  missing", 277
Reserved memory, 162
RESTORE command, 99,
  108-110
Restoring files, 6
  after BACKUP, 110
  after MS Backup, 111
RFT, 303
RGB, 303
Ring, 303
ROM, 164, 303
Root directory, 21, 61, 303

"Root directory of your hard disk contains some of your original DOS files", 21
RS-232C, 304
RTF, 304
Runtime version, 304

S

ScanDisk, 51, 60, 69, 110, 254, 304
Scanner, 304
Screen display
  enlarging, 92
  printing out, 84
  setting, 205-206
Screen saver, 91-92, 304
Script files, 304
SCSI, 304
SCSI hard drives, setting up, 27
.SDF files, 304
Selective backup, 304
Separation, 304
Serial cable connections, table of, 218
Serial data, 305
Serial port, 305
Server, 250
SET command, 257
Setup, 11-38 (*See also* Installing)
  compatibility, 12-13
  computer models and, 28
  and disk-compression programs, 26
  disk space required by, 30-31
  drive specifications, 24
  files in the root directory, 21

and finding the hard disk, 16-17
free copies of, 33
free space to install DOS, 17-18
hard drive compatibility, 31-32
hardware compatibility, 15-16
interrupting, 14-15
on a new hard drive, 36-37
process of, 11
prompting for a second disk, 236-237
and QEMM386, 27-28
running from drive D, 25
and SCSI drives, 27
single disk upgrade, 35
and Uninstall, 30
and virus checking, 17
Setup disk, 12-13
SETVER command, 107, 258-259
SHARE command, 183-184
Shareware, 230
Shell. *See* DOS Shell
Shielding, 305
SIMM, 305
"Size of expanded memory pool adjusted", 174
Slowed down system
  display from DIR or TYPE, 90
  and DoubleSpace, 149
SMARTDrive, 8, 139-140, 195-196, 305
"SMARTDrive cannot cache a compressed drive", 219
Software. *See* Applications; Programs
Software cache, 194
Source code, 305
Spreadsheet, 305
SQL, 305

Stacker
  drives, 242
  and file locations, 178-179
  Stacker-to-DoubleSpace
    conversion, 134
Stand-alone program, 306
Standard deletion protection,
  100
Star, 306
Startup. *See* Booting (bootup)
Stepup, 9, 22-23
Stopping a command, 78
SUBST, 189
Switches, memory, 171
Switching between programs
  in DOS Shell, 122-123,
  128-129
SYLK, 306
Synchronous, 306
"Syntax error", 277
SYS command, 90-91
System disk, 193
System time, changing, 78

T

Tandy computers, 28
"Target disk bad or
  incompatible", 277
Task swapping (DOS Shell),
  123, 128-129
Temporary files, 57-58, 118,
  204-205
10Net, 253-254
Terabyte (Tb), 306
Terminal, 306
Terminal emulator, running,
  184
Terminate-and-stay-resident
  programs (TSRs), 172-173,
  230, 306

Text attributes, screen display,
  206
Text files
  combining, 75
  DOS Editor, 107
"There is not enough free
  conventional memory", 271
"There is not enough free
  space on drive C to install
  MS-DOS", 17-18
Time (system), changing, 78
.TMP files, 57-58, 118
Token passing, 306
Token-ring, 306
"Too many block devices",
  220-221
"Too many parameters", 277
"Too Many Primary
  Partitions", 33-34
Topology, 306
Toshiba computers, 36
TSR programs, 172-173, 230,
  306
TTY, 306
Turning on the computer,
  48-49
TWAIN, 306
Twisted pair, 307
TYPE command, 88-90

U

UMA, 209-210, 307
UMB, 307
"Unable to create directory",
  277-278
"Unable to load
  COMMAND.COM or
  DOSSWAP.EXE", 128, 278
"Unable to open source",
  55-56

"Unable to update
DOSSHELL.INI", 121
"Unable to write BOOT", 278
Uncompressing a disk, 140,
142
Uncompressing a drive, 143
Undelete, 23, 41-42, 62, 76
UNFORMAT command,
49-50, 76
Uninstall, 30-31
Uninstall disk, 13
UNIX, 307
"Unrecognized command in
CONFIG.SYS", 197, 278
"Unrecoverable read/write
error", 278
Updating files, 9
Updating files with Stepup,
22-23
Upgrade disk for Setup, 35
Upgrades, getting behind on,
230
Upgrading, 13-14
Upload, 307
UPS, 307
Utilities, 97-114, 307
installing for DOS and
Windows, 19
installing manually, 18
summary of, 98
using with other DOS
versions, 112

V

VCPI, 307
VDISK, 307
Vector graphics, 307
VER command, 80
Verifying file integrity, 107
Version of DOS, displaying, 80

Versions of DoubleSpace, 132
Versions (old), using new
utilities with, 112
VGA, 307
Video RAM, 173
Viewing hidden files, 144
Virtual 8086 mode, 308
Virtual memory, 308
Virus-detection programs, 4-5,
17, 103-104, 108, 239,
246-247
Viruses, 103, 308
"Volume in drive C is MS-DOS
5", 80
Volume labels, disk, 61, 80,
308
Vsafe, vs. MSAV, 108

W

"WARNING: EMM386 installed
without a LIM 3.2
compatible page frame",
185-186, 279
Whatsnew feature, 29-30
Wildcard, 308
WINA20.386, 244
Windows
slowed down, 232-233
starting, 240-241
Word processor, 308
Workstations, 251, 308
"Write failure. Diskette
unusable", 279
"Write Fault error
reading/writing to device
XXX", 279
"Write Protect Error", 279
Write-protected, 308
WYSIWYG, 309

X

XCOPY command, 67-68, 81, 104-105
Xmodem, 309
XMS, 309
XON/XOFF, 309
XtraDrive disk compression, 135

Y

Ymodem, 309
"You must have the file WINA20.386 in the root of your boot drive", 244
"You must specify the host drive for a DoubleSpace drive", 139-140, 279-280

"Your computer might be running software that is incompatible with DoubleSpace", 138-139
"Your computer uses a disk-compression program", 26
"Your version of DOS cannot be upgraded with Setup", 28

Z

Zenith SuperSport computer, 247
Zoom, 309

Have we answered all your questions?

If you would like to **speak to the experts** who wrote this book, **call** Corporate Software's DOS answer line! Trained specialists will answer your DOS questions including installation, configuration, standard utilities and DOS command usage.

1-800-477-7718 $20 per problem. (Major credit cards accepted)

1-900-555-2003 $1.75 per minute. (First two minutes free)

Support is for versions 3.3 and greater!